SEEING WITH THE MIND'S EYE

SEEING WITH

Mike Samuels, M.D.
Nancy Samuels

THE MIND'S EYE

The History, Techniques and Uses of Visualization

A RANDOM HOUSE · BOOKWORKS BOOK

First printing, September 1975	**25,000 copies in paperback**
Second printing, November 1976	**10,000 copies in paperback**
Third printing, August 1977	**10,000 copies in paperback**
Fourth printing, May 1978	**10,000 copies in paperback**
Fifth printing, April 1979	**15,000 copies in paperback**
Sixth printing, October 1980	**10,000 copies in paperback**
Seventh printing, September 1981	**10,000 copies in paperback**
Eighth printing, April 1982	**7,500 copies in paperback**
Ninth printing, January 1983	**10,000 copies in paperback**

Cover photograph by the authors.
Typeset in Photographic Palatino by Vera Allen Composition Service, Castro Valley, California
    (with special thanks to Vera and Dorothy)
Printed and bound under the supervision of Dean Ragland, Random House

This book is co-published by   Random House Inc.
                                  201 East 50th Street
                                  New York, N. Y. 10022

                                  The Bookworks

Distributed in the United States by Random House, and simultaneously published in Canada
by Random House of Canada Limited, Toronto. Booksellers please order from Random House.

Library of Congress Cataloging in Publication Data

Samuels, Mike.
    Seeing with the mind's eye.

    "A Random House Bookworks book."
    Includes index.
    1. Visualization. I. Samuels, Nancy, joint author. II. Title.
BF367.S28   153.3'2   75-10316
ISBN 0-394-73113-1 pbk.

Manufactured in the United States of America

This book is dedicated to
our publisher and editor
Don Gerrard
who first visualized this book
and who gave us help and support
in its completion

We would like to thank all the people who helped with various aspects of this book. Lyn and Daniel Camiccia, Jane Deer and Joey, Sandy and Danny Harrington, Ginger McNew and Niko, Donna and Suzanna Staples, and Karen and Erica Willig—the mothers and children of the playgroup who provided us with most of the time for writing this book. Florence and Iggy Samuels for taking care of Rudy while we looked for illustrations in New York and went to the typesetter's in California. Judy Lubar Roth who entertained Rudy in Berkeley while we met with our publisher.

We would also like to thank people who helped us with their ideas and advice. James Surls with whom we have had many discussions on creative visualization. Schuyler Harrison for advice on the manuscript and on illustrations. Hal Bennett for good book talk.

Thanks to Susan Smith for the tremendous thought and loving care that went into the illustrations she drew—which hardly needs expressing because it is reflected in the illustrations themselves.

And thanks to Vera Allen who took such care in the layout of the book, who understood our visualization of how the book should look, who always had more done than we expected, and who was a pleasure to work with.

The use of the pronouns ''he'' and ''she'' was maintained merely so that readers would not be distracted by unconventional grammar. The pronouns ''he'' and ''she'' were not used to connote gender. We regreted using ''he'' and ''she'' in general situations, and only chose to do so after much thought and rewriting. It is regrettable that the English language does not have a singular pronoun for the third person that does not imply gender.

hi Roo! Photograph by Michael Samuels.

To Rudy who lives in a world of
visualization and who bore with his
parents during the writing of this book.

Books by Mike Samuels (with Hal Bennett)

The Well Body Book, 1973
Spirit Guides, 1974
Be Well, 1974

PREFACE

The human mind is a slide projector with an infinite number of slides stored in its library, an instant retrieval system and an endlessly cross-referenced subject catalog. As your eyes read these words you can easily see your bedroom in your mind, go to your bed and turn back the covers. In another instant you can sit behind the wheel of your car in traffic. Then you can be in your office looking through a file drawer. And now in a supermarket pushing a shopping cart up to the checkout stand; finally walking down a windswept, deserted beach last summer. You can move from image to image as rapidly as you read. You can 'see' any part of your life effortlessly as often as it is suggested to you. What is this inner seeing? Avoided by the standard educational process, the importance of visualization in our lives has yet to be adequately explored. This book plugs in your slide projector and pulls down the screen. And soon you will begin to show yourself magic slides!

If there are two important 'new' concepts in 20th century American life, they are meditation and visualization. Meditation clears and concentrates the mind; visualization puts an image in it which can profoundly affect the life.

In a sense man has long been in conflict between the power his visual images have over him and the control he can exert over his environment through the spoken word. Both of these faculties, the visual and the verbal, are basic mental processes. Man sees; he also talks. When he talks to others, he calls it communicating; when he talks to himself, he calls it thinking. When he sees the world around him, he calls it reality; when he sees in his mind's eye, what is it?

It is only recently that this powerful, often fearful, question is beginning to be answered. What is it that goes on when we see in our mind's eye? Are we going crazy? Are demons possessing us? Are repressed terrors from the night, from our past, haunting us? These questions are so anxiety-provoking that the rise of civilization in the last 2000 years reads like a history of the social suppression of visualization and therefore a denial of one of our most basic mental processes. For visualization *is* the way we think. Before words, images were. Visualization is the heart of the bio-computer. The human brain programs and self-programs through its images. Riding a bicycle, driving a car, learning to read, bake a cake, play golf — all skills are acquired through the image-making process. Visualization is the ultimate consciousness tool.

I have worked with Mike Samuels since 1972, witnessing the evolution of his learning process as he has moved from human physiology in THE WELL BODY BOOK (1973) to BE WELL (1974), which describes the basic wiring connecting the body with the brain, called the homeostatic principle, to SEEING WITH THE MIND'S EYE (1975) an exploration of consciousness itself. In this trilogy the interested reader is shown a direct path between mind and body, consciousness and experience.

Visualization, as presented in this book, is a set of concepts and techniques drawn from historical as well as contemporary sources, in every aspect of life, that seeks to reinstate the reader to an understanding of the nature of his visual processes and their importance in his life. Visualization is the other side of human nature, the primitive darkness, the energizing non-rational flow, the connection to the Source, the artist's inspiration, the path in the right hemisphere of the brain, the Dionysus to civilization's Appolonian rigidity, the door to the fountainhead. Visualization is not just an idea; it is one half of consciousness. It is one way we think, perhaps the more basic way.

This book cannot teach you to visualize. You already do. You may want to rediscover this part of yourself, missing for centuries.

Don Gerrard
Editor and co-publisher
June 1975

Contents

All that we see are our visualizations.
We see not with the eye, but with the soul.

SECTION I

THE NATURE OF THE IMAGE

Twentieth century man travels in two directions—outward to space and inward to the mind. Traveling outward he uses space craft, traveling inward he uses images. The remarkable scene in this picture could be an artist's portrayal of an inner image, but actually it is a photograph of the Orion Nebula (NGC 1976) and NGC 1977 taken with a Crossley reflector by Lick Observatory. At the edges of the universe inner and outer become one.

INTRODUCTION

We see this book as an adventure story. All of us have read stories of adventures in lands where few men had been before—stories like *The Heart of Darkness* by Conrad or *20,000 Leagues Under the Sea* by Jules Verne. These adventure stories gripped us because in them man faced the *unknown.* And while reading these stories, we've become so involved as to momentarily lose touch with events around us, to not notice sounds or the conversation of people in the room where we were. We felt so involved in the scenes we were reading about that they almost felt more real to us than our surroundings. We could often hear the river slapping against the boat, see the darkness of the forest, and smell the damp odors of the jungle.

This book is an adventure story because it deals with an area which throughout history has been feared for its dangers and lauded for its power: the human mind. The vehicle for the journey is neither a boat nor a submarine. It will be the image. Just as we describe travel by space ship as flying, so we speak of travel into the mind through image as visualization.

Occasional travelers have journeyed deeply into the mind from the beginning of recorded time and have brought back chronicles of their journeys which will be useful to us. Just as a time came to discover the uncharted areas of the earth, the time has now come to journey into uncharted areas of the mind. The rewards reaped by the explorers of the earth were earthly; the rewards reaped by explorers of the mind can be heavenly as well.

When people's eyes are open, they see landscapes in the outer world. When people's eyes are closed, they see landscapes with their mind's eye. People spend hours looking at outer landscapes, but there is just as much to see in inner landscapes. The landscapes are different, but they are equally valid. Top: Michael Samuels. *Landscape (Foal Field)*. 1975. Photograph Bottom: Joan Miro. *Landscape (The Hare)*. Oil on canvas. The Solomon R. Guggenheim Museum, New York.

Chapter 1

INNER AND OUTER—FANTASY AND REALITY

When people's eyes are open, they are drawn to scenes that they perceive outside their bodies. They see the contents of the room they're in, and other people—scenes which change as they shift their eyes. Most people take for granted the fact that the objects they perceive are real and separate from them.

When people's eyes are closed and there is silence, images and thoughts come to them that appear to be within their mind. In their mind's eye people "see" memories of past events, imagine future situations, daydream of what may be or might have been, dream of vividly textured happenings beyond the bounds of space and time. Many people accredit little importance to these inner events, even to the point of denying that the experiences are real. In their view, reality—that is external reality—is the ground upon which people must work out their existence, whereas inner reality is at best pleasantly irrelevant and, at worst, may actually endanger their existence.

Similarly, most people feel that they know a great deal about the outer world, the world beyond their body, and very little about the inner one. In fact, some people are so involved with external reality that they are only fleetingly, if ever, aware of inner events. In modern society, stimulation from the outer world has become so intense that people are daily, hourly, bombarded with a flood of visual and auditory stimuli—bombarded so continuously that they have to make a conscious effort to shut out the outer world, in order to become aware of inner experiences.

While most people are convinced of the separateness of these two worlds, these two realities, the scientist is finding it more and more difficult to maintain the distinction between them. Psychologists have conducted some interesting experiments to see whether people can truly distinguish between their inner and outer worlds. In 1964 the American psychologists Segal and Nathan showed a

The outer world constantly bombards people with visual stimuli. Visualization provides people with a means of getting in touch with inner stimuli. Richard Estes. *The Candy Store*. 1969. Oil and synthetic polymer on canvas. 47¾ × 68¾ inches. Collection of Whitney Museum of American Art. Gift of the Friends of Whitney Museum of American Art.

number of subjects a blank screen on which they were told to imagine an object such as a lemon.[1,2] The experimenters then projected a similar shape from the back of the screen, at very low intensity. Most of the subjects were unable to tell the difference between the shapes they imagined and those projected by the experimenters. Sometimes subjects thought that they had imagined the image that the experimenters had projected. Other times, they thought that they saw images projected on the screen when actually the images were the subjects' own imagined ones. Finally, subjects sometimes described seeing images which involved a combination of their own inner image and an image the experimenters had projected.

For example, a subject told to imagine a yellow lemon, and shown a barely perceptible image of a purple flower, might report seeing a purple flower with a yellow center. All that the psychologists were able to determine was real to these observers was the image that they held in their mind's eye—whether or not a real object was being perceived.

What people "see" when they look at an external object is dependent upon who they are and what they are interested in at that moment. For example, a butcher might look at a bull and see beef steaks, a county judge might see the bull's good or bad lines, and a city dweller might see the bull as an object of sheer terror.

For the physicist, the difference between ex-

Ignorant of the nature of a rope lying in the road, one may perceive a snake."[7] People are constantly fooled by their senses; they "see" what they expect to see. If something (an object, people, a situation) is out of its familiar context, people may mistake it for something else. Thus inner reality structures outer reality. Illustration by Susan Ida Smith.

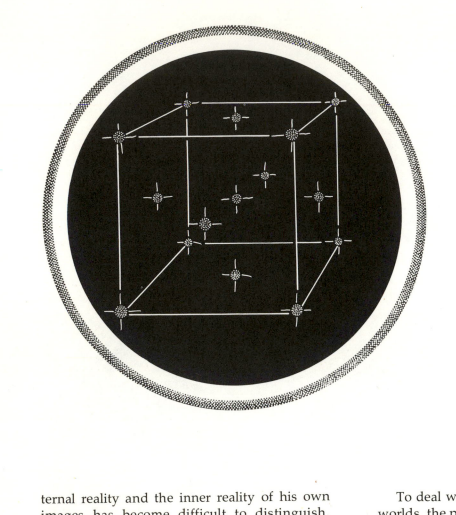

A layman "sees" a metal cube as solid. This is one level of reality—a reality based on a sensory model. The physicist, using another model, "sees" a metal cube as largely composed of empty space between the atoms that make up the cube. Both models are valid; both are "real" and can be proved through experiments. There is no single valid external reality—reality is multi-faceted. Illustration by Susan Ida Smith.

ternal reality and the inner reality of his own images has become difficult to distinguish. Whereas a layman "sees" a metal cube as a solid object, a physicist has an image in his mind of the cube as something like the nighttime sky—being made up mostly of space between atoms. And whereas the layman "sees" the cube as stationary, the physicist "sees" the cube as so many rapidly moving electrons whose position in space can only be fixed as a matter of mathematical probability.

Furthermore, for the physicist, the whole question of the structure of matter is studded with paradoxes. Light, the very substance that allows people to perceive external objects, is believed to behave both as a wave and as a particle—as both energy and matter. Also, the physicist now believes that time is relative to the speed at which an observer is moving. He no longer recognizes one fixed external reality; he believes that a perceived reality is inseparable from the mind of the observer.[3,4]

To deal with this paradox of inner and outer worlds, the psychiatrist Carl Jung developed the concept of *psychic reality*. He said, "All that I experience is psychic . . . [including] my sense impressions . . . [psychic images] alone are my immediate experience, for they alone are the immediate objects of my consciousness . . . it seems to us that certain psychic contents or images are derived from a material environment to which our bodies also belong, while others, which are in no way less real, seem to come from a mental source which appears to be very different. . . . If a fire burns me, I do not question the reality of the fire, whereas if I am beset by the fear that a ghost will appear, I take refuge behind the thought that it is only an illusion. But just as the fire is the psychic image of a physical process whose nature is unknown so my fear of the ghost is a psychic image from a mental source; it is just as real as the fire, for my fear is as real as the pain caused by the fire."[5]

8

Carl Jung believed that psychic happenings constitute man's only reality. These psychic happenings, as mental images, can come from either external or internal sources. The fear-arousing apparition and the terror it causes are as real as mental images derived from external sources. Francisco Goya. *Nun Frightened by a Ghost*. Wash drawing in sepia. The Metropolitan Museum of Art, Harris Brisbane Dick Fund, 1935.

Some cultures have even accredited events of the inner world with greater importance than events of external reality. Among American Indians the inner reality of dreams and visions has played a decisive role in their culture. In *Black Elk Speaks*, the Oglala Sioux chief Black Elk recalls a dream in which he was taken up into the sky with a herd of wild horses. The events of this dream profoundly influenced his understanding of his place in the creative scheme and were the basis on which he became a chief.[6]

FOOTNOTES

1. Segal, S. "The Perky Effect: Changes in Reality Judgements With Changing Methods of Inquiry," *Psychon. Sci.*, 12:393–394, 1968.

2. Perky, C. W. "An Experimental Study of Imagination," *American Journal of Psychology*, 21:422–452, 1910.

3. LeShan, L. *The Medium, the Mystic, and the Physicist*, New York, Ballantine Books, 1975, pp. 61–78.

4. Jung, C. G. *Man and His Symbols*; Garden City, N.Y.; Doubleday and Co.; 1968; p. 308, from M. L. von Franz, "Science and the Unconscious."

5. Jung, C. G. *Modern Man in Search of a Soul*; New York; Harcourt, Brace & World, Inc.; 1933; p. 190.

6. Neihardt, J. *Black Elk Speaks*, Lincoln: University of Nebraska Press, 1961.

7. Campbell, J., ed. *Philosophies of India*; New York; Meridian Books, Inc.; 1960; p. 19.

In this picture the artist Paul Gaugin (French, 1948-1903) portrays man in a state of union with nature. The whole family of man is depicted in a primeval setting. The figure of an idol in the left hand background fits in harmoniously with the other figures and conveys a feeling of the natural interaction between man and his spirits. The title *D'ou Venons Nous . . Que Sommes Nous . . Ou Allons Nous? (Where Do We Come from? What Are We? Where Are We Going?)* is a verbal comment on modern man's separation from this primitive state of harmony in which visualization connected man with his world. Canvas 54¾ × 147½ inches. Courtesy, Museum of Fine Arts, Boston. Tompkins Collection, Arthur Gordon Tompkins Residuary Fund.

Chapter 2

VISUAL IMAGES AND THE WORD

The history of man's understanding and use of visualization is unusual because, although it is marked by external events, the real record has unfolded at a different level. The history of visualization deals with inner events. To be more exact, it deals with the waxing and waning of two basic mental processes: verbal thought and visual thought. Throughout man's history these two processes have, in turn, eclipsed each other in importance.

Primitive, pre-civilized man in every part of the world lived his existence in integral connection with his environment. He saw and interacted with spirits and gods in every animal, tree, stone, and cloud. Every event and natural force was animated with primitive man's inner vision. His basic consciousness was visual. He thought, felt, lived visually. Often little distinc-tion was made between sleeping and waking activities, between visions and perceptions. Dreams and fantasies were valued more than cognitive thought. In this period of union, man lived in nature. Primitive man did not need to be made aware of visualization; it was the way in which he related to the world.

With the development of language and a written system for recording it, rational thought came to dominate. Words came to function as labels, allowing man to detach himself from his experience and analyze it, as well as causing man to separate himself from nature. With these changes came the birth of civilization, law and order, the development of philosophical and moral systems, and the growth of mathematics and the sciences. As knowledge and communi-cation increased people began to live out

11

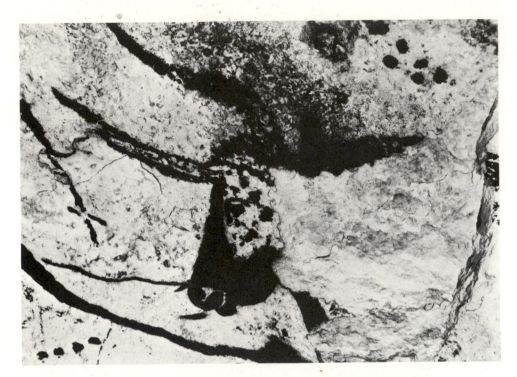

The cave painting of Lascaux are believed to have functioned ritually. They gave man power over the spirits of the animals portrayed and thereby insured the success of the hunt. These earliest of recorded visualizations took man into an inner world which united him with the outer world. Courtesy of the French Government Tourist Office, New York.

highly-specialized social roles, carrying the sense of separation and alienation from nature to its extreme.

During this long historical period some men discovered techniques that helped to re-unite them with their natural world. These men were shamans of primitive tribes, priests of Hellenic civilizations, alchemists and saints of medieval times, and mystics, artists and psychics of all ages. They have all employed techniques deliberately designed to produce an inner state in which their visual powers were enhanced. Achieving this state, variously described as relaxation, oneness of mind, reverie or ecstasy, gave them abilities to affect the outer world, to heal and to become one with God or "the source."

It is interesting that the creation mythology of almost every major civilization contains elements that reflect this fall from "grace" and a subsequent search for "redemption." The price of civilization for man has been the loss of his sense of wholeness and a search for the missing pieces.

The earliest record of visualization experiences is in the form of pictures, visual images. During the Ice Age—60,000 to 10,000 B.C.—cave dwellers in France, Spain, Africa and Scandanavia painted on the walls of their caves representations of the images that they saw. Most of these paintings are of animals that the people hunted. We can imagine these cave dwellers gathered together around communal fires, staring at these animal images, reliving the events of a great hunt, anticipating even greater kills to come. Some of these rock images are even scarred with spear marks. It has been speculated that the Ice Age hunters believed that they ritually insured the success of forthcoming hunts by spearing the rock images which they visualized as the souls of the animals they would slaughter.[1]

A second kind of image that has been found in these caves is pictures of men wearing animal masks. Anthropologists have theorized that these paintings depict tribal shamans—priest-magician-healer figures common to many non-literate cultures. Among such cultures it is believed that the shaman, in putting on the mask of an animal, becomes one with the animal and gains power over it.[2] When a person holds such an image in his mind he is compelled to participate in its reality. All his senses are awakened: he "sees," "smells," "hears," and "feels more intensely." And since extremely vivid internal images cannot be distinguished from an external experience, the imager and his image become one. Levy-Bruhl, a contemporary anthropologist, has called the state in which the subject or imager does not separate himself from the object or image *participation mystique*.[3] He feels that this state is characteristic of "primitive" man who did not separate himself from the plants and animals in his environment. As Carl Jung has stated, "Plants and animals then behave like men; men are at the same time themselves and animals also, and everything is alive with ghosts and gods."[4]

Primitive man saw himself as part of a unity encompassing both the physical and the spiritual, the visible and the invisible. Everything in his life was integrally tied to his view of the universe. For the American Indian, like primitive man, animals, cornstalks, stones, and mountains, all were alive, all were symbols of spirits that gave form and life. Images such as these linked the people to the earth and established their place in the schema of the universe. This feeling is evoked by a statement Ochwiay Biano (Mountain Lake), a chief of the Taos Pueblo, once made to Carl Jung: "We are a people who live on the roof of the world; we are the sons of Father Sun, and with our religion we daily help our father to go across the sky. We do this not only for ourselves, but for the whole world. If we were to cease practicing our religion, in ten years the sun would no longer rise. Then it would be night forever" Jung has said of this remark, "Knowledge does not enrich us, it removes us more and more from the mythic world in which we were once at home by right of birth."[5]

It would seem that the use and development of visualization has occurred in inverse proportion to the development of language and a written structure for recording it. Initially, language was based on images. Words functioned to evoke particular images; words enabled one person to share with another an experience at which the second had not been present. Among the American Indians words, like images, originally were considered to have the power to

This picture shows a Zuni eagle fetish. The Zuni Indians believe that a fetish contains a living power which can help the owner of the fetish. Fetishes are treated as living things: they are fed and taken care of. They are used in hunting, in medicine, and in relating to spirits. The eagle is one of the hunter gods. Collection, Dr. and Mrs. I. Samuels.

This *boli* made by the Bambara of Mali is a sacred altar. It is made of wood covered with a crust of dried blood from sacrificial animals and saliva from Bambara tribesmen. The boli is a visualization of the universe (the wood) and the Bambara people's relation to it (the saliva), a visualization which literally connects the Bambara with the universe. Courtesy of The Museum of Primitive Art, New York.

Ochwiay Biano, a chief of the Taos Pueblo, believed that his people helped the sun to cross the sky each day. This visualization gave the people a reason for being. This photograph of Taos pueblo evokes the interconnectedness of earth and sky, man and heaven. Photograph by Dr. Isidore Samuels.

evoke action. And for that reason, they were considered sacred. The Hopi Song of Creation illustrates how words function as triggers of mental images to produce a sacred feeling:

"The dark purple light rises in the North,
A yellow light rises in the East.
Then we of the flowers of the earth come forth
To receive a long life of joy."[6]

This use of the word to show both reverence for life and a feeling of man's at-oneness with his world is beautifully conveyed in the narrative of Ishi, the last of the Yana Indians of northern California. Ishi evokes the mood of storytelling, of weaving verbal tapestries rich with images. "Winter was also the time for retelling the old history of the beginning of the world and of how animals and men were made, the time to hear over again the adventures of Coyote and Fox and Pine Marten, and the tale of Bear and Deer. So, sitting or lying close to the fire in the earth-covered house, and wrapped in warm rabbitskin blankets, with the rain falling outside and the snow moon bringing a light fall down Waganupa as far even as Deer Creek, the Yana cycle of changing seasons completed another full turn."[7]

As language developed words came to serve not only to evoke images or experiences but to enable the speaker to establish distance between himself and his experience, to separate himself from the experience and externalize it. When this happened words no longer carried the physical immediacy of a situation; they became a tool which functioned for a different end. Language as a whole became so removed from experience that words no longer readily triggered the sensations of the objects to which they referred. Words became tools which enabled a person to rapidly categorize objects as either recognizable or unknown, threatening or not threatening, useful or irrelevant. This function of the word became, in time, of greater importance that the sensation-sharing function.

These American Indian pots show cornstalks, animals, spirits—the basic elements of the Indians' visualization of the universe and their place in it. Lefthand pot by Grace Medicine Flower. Righthand pot by Camilio Sunflower Tafoya. Both from Santa Clara Pueblo, New Mexico. Collection, Dr. and Mrs. I. Samuels.

17

The Alaskan Eskimo constructed masks of wood and feathers. These masks were worn during ceremonies which brought the Eskimo closer to the supernatural. The masks showed supernatural figures such as deities, animal spirits, and shamans' guardian spirits. The shaman saw the spirit and carved the mask as a concrete form of his visualization. The mask shown here represents the moon or man in the moon (deity) and is from St. Michaels, Alaska. 19th century. M. H. de Young Memorial Museum, San Francisco, Gift of Mrs. Edwin R. Diamond.

Communication was now directed to oneself, and perception became a matter of identifying objects in terms of labels.

As the New York psychoanalyst Ernest Schachtel says, "The usual perceptual experience is one of recognition of something either already familiar or quickly labeled and filed away in some familiar category. It does not enrich the perceiver, but it may reassure him —usually without his awareness—that everything is 'all right' . . . Compared with this the fullest perception of the object . . . is characterized by an inexhaustible and ineffable quality, by the profoundest interest in the object, and by the enriching, refreshing, vitalizing effect which the act of perception has upon the perceiver. [The] perception (especially of nature, people, and great works of art) always breaks through and transcends the confines of the labeled, the familiar, and establishes a relation in which a direct encounter with the object itself, instead of with one or more of its labeled and familiar aspects, takes place."[8]

The desire to break through the labels and abstractions that enclose literate man has prompted him to rediscover the importance of visualization. For visualization enables him to be at one with his world once again.

FOOTNOTES

1. Jung, C. G. *Man and His Symbols*; Garden City, N.Y.; Doubleday and Co.; 1968; p. 235, from A. Jaffe, "Symbolism in the Visual Arts."

2. Jung, C. G. p. 236.

3. Jung, C. G. p. 24.

4. Wilhelm, R., trans. *The Secret of the Golden Flower*, London, Routledge & Kegan Paul, 1969, p. 123, from C. G. Jung, "Commentary."

5. Jung, C. G. *Memories, Dreams, Reflections*; New York; Vintage Books, 1963; p. 252.

6. Waters, F. *Book of the Hopi*, New York, the Viking Press, 1963, p. 6.

7. Kroeber, T. *Ishi in Two Worlds*; Berkeley, Ca.; University of California Press; 1961; p. 39.

8. Schachtel, E. *Metamorphosis*; New York; Basic Books, Inc.; 1959; p. 177.

OTHER READING

1. Teilhard De Chardin, P. *The Phenomenon of Man*; New York; Harper & Row, Publishers; 1965.

2. McLuhan, M. *Understanding Media: The Extensions of Man*, New York, Signet Books, 1964. McLuhan writes of our age as the age of the camera, movie, and TV, in which the visual image replaces the word as a primary means of communication. McLuhan describes this visual age as tribal, mythic, and closer to perceptions of preliterate cultures.

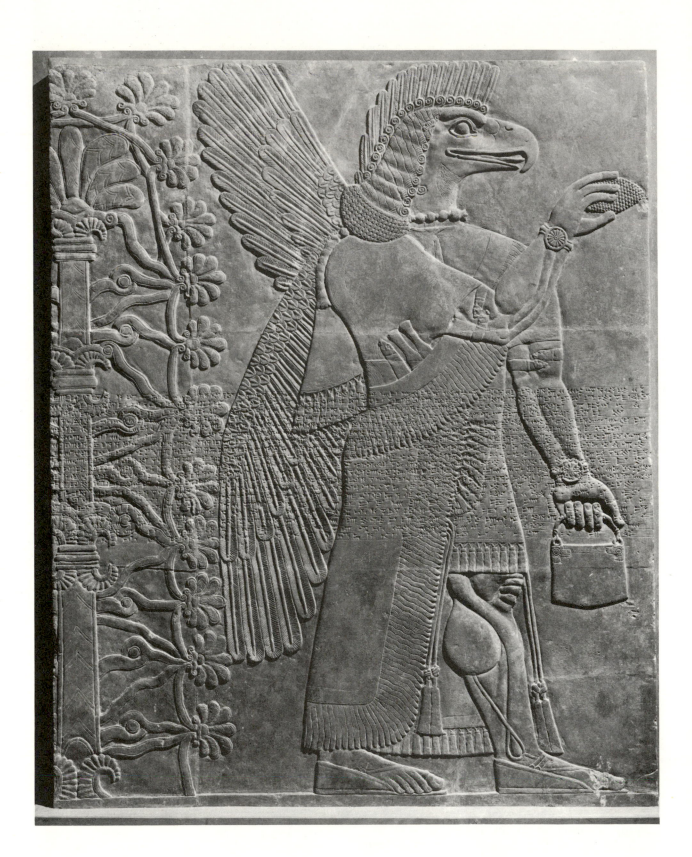

A visualization of an Assyrian fertility god rendered in stone. Art of this kind enabled ancient man to participate in a sacred communal vision. Fertility gods were believed to bring about abundant harvests. In this way the image affected the environment.
9th century B.C. Eagle-headed, winged being pollinating the sacred tree: wall panel. Alabaster. From the palace of Ashur-Nasir-Apal II, King of Assyria at Kalhu, modern Nimrud. The Metropolitan Museum of Art. Gift of John D. Rockefeller, Jr., 1913.

Chapter 3

A BRIEF HISTORY OF IMAGERY

In the last hundred years specialists in different fields have begun to rediscover the existence and meaning of visualization. Historians, religious scholars, archaeologists, physicians, and psychologists have begun to study the nature of the inner image as it relates to their area of specialization.[1] There is no widely-accepted overview of visualization at this time. There is only a general striving toward understanding in many fields, from many viewpoints. We present here some of the specialized approaches to visualization, synthesizing them into a small history of inner vision.

Philosophers and priests in every ancient culture used visualization as a tool for growth and rebirth. The Egyptian Hermes Trismegistres believed that THE ALL creates the Universe mentally, in a manner similar to the process whereby man creates mental images.[2] Beginning with Hermes, a spiritual philosophy was born based on primacy of mind, as opposed to primacy of matter. This philosophy stated that images held in the mind affect the physical universe. The corollary to this thought is that a particular image held in the mind will bring about a particular effect.

Hermetic philosophy (which later gave rise to alchemy) believed in *transmutation,* a process of transformation and spiritual development by which people can change their mental state from hate to love, from fear to courage. Hermes believed that thoughts have characteristics similar to the physical world, that thoughts have vibrational levels and energy levels which bring about changes in the physical universe. Learning to control mental images is one method used to produce such transmutations.[3]

Since the time of the cave paintings, man has externalized his spiritual visualizations in the form of art. Objects of art give concrete form to mental images and allow everyone to participate in the vision. In creating a work of art the artist

This Egyptian sculpture of the XXX Dynasty depicts the Hawk-God Horus protecting the smaller figure of King Nectanebos. Horus was the Egyptian god of the daytime and he was associated with healing. Tiny likenesses of Horus were believed to frighten off evil demons which were thought to be disease-causing. The Metropolitan Museum of Art, Rogers Fund, 1934.

holds a sacred image in his mind for a sustained period of time, concentrating on and working out its details. Viewers concentrate on the same image as they look at the sacred work of art, both firsthand and later in their memory.

From a Hermetic point of view, the person who holds a sacred image in his mind experiences the effects produced by the specific energy of that image, effects which extend to the world around him.

Starting with the river-basin cultures of Summaria, Assyria, and Babylonia (4,000-1,000 B.C.) images of fertility gods were externalized in the form of sculptures. It was believed that the presence of these gods would induce the fertility that people needed—rich fields, abundant harvests, and healthy children. The life of the people was intimately bound up with these sculptures in rites as well as in beliefs. Similarly, the Egyptians, from 3,000 to 300 B.C., represented their gods in both sculpture and painting.

Visualization in the form of concentration on an image was employed as part of Indian yogic practices in very ancient times. The Yoga Sutra of Patanjali, written in approximately 200 B.C., brought together ascetic practices used in India from time immemorial. Primary among these were *dharana*, the focusing of one's attention on a particular place, either inside or outside of the body; *dhyana*, the continued focus of attention aided by supportive suggestions; and *samadhi*, the union between the object and the person concentrating upon it. The Yoga Sutras say that when a person has achieved union with the object he sees the truth of the object and consciousness flows blissfully and calmly.[4] Southern Buddhists visualize simple objects such as colors or elements. They use such exercises to develop their powers of concentration.[5]

Tantric Yoga is the most highly developed system man has achieved for holding images in his mind to achieve an effect. Tantric thought became popular in India around the sixth century A.D. and permeated both Buddhism and Hinduism. It is interesting to note that Tantrism developed in the outlying, rural provinces, where the influence of aboriginal cultures was strong. Tantrism rediscovered for Indian thought the religion of the Mother, mother earth, generation and fecundity. According to

Indian thought, Tantrism was developed to meet the needs of the *Kali-Yuga,* or dark age, a time in which man's concentration centers in his body rather than in his spirit.[6] Tantrism clearly applies to modern man who is not in direct contact with the truth, who is separated from the truth by his habitual use of labels. A person studying Tantrism is taught "to 'visualize' a divine image, to construct it mentally or, more precisely, to project it on a sort of inner screen through an act of creative imagination . . . There is . . . no question of abandoning oneself to a pure spontaneity and passively receiving the content of . . . the individual or collective unconscious; it is a question of awakening one's inner forces, yet at the same time maintaining perfect lucidity and self-control. The aspirant must visualize what has been 'seen' and prescribed and codified by the masters, not what his personal imagination might project."[7] Visualization is the step which precedes actual identification with, and union with, the divinity. Visualization as used in Tantrism is not an intellectual exercise, it is a matter of experience. In addition to visualizing the deities, Tantric students project the image of the divinity into parts of their body to free the energies there. A similar technique called *dkihr* is used by the Moslems and the Sufis. Tantric students also project colors and shapes to specific areas of the body.

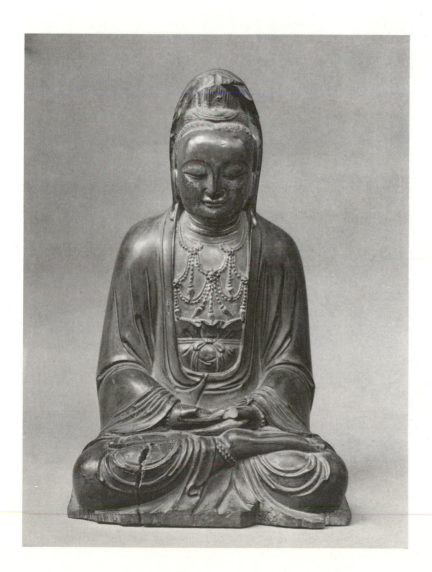

17th century Chinese sculpture from the Ming Dynasty. The figure is Kuan Yin, a Bodhisattva, an enlightened person whose role is to help people. As depicted here, the figure epitomizes the bliss and inner peace that can accompany meditation. The Metropolitan Museum of Art, Fletcher Fund, 1936.

23

This 18th century Tibetan tanka depicts Mañjuśrī, the Bodhisattva of transcendant wisdom. Mañjuśrī is shown in a full lotus position, the most common meditation pose. He is seated on a blue lion and holds aloft a sword to dissipate the clouds of ignorance. In his left hand is a pink lotus on which rest a book and a flaming pearl. In the lower righthand corner an attendant Lama, or Tibetan holy man, makes an offering of dough. Asian Art Museum of San Francisco. The Avery Brundage Collection.

The Tantric mandala symbolizes the universe and creation. The yogin meditates on the image and thereby approaches his own center. Mandalas are drawn on cloth and serve as an altar, a sacred space. Asian Art Museum of San Francisco. The Avery Brundage Collection.

This superb painting, *The Virgin With St. Inés and St. Tecla* by El Greco, gives substance to the kind of visions experienced by Roman Catholic mystics in 16th century Spain. The angels surrounding the Virgin and Child are portrayed in cloudlike forms which look as though they are emanations of thought. El Greco's visionary paintings allow many people to participate in the mystical experience. National Gallery of Art, Washington. Widener Collection, 1942.

Duccio's *Temptation of Christ* shows Jesus being tempted by Satan, whose dark, frightening apparition appears to the left of Christ. This is one of a number of visionary experiences described in the New Testament. Copyright, The Frick Collection, New York.

Another Tantric visualization practice involves the use of a mandala, a circular design containing geometric shapes in the center. The person meditating on the mandala mentally concentrates on that image and becomes one with it. Mandalas have been used by many cultures to represent the creation of the universe. Carl Jung has theorized that mandalas represent centering, the unification of parts of the psyche.[8]

Fertility goddesses and idols, which are externalizations of inner images, were rejected by the Biblical Jews. In their place the Jews looked to an abstract god for whom there was no concrete visualization. But the Jews frequently recorded experiencing other forms of visualizations—visions and visionary dreams. These examples of visualization can be characterized by the visualizer's feeling that he exercises some control over his inner images. That is, the visualizer does not have the choice of whether or not to continue to concentrate on the image. Dreams and visions are unique in that they come and go unbidden. Also, visions and, to a lesser extent, dreams can be extraordinarily vivid. Frequently following a dream or vision the person feels that the experience must have taken place in the external world, because it was so vivid. Like other visualizations, visions and dreams are psychic experiences which can affect the person and the world around them. Most people who experience visionary states are profoundly affected by their experience; the course of their lives is often changed as a result.

The Old Testament is a rich source of such visions and dreams. Perhaps the most familiar dream story is that of the Egyptian Pharaoh who dreamed of seven sleek, fat cows who were devoured by seven lean and gaunt cows, then dreamed again of seven full and ripe ears of corn which were swallowed up by seven thin and gaunt ears. These dreams were rightly interpreted by Joseph as foretelling seven years of plenty for Egypt, followed by seven years of famine.

Most religions have used visualization as one of their basic techniques for helping people to realize their spiritual goals. Visualization intensifies any experience. The visualizer lives, or relives, the experience with great involvement. Visualization enables a person to incorporate into his body or being in a concrete way what must otherwise be an abstract idea. The Christian Communion service is an example of this. It combines outer and inner reality. The service begins with concrete objects—bread and wine—in a physical ceremony. From this literal experience, the Christian is asked to visualize the Last Supper that Christ shared with his disciples and to be purified by it. In the Roman Catholic faith the bread and wine are believed to *become* the body and blood of Christ, that is, they are believed to be *transmuted, transsubstantiated*, in the ceremony.

"For in the night in which he was betrayed, he took Bread; and when he had given thanks, he brake it, and gave it to his disciples, saying, Take, eat, this is my Body, which is given for you; Do this in remembrance of me. Likewise, after supper, he took the Cup; and when he had given thanks, he gave it to them, saying, Drink ye all of this; for this is my Blood of the New Testament, which is shed for you, and for many, for the remission of sins; Do this, as oft as ye shall drink it, in remembrance of me."[9]

Visualizations based on rituals involving concrete objects seem uniquely suited to the Western mind, which has been steeped in the material rather than the spiritual, in visible rather than invisible, in body rather than mind:

"Grant us therefore, gracious Lord, so to eat the flesh of thy dear Son Jesus Christ, and to drink his blood, that our sinful bodies may be made clean by his body, and our souls washed through his most precious blood, and that we may evermore dwell in him, and he in us."[10]

One of the central visualizations of Christianity is portrayed in this unusual trefoil panel. In the foreground Christ is seen struggling with the cross, while in the background the crucifixion has already taken place. Medieval artists traditionally portrayed consecutive events in one scene. Visualization enables a person to transcend time and space in a similar way. *Christ Carrying the Cross,* Juan de Flandes (Flemish, active in Spain, d. 1519) M. H. de Young Memorial Museum, San Francisco. Gift of Mr. and Mrs. George T. Cameron.

In addition to using visualization for spiritual goals, man has also used it for more materialistic ones. The cave paintings we discussed at the beginning of this chapter are believed by some anthropologists to have played a role in insuring the success of the hunt. Similarly, the fertility gods of both ancient and more recent times were believed to bring about abundant harvests.

One of the most basic uses of visualization is that of healing the body. The *shaman,* or healer often visualized himself going on a journey, finding the sick person's soul, and returning it to him. The shamanistic philosophy of healing sees the cause of illness as a disharmony in the sick person's world. Thus it follows that the shaman seeks to visualize the reuniting of the patient with his soul, rather than seeking to isolate a physical cause of disease. Among the Navaho Indians elaborate, concrete visualizations, in which a number of people participate, are used for healing a sick person. The rite helps the patient visualize himself as healthy, and it helps the healer visualize the patient as regaining a harmonious place in the natural schema.

For the Egyptian followers of Hermes, who believed that everything is mind, disease was thought to be cured by visualizing perfect health. Holding in mind the image of a healing god was believed to bring about a state of health in the physical world.[11] Hermetic principles of healing with the mind influenced ancient

An ancestor figure from Tamberan House in New Guinea. The ancestor represented by the figure was honored by the Abelam in a ritual. Aspects of the ancestor were believed to inhabit yams and make them grow. Prestige and authority were accorded to the tribesmen who were able to grow the largest yams. Tribesmen not only used visualization to increase the growth and size of their own yams, they also used magic to try to cause rival tribesmen's yams to stop growing or rot in the ground. M. H. de Young Memorial Museum, San Francisco. Gift of Mr. Victor Bergeron.

A shaman's guardian figure from the American Northwest coast. It is believed to help the shaman contact supernatural figures. M. H. de Young Memorial Museum, San Francisco. Gift of Captain William Noyes.

The Headache

Illness has often been visualized as a demon. These two 18th century prints show visualizations for two common ailments. Above, *The Headache* by George Cruikshank, 1819. Below, *The Gout* by James Gillray, 1799. Reproduced from *Medicine and the Artist (Ars Medica)* by permission of the Philadelphia Museum of Art. Courtesy, Dover Publications, Inc.

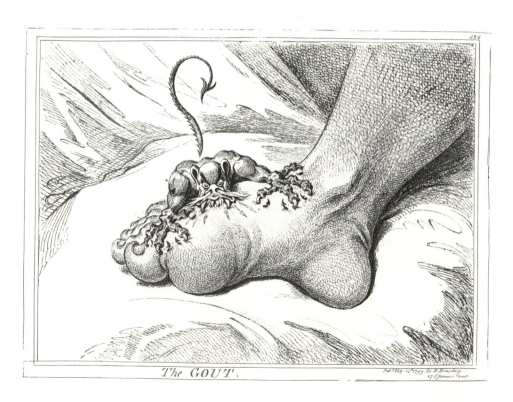

The GOUT.

Greek, medieval, and some modern forms of healing. The Greek healer had patients dream of being healed by the gods. Paracelsus, a Swiss alchemist and physician of the sixteenth century, believed that "The power of the imagination is a great factor in medicine. It may produce diseases in man and it may cure them."[12]

In the late 1800's Mary Baker Eddy discovered Christian Science. Christian Science is based on the concept of God as infinite, divine Mind. Disease is essentially a product of the human mind and through deep, consecrated prayer the action of this divine Mind is brought to bear in human experience to heal physical disease. The following quotations from the Christian Science textbook, *Science*

and Health with Key to the Scriptures, by Mary Baker Eddy expresses some of its theology. For more about Christian Science we suggest reading *Science and Health*.

"Science not only reveals the origin of all disease as mental, but it also declares that all disease is cured by divine Mind." (p. 169)

"Christian scientific practice begins with Christ's keynote of harmony, 'Be not afraid!'" (p. 410)

"When fear disappears, the foundation of disease is gone." (p. 368)

"To prevent disease or to cure it, the power of Truth, of divine Spirit, must break the dream of the material senses. To heal by argument, find the type of the ailment, get its name, and array your mental plea against the physical. Argue at first mentally, not

Visualizing body systems as healthy and working harmoniously helps to prevent and cure disease. Images such as these can serve as suggestions for such visualizations. Left, *The Ninth Plate of Muscles* from the workshop of Titian. Right, *A Chart of Veins* from the workshop of Titian. (The latter picture was made before Harvey's discovery of the heart's role in circulation.) Both illustrations were originally from the famous anatomy book *De Humani Corporis Fabrica* by Vesalius, 1543. Reproduced from *Medicine and the Artist (Ars Medica)* by permission of the Philadelphia Museum of Art. Courtesy, Dover Publications.

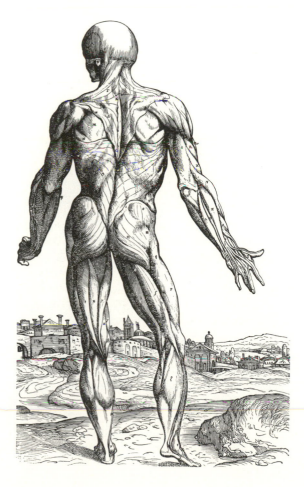
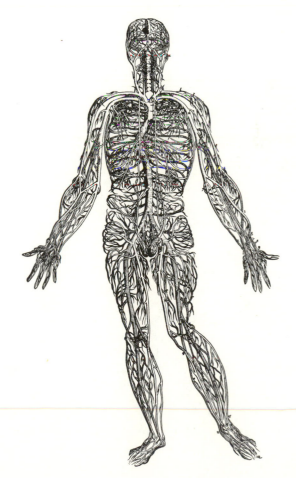

audibly, that the patient has no disease, and conform the argument so as to destroy the evidence of disease. Mentally insist that harmony is the fact, and that sickness is a temporal dream. Realize the presence of health and the fact of harmonious being, until the body corresponds with the normal conditions of health and harmony." (p. 412)[13]

Other religious denominations and groups such as the Rosicrucians have also used visualization in healing.

Modern Western medicine is rediscovering visualization as a healing tool. The American physician and physiologist Edmund Jacobson did experiments in the 1920's which proved that when people pictured themselves doing an action such as running, the muscles in their body associated with that action contracted in small, but definite amounts.[14] Also in the 1920's, a German physician named J. H. Schultz developed a healing technique called "Autogenic Training," which uses relaxation, autosuggestion, and visualization in the treatment of diseases.[15] Since that time a number of people have conducted research into and developed other techniques for healing which use visualization. We will talk more about them in the chapter *Medicine and Healing*.

Psychologists and philosophers have long accorded inner images and visualization primary importance in their thinking. Aristotle believed that thought itself was composed of images. He also believed that images have the power to stimulate a person's emotions and motivate him to effort. Locke, a philosopher of the late 1600's, believed that thought consisted of images derived from perceptions of the outer world.

Up until the early 20th century the science of psychology had accepted as self-evident the validity and existence of images and inner experience. Pioneering psychologists like William James, Francis Galton, and Edward Titchener believed that the image was a fundamental concept in psychology. Then, American psychologists, led by the behaviorist John Watson, became preoccupied with the scientific methodology of the physical sciences. That is, they turned their attention toward only those areas in which quantified measurements could be made, duplicated, and predicted: neurophysiology, perception, learning, conditioning and reinforcement.

John Watson was opposed by E.B. Titchener, a Cornell University psychologist of the "European school" who believed in the existence of internal images and who was, himself, an exceptional visualizer. Titchener's world was so rich with mental images that he refused to deny their existence even if, as Watson claimed, they could not be measured.

But the lure of becoming a hard science —rather than an area of philosophy—was too great for the mainstream of psychology. And psychology, under Watson's leadership, became the science of behavior rather than the study of inner processes. In the United States psychology became so overwhelmingly behaviorist-oriented that virtually no further works were published on mental imagery for fifty years.[16]

In the 1960's psychologists again became interested in the more abstract inner processes of the mind. In 1964 the American psychologist Robert Holt wrote a paper entitled, "Imagery: The Return of the Ostracized," welcoming back imagery—visualization—as an important area of scientific pursuit.[17] The growth of interest in visualization since the 1960's is part of a new climate of thought in the West. This new climate has manifested in an interest in all forms of imagery, in the experience of Eastern religions and philosophy, in hypnotism, and in hallucinogenic drugs and altered states of consciousness in general.

From its beginnings in the late 19th century psychiatry has used techniques based on people's ability to visualize. Since Freud's time, psychotherapists have asked patients to form spontaneous images in their minds, believing that as patients examine their personal images—whether of memory or of imagination—their mental state will improve. Regardless of whether the psychiatrist comments on the image, his objective support is considered an important part of the therapeutic process. The Freudian psychiatrist tends to analyze images "in terms of underlying defense motives . . . sexual and aggressive impulses or derivative childhood memories."[18] Jungian therapists also use visualization to help a person

Many philosophers and psychologists believe that thought itself is composed of images. They believe that perceptions are stored in the mind in the form of images and can later be recalled. Illustration by Susan Ida Smith.

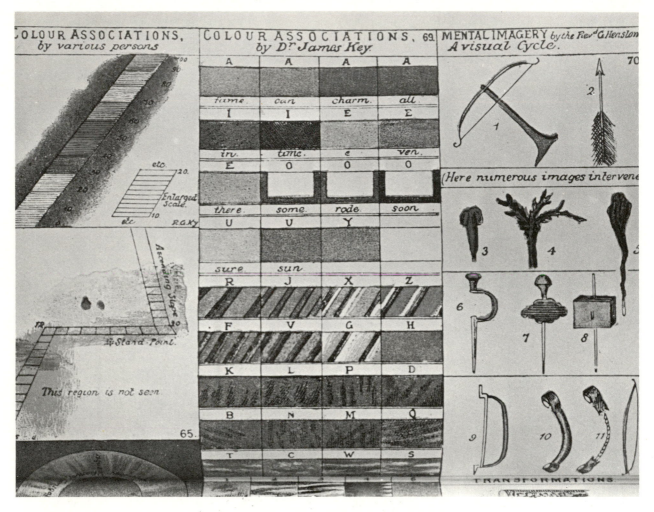

One of the earliest imagery researchers, Sir Francis Galton, demonstrated the variety of imagery and styles of thought experienced by people. This illustration from *Inquiries Into Human Faculty and Its Development* (1883) shows some of the modes of imagery studied by Galton. The lefthand column shows images seen by people when they thought of particular numbers. For example, the middle left shows the spatial landmarks associated with numbers: twenty and above were seen as an ascending slope. The middle column shows colors and patterns that were seen when people thought of specific words or letters. The righthand column showed a series of images seen by the Rev. G. Henslow. The images represent a visual cycle in which one image spontaneously gave rise to another.

get in touch with his unconscious. Like Freudians, the Jungian therapist encourages the patient to become a passive receiver, letting go of organized thought. "In this state, previously hidden contents emerge . . . often in the form of visual images."[19] The patient and the therapist work together in analyzing the images that emerge. Jung called this process *active imagination*. He believed that the images that people received in the state of active imagination were often archetypal figures such as witches, devils, sorcerers, heroes, and wisemen. Jung encouraged his patients to allow these images to develop further.

Currently, visualization is being used in a number of different psychotherapeutic techniques—including Guided Affective Imagery, directed daydreams, Psychosynthesis, and behaviorist desensitization. We will discuss these therapies in the chapter *Psychology*.

Throughout history people have been exposed to the power of mental images, an idea that dates back, as we have seen, to earliest man. In this book we will bring together theories of how visualization works, visualization techniques from many disciplines, and examples of how people can use visualization effectively in all areas of their lives.

A A Witch. B A Spirit raised by the Witch.
C A Friar raising his Imps. D A Fairy Ring.
E A Witch rideing on the Devill through the Aire.
F An Inchanted Castle.

Jung believed that the images a person saw during therapy were often archetypal. This *frontispiece* from *Devil's Cloyster Pandremonium* by R. Gent, 1684, shows a group of archetypal figures especially common to the 17th century.

FOOTNOTES

1. See references after each chapter in Section III.
2. _____ *The Kybalion, A Study of the Hermetic Philosophy of Ancient Egypt and Greece*; Chicago, Ill.; The Yogi Publication Society; 1940; p. 69.
3. _____ The Kybalion, p. 47.
4. Mishra, R. *Yoga Sutras*; Garden City, N.Y.; Anchor Press; 1973; pp. 297–305.
5. Eliade, M. *Yoga: Immortality and Freedom*, New York, Pantheon, 1958, p. 195.
6. Eliade, M. p. 202.
7. Eliade, M. pp. 207–208.
8. Jung, C. G. *Collected Works, Vol. 9*; London; Routledge & Kegan Paul.
9. _____ *The Book of Common Prayer*, New York, The Church Pension Fund, 1945, p. 80.
10. _____ *The Book of Common Prayer*, p. 82.
11. Jayne, W. *The Healing Gods of Ancient Civilizations*, New Haven, Yale Univ. Press, 1925.
12. Hartmann, F. *Paracelsus: Life and Prophecies*; Blauvelt, N.Y.; Rudolf Steiner Publications; 1973; p. 129.
13. Eddy, M. B. *Science and Health*; Boston, Mass.; First Church of Christ, Scientist; 1934; pp. 169, 410, 368, 412.
14. Jacobson, E. *Progressive Relaxation*; Chicago, Ill.; University of Chicago Press; 1942.
15. Luthe, W. *Autogenic Therapy*, New York, Grune & Stratton, 1969.
16. Klinger, E. *Structure and Functions of Fantasy*, New York, Wiley-Interscience, 1971, pp. 11–13.
17. Holt, R. "Imagery: The Return of the Ostracized," *American Psychologist*, 19:254–264, 1964.
18. Horowitz, M. *Image Formation and Cognition*, New York, Appleton-Century-Crofts, 1970, p. 296.
19. Horowitz, M. p. 296.

A striking visionary image by the 18th century English poet and printmaker William Blake. This etching, *The Whirlwind of Lovers* illustrates Canto V of Dante's *Inferno,* in which souls of the lustful are tossed for all eternity on a howling wind. Both Blake and Dante were known for the vivid imagination images they created. The Metropolitan Museum of Art, Rogers Fund, 1917.

Chapter 4

VARIETIES OF VISUALIZATION EXPERIENCE

Since the time man began analyzing his experiences he has tried to define and explain the interior processes of his mind—all those experiences which are invisible to another person because they do not have physical referents. Philosophers have speculated at length on the nature of mental imagery, and scientists have found the phenomenon difficult to verify or measure. Indeed, behavioral psychologists of the 1920's went so far as to say that mental images simply did not exist.

Since 1960 psychologists have done a great deal of work exploring and categorizing mental imagery and inner processes. Contemporary psychologists distinguish several types of images. Probably the most common kind of visualization that people experience is *memory*. If a person tries to remember a friend, the bed in his room, or what the dashboard of his car looks like, he immediately sees an image in his mind. People refer to this experience as forming a mental picture or seeing with their mind's eye. Some people feel that they do not "see" the scene, but that they simply have a strong sense of the scene and "know" what it looks like.

Each person can experience the visual nature of remembering by simply picturing in his mind's eye the room in which he slept as a child or teenager. A person can count the doors and windows and see the walls and furniture in the room. Most people, without trying, imagine that they are *in* the room. And they act as if they're in the room, in that they find themselves looking around the room, scanning the walls with their eyes. In fact, if a person is watched carefully while he remembers in this way with his eyes closed, his eyelids will probably be seen to flicker and his eyes may be seen to move beneath their lids. People often begin to notice a change in the way they feel during memory recall. They may feel relaxed, dreamy, nostalgic, or unhappy.

Childhood photographs often stimulate vivid memory images of events, places, and people that have been long forgotten. Photograph by Dr. I. Samuels.

If people think back over a typical day they realize that memories frequently come to their mind. The memories may be ones from the distant past or ones recently formed. For example, as a person drives down a familiar road he briefly visualizes a sharp turn ahead and automatically begins to slow for it. Or as he is shopping at the market he suddenly sees himself throwing out an empty wrapper of bread the day before and realizes that he needs to buy another loaf. When he speaks to his sister on the phone he sees images of her face, her house, her family. In each case a visual image comes to mind.

Psychologists call these *memory images.* Mardi Horowitz, a California research psychiatrist, defines a *memory image* as "a reconstruction or resurrection of a past perception."[1] A memory image may be experienced spontaneously or it may be summoned—as for example, when a person tries to remember where he left something. Psychologists use two concepts in describing images: vividness and controllability. Memory images may span the range of vivid-

ness, from vague and fuzzy to clear and detailed. The Austrian psychologist Alan Richardson says that memory images are typically hazy, unstable, incomplete, and of brief duration.[2] No matter how vivid memory images are, they are rarely mistaken for an actual experience in the outside world. And, in general, memory images are controllable—that is, they can be summoned at will and those that arise spontaneously can be stopped whenever the person desires.

Some people are able to call up a memory image of a particular page in a book and read off, word by word, what is written on the page. Other people will be able to see in their mind's eye where in the book the particular page lies, but they will not be able to "read" the words. One person may immediately see an image clearly and in rich detail; another person may recall the same details slowly, one after another, as he mentally "looks" at the image. Some people, when looking at a memory image, are easily able to control the image in space; they can "move" around a remembered object, "seeing" the object from different vantage

People can remember visual images from their childhood. One of the easiest memory images for them to evoke is their childhood room. Often when people visualize their childhood room certain objects stand out sharply. Illustration of a memory image by Susan Ida Smith.

Through imagination imagery, people can invent a new reality. People can see themselves doing things that are ordinarily impossible. Illustration of an imagination image by Susan Ida Smith.

points. Other people may at first be able to see the image only from one vantage point.

Often memory images involve one or more of the senses in addition to the visual component, although the visual part of a memory is generally the central aspect. A person may recall a distinct smell, "hear" a specific sound that was connected with the image, or re-experience a particular emotion that was related to the scene. Memory images are frequently evoked by a sensory impression—often a specific smell or touch. For instance, the smell of a particular combination of ink and paper in a magazine unfailingly triggers in my (Nancy) mind an image of myself—at a time before I had learned to read—sitting in my parent's living room *pretending* that I was reading as I looked at the pictures in a magazine. Richardson comments that "memory images are usually linked to particular events or occasions having a personal reference."[3]

Eidetic images are an especially vivid form of memory image. The experience of eidetic imagery is similar to the phenomenon people refer to as photographic memory. A person who experiences eidetic images can perform amazing feats of memory. For example, he can look at a complicated picture, then close his eyes and see a vivid replica of that picture in his mind's eye. Some people may only see the mental image for a matter of seconds; others may be able to recall the image for years. An eidetic imager can scan the picture in his mind and report back precise details as if he were still looking at the external image. A striking example of this phenomenon is provided by the Russian psychologist A.R. Luria who reported on a subject's ability to remember many random numbers, letters, or nonsense syllables arranged in a checkerboard fashion. The subject did this by recalling the image exactly as he had seen it and then reading off the figures from his mental image.[4]

The most striking experiment done on eidetic imagery involved showing subjects a pair of random, computer-generated dot patterns, each one composed of over a million dots. When viewed singly neither pattern revealed a figure; when viewed through a stereoscope, which simultaneously presents one pattern to each eye, an identifiable figure emerged. It was found that subjects with eidetic ability were able to combine the images and see the figure in their mind hours after they saw the random dot patterns.[5]

Psychologists have found that eidetic images are most frequently experienced by school-age children. Child development researchers believe eidetic imagery is an underlying phenomenon of the learning process and tends to diminish in adolescence—when abstract thought and higher verbal skills develop. Most children are neither encouraged to maintain their eidetic skills nor to expand them. Our culture places more value on the ability to label and categorize an experience such as going shopping, than on being able to recall all the myriad images of a single visit to the supermarket. People tend to perceive and log their experiences in terms of a goal-oriented model. For instance, a woman at the market considers it important to remember what's on her shopping list, but she doesn't consider it important to remember the image of a child eating an ice cream cone.

Another common visualization experience is that of imagination. For example, a man might imagine how his room would look if he moved a chair next to the window. A woman might imagine how she would look if she had her hair cut short, or how her husband would look if he grew a mustache. Through imagination imagery a person can create a dog with duck's feet, a sky with two suns or other images that don't exist in external reality. A person can create someone they've never met, such as a childhood imaginary playmate. An *imagination image* may contain elements of past perceptions, but arranged in a different way than when they were originally perceived. A continuum exists among imagination images from those which rely heavily on past perceptions to those which are largely made up of newly created material. As opposed to memory images, imagination images generally have no fixed reference point, that is, they are not tied to a specific occasion. Richardson says that imagination images tend to be "substantial, vividly colored . . . and involve concentrated and quasi-hypnotic attention with inhibition of associations,"[6] that is, they are free of intruding thought.

Imagination images such as this one often illustrate books for children. Children readily accept a world of fantasy and participate in it. W. Heath-Robinson, British, 1872-1944. *Over farms & fields & rivers & ponds.* Drawing for "Cosey Hokey" in *Topsy-Turvy Tales.* The Metropolitan Museum of Art, The Elisha Whittelsey Fund, 1967.

Through imagination images, people can glimpse creatures visible only to the mind's eye. Morris Graves. *Little-Known Bird of the Inner Eye.* (1941). Gouache, 20¾ × 36⅝ inches. Collection, The Museum of Modern Art, New York. Purchase.

For centuries people have travelled into space in imagination and seen fantastic other worlds. Etching from *Incredible Things Seen by J. Wilkins on his Famous Voyage to the Moon* by Filippo Morghen, Italian, born about 1730. The Metropolitan Museum of Art, Harris Brisbane Dick Fund, 1932.

In imagination images, disparate elements can be put together to form new wholes. *Here Everything Is Still Floating* (1920) by Max Ernst. Pasted photo-engravings and pencil, 4⅛ × 4⅞ inches. Collection, Museum of Modern Art, New York. Purchase.

Pastoral country scenes stimulate daydreams. *Wivenhoe Park, Essex* by the artist John Constable shows the English countryside in the early 1800's. National Gallery of Art, Washington. Widener Collection, 1942.

Far from being whimsical or unimportant, this kind of visualization is the stuff of which creativity is made. Imagination images are the source of solutions to problems. Writers often visualize their characters acting out scenes. Painters see visual images, architects envision buildings, mathematicians see pictures of geometric shapes and surfaces. These visualizations are the basis of new work for the creative person. We'll say more about such images in the chapter on *Creativity*.

Daydreams and *fantasy* are a special case of imagery made up of a combination of memory and imagination images. In a daydream people picture scenes, objects, and other people in ongoing situations. The objects or people may be known or unknown, and the situation may have occurred, in part, in the past or it may not. For example, while sitting at her office desk, a woman might imagine lying on a sunny beach. Imagination frequently and typically comes into play in anticipatory experiences. A simple example of such imagery is a man daydreaming about a boat he hopes to buy. He may picture buying the boat, sailing it in the bay with friends, then trailering it home at the end of the day.

Daydreams may be past as well as future oriented. A person may imagine what he wished he had done in a past situation, as well as what he will do if a certain situation arises. Daydreams introduce a time factor into inner imagery. In general, daydreams deal with a series of images, more or less in chronological order, in which events take place. You could say that the images are part of an internal continuum, as in a film. In fact, a number of recent films have portrayed various aspects of personal imagery in flashbacks and in the use of still pictures. As time and action become part of his imagery, a person tends to forget himself, to become engrossed. While people are absorbed in daydreams, they are less likely to analyze or separate themselves from their images. The daydream experience bears more similarity to events in external reality than memory images do, and a person is less likely to apprehend the experience as a visualization.

Daydreams serve to release people from the pressures of everyday life. *Breezing Up* by the American painter Winslow Homer conveys the feeling of daydreaming about leisure activities. National Gallery of Art, Washington. Gift of the W. L. and May T. Mellon Foundation, 1943.

Jerome Singer, a Yale University psychologist whose main interest is daydreams and fantasy, says that 96 per cent of the subjects he studied reported having daydreams. Singer describes a number of different varieties of daydreams: daydreams about fear of failure, about hostility, about achieving success, about sex, about heroic activities, about problem-solving, about a sense of well-being.[7]

One imagery experience people are often unaware of occurs in the twilight state between sleep and waking. Psychologists call these images *hypnagogic* when they occur preceding sleep and *hypnopompic* when they occur just after sleep, before becoming fully awake. These reverie images tend to be vivid, detailed and beyond the reach of conscious control. People in hypnagogic states have described seeing images of light flashes, sparks, geometric forms, faces, even whole scenes. The experiences are vivid enough to seem real, but in general people know the images are internal.

One of the most important categories of imagery is *dreams*. In his sleep a person may dream of people, places and objects—familiar and unfamiliar images jumbled together, one following another. Psychologists have found that everyone dreams. In fact, the average sleeper studied had three to five discrete dreams per night.[8] Yet people often report that they do not dream or do so only rarely. In fact, they simply do not remember their dreams. Psychologists have divided sleep into different phases based on their studies of eye movements and brain waves. Dreaming has been found to be associated with rapid eye movements (REM) and

Dreams may contain vivid but enigmatic images that visually express profound relationships. Here memories coalesce with wishes and imagination, and everyday events are seen in a new light. *A Father and Daughter Dream.* Photograph by Michael Samuels.

In the twilight state between waking and sleeping people frequently see images of whole scenes transfixed in time and space. The images are sometimes accompanied by unusual lighting that is brilliant, flashing or vividly highlighted. *Star Woman.* Photograph by Michael Samuels.

4-6 cycles/second brain waves. When a person who does not frequently report having dreams is awakened during REM sleep, they report "visual-image events of fantasy-like quality."[9] Sleep studies have shown that people dream throughout sleep, but are most likely to report visual images during phases of REM sleep.

Dream contents vary greatly, from those about the day's events to those about food, sex, childhood, and people or abstract ideas. Dreams, like daydreams and hypnagogic imagery, contain varying amounts of past perceptions (memory images) and imagination images. Most people experience dreams predominantly in terms of visual images, but dreams may contain elements of any of the other sensory modalities. Whereas most people feel they have some element of control over their daydreams, they feel they have little or no control over images in their dreams.

Dreams break all the laws of causality, of time and space chronology, of rational thought. A dreamer can fly through the air unaided, be a child one second and an adult the next, travel thousands of miles in a moment, all with no break in the dream's inner logic.

Of all the types of imagery we've discussed, dreams can have the most compelling sense of reality. We've already noted that visual images work differently than rational, verbal thought; that there is less analysis, less separation between subject and object in the visual image and a greater sense of participation. This is especially true of the dream state. As people dream, they believe that what is happening in the dream is actually taking place. In particularly vivid dreams, people may even believe dream events have transpired after they've awakened. Probably everyone at one time or another has had the experience of saying, "But it seemed so real; I can't believe it was a dream. Are you sure it didn't happen?" This is an example of not being able to distinguish between inner and outer reality, which we discussed in the first chapter.

A person's body can react to the inner images of a dream as surely as it reacts to events in the outer world. Everyone who has experienced a particularly vivid and frightening nightmare knows what it feels like to awaken with his heart in his mouth and a quickened pulse. Just as the images in a dream can affect a person's body, they can have striking effects on the outside world as well. Dreams sometimes provide the answer to a problem with which a person has been struggling. One of the most famous examples of this phenomenon comes from the chemist, Kekulé, who dreamt of a snake holding its tail in its mouth, which gave him the idea for understanding the structure of the benzene ring. The prophetic dream is an equally striking example of the inner image being connected to outer reality. As we mentioned, in the Bible the Pharaoh had such a dream—a dream of fat ears of corn being consumed by lean ones, of fat sleek cows being eaten by thin ones.

A less frequently experienced kind of visualization is the *hallucination* or *vision*. The person who experiences a vision believes that it is occurring in the outer world, although another person who was with them would not necessarily agree. Obviously, a vision is an extremely vivid image. Psychiatrists sometimes diagnose people who have visions or hallucinations as psychotic. People praying or meditating, people under the influence of certain drugs, people deprived of sleep or food, and people who have been in sensory deprivation chambers often experience visions or hallucinations. Other conditions which are associated with hallucinations are fever and boring, repetitive situations such as night driving. Regularly repeated auditory "bleeps" or flashing lights may also induce hallucinations.

Hallucinations and visions differ from other forms of visual imagery in what a person perceives the source of the image to be. In an hallucination, a person believes the image he sees is external to himself. If he changes his mind and decides that what he "saw" was actually a vivid internal picture, then his experience is termed an imagination image rather than an hallucination.

50

In this pen-and-ink drawing Susan Ida Smith illustrates a recurrent dream that she had as a child. In the dream she was in an old museum at closing time and entered the elevator to leave. In the elevator she felt the presence of large shapes on either side of her. She looked around and saw the lion-like figures.

Religious mystics of all faiths have always sought to experience visions. In this 19th century picture Wilhelm von Kaulbach shows a number of Crusaders overcome by a heavenly vision. The Crusades represented the joining of religious and political, inner and outer visualizations. The Metropolitan Museum of Art, Bequest of Catharine Lorillard Wolfe, 1887.

Both the Old and New Testments are filled with visions. This picture illustrates the annunciation of Christ's birth to the shepherds. Illumination from the 15th century French manuscript *The Belles Heures of Jean, Duke of Berry*. The Metropolitan Museum of Art, The Cloisters Collection, Purchase, 1954.

This picture of *Faust in his Study* by Rembrandt Van Rijn shows the medieval alchemist, magician and astrologer conjuring up a vision of the spirit of knowledge. Courtesy of the University of Kansas Museum of Art, Lawrence, Kansas.

Many artists have been inspired by mystical visions. *The Ancient of Days* shows a vision seen by William Blake. Courtesy of The Whitworth Art Gallery, University of Manchester, England.

Like imagination images, hallucinations and visions are often the source of creative inspiration. An extreme example of this occurred in the life of the 18th century poet, William Blake. For a week Blake saw a vision of a man above the stairs in his house. He recorded this vision in a painting called, "The Ancient of Days."[10]

Another common type of visual experience is the *after-image*. This image typically takes place after looking at a bright object against a dark background, such as a bolt of lightning seen at night. If a person closes his eyes right after the flash, he will continue to see a light flash against a dark background. The original image lasts only a few seconds. It is followed by a negative after-image. If the original image is seen in black and white, the tones of the after-image are reversed. If the original image is in color, the negative after-image is seen in the complimentary colors. After-images cannot be scanned, that is, the image shifts as a person moves his eyes. Most people are not aware of after images until they are told of their existence. Then, with practice, they are able to see them.

People who spend prolonged periods staring at the same scene, for instance looking through a microscope, often experience a *recurrent image*. This image may occur immediately after looking at the original scene, or several hours later when they close their eyes to rest. People usually have little control over the appearance and disappearance of these images. A person who picks strawberries all day and later sees spontaneous images of strawberries is experiencing a recurrent image. Recurrent images also occasionally occur in people who have taken hallucinogenic drugs. In this case the image may recur long after the drug has worn off.

Memory, imagination, dreams, and visions all share a common link—visual images—and they can be looked upon as a continuum, rather than as entirely separate experiences. These divisions of visual activity are arbitrary and tend to overlap. But visual experiences do differ in details. Psychologists have found the divisions to be useful for exploring visualization. Learning about the differences between the kinds of images helps people to become aware of their own inner processes.

FOOTNOTES

1. Horowitz, M. *Image Formation and Cognition*, New York, Appleton-Century-Crofts, 1970, p. 22.
2. Richardson, A. *Mental Imagery*, New York, Springer Publishing Co., 1969, p. 43.
3. Richardson, A. p. 93.
4. Luria, A. *The Mind of a Mnemonist*; New York; Basic Books, Inc.; 1968.
5. Stromeyer, C. "Eidetikers," *Psychology Today*, 4(6) 76–80, 1970.
6. Richardson, A. p. 94.
7. Singer, J. *Daydreaming*, New York, Random House, 1966.
8. Horowitz, M. p. 33.
9. Horowitz, M. p. 23.
10. McKellar, P. *Imagination and Thinking*, London, Cohen & West, 1957, p. 2.

OTHER READING

1. Sheehan, P., ed. *The Function and Nature of Imagery*, New York, Academic Press, 1972.
2. Arnheim, R. *Visual Thinking*; Berkeley, Cal.; University of California Press; 1972.
3. Segal, S. J. *The Adaptive Functions of Imagery*, New York, Academic Press, 1971.
4. McKim, R. *Experiences in Visual Thinking*; Monterey, Cal.; Brooks/Cole Publishing Co.; 1972.

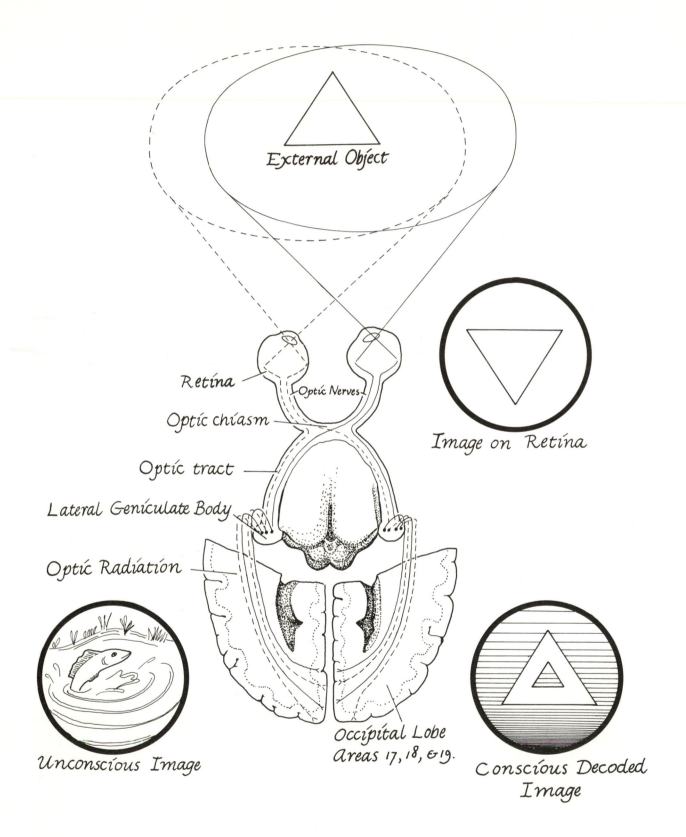

External Object

Image on Retina

Retina

Optic Nerves

Optic chiasm

Optic tract

Lateral Geniculate Body

Optic Radiation

Occipital Lobe
Areas 17, 18, & 19.

Unconscious Image

Conscious Decoded
Image

A diagram of the pathways of perception. Illustration by Susan Ida Smith.

Chapter 5

VISUALIZATION AND PERCEPTION

It has been found that mental images have many of the same physical components as open-eyed perceptions. For example, researchers have found correlations between a person's eye movements and the moment when he was dreaming of climbing stairs.[1] In another study, it was found that people scanning their eidetic images moved their eyes just as if they were still viewing the external picture.[2] The American physiologist Neisser has said that "visual images are apparently produced by the same integrative processes that make ordinary perception possible . . . Visual memory differs from perception because it is based principally on stored, rather than on current information, but it involves the same kind of synthesis."[3]

A person's vision of an external object begins with rays of light, which are made up of photons. The rays come from a light source, strike the object, are reflected by it, and fall on the eye. The cornea and lens of the eye focus the rays to form an image on the retina. This retinal image is inverted, vertically and horizontally. The retinal surface is made up of two types of cells: the rods, which are stimulated by low intensities of light and register only shades of gray; and the cones which are stimulated under bright light and register color. A photochemical reaction takes place in these cells which triggers nerve impulses that are eventually conducted to the visual area of the brain's cerebral cortex.

Surrounding this visual area is the visual association zone. The visual area registers electrical stimuli received from the retina as meaningless patterns of light. The visual association zone decodes and makes sense of the impulses registered in the visual area, but it does not form an actual image from the impulses. There is no inner eyeball that "sees" a pictorial representation in the brain. This decoding process is a learned ability. People blind from birth whose sight is restored through surgery only perceive

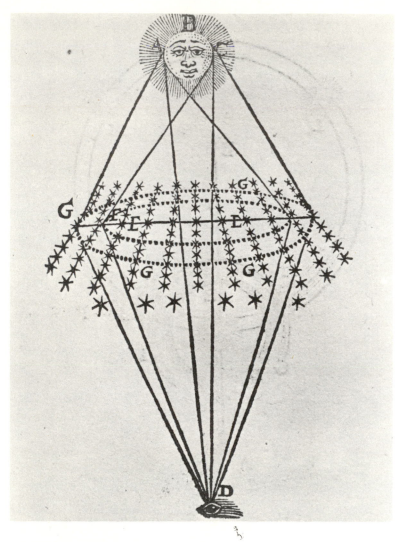

Photons of light from the sun strike an object, bounce off, and strike the eye. An illustration from *Henrici Regii's Philosophia Naturalis*, 1661.

The lens of the eye (E) forms an image on the retina which is inverted vertically and horizontally. The brain interprets the image as right side up and re-inverted horizontally. An illustration from *Henrici Regii's Philosophia Naturalis*, 1661.

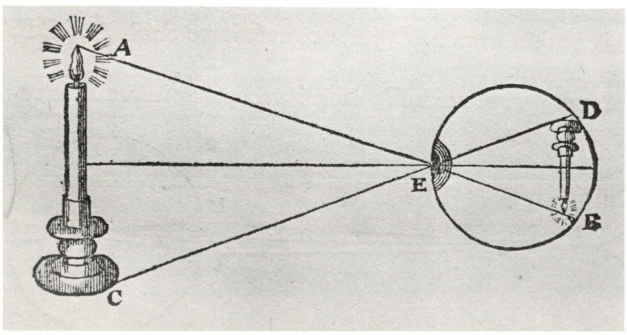

light. They have to learn to turn light patterns into meaningful images.[4]

Next to the visual association zone in the brain is an extensive, "relatively 'silent' area of the temporal lobe in which visual and auditory sensory experiences apparently are placed in storage as if they had been permanently recorded on sound film. It is here that the unknown mechanisms of memory, hallucinations, and dreams may be located."[5]

From the eye to the visual area, the system functions much like a complex switchboard or a computer. "Beyond this stage virtually nothing is known about the evolving patterns of cortical activity."[6] The British neurophysiologist Eccles postulates that visual memories must be made of "a congealed neuronal pattern or 'engram' ready to be replayed by an appropriate input."[7] Eccles goes on to say that literally millions of brain cells or neurons are involved in a single memory. He sees the "working of the brain as a patterned activity formed by the curving and looping of wavefronts through a multitude of neurons, now sprouting, now coalescing with other wavefronts, now reverberating through the same path."[8] It follows from this that all people need to experience an image is for the right neuronal pathways to fire. It does not matter whether they fire because of stimulation to the retina or other sense organs, or because of an internal stimulus. In the course of surgery on epileptic patients, Dr. W. Penfield, an English neurosurgeon, was surprised to discover that an electrode placed in the 'silent area' of a patient's temporal lobe would stimulate the patient to experience vivid visual images. Patients, although aware that they were in surgery, experienced almost lifelike visual images of scenes from their past.[9]

Because the processes of perception and visualization are similar, many phenomena associated with perception also apply to visualization. Psychologists have found that if a person's gaze becomes absolutely fixed while looking at an object, the image of the object will extinguish within seconds.[10] Most people are unfamiliar with this phenomenon because in the course of normal seeing they unconsciously move their eyes continuously. Studies have shown that people move their eyes in small, jerky, scanning movements even when they are looking at an object that is not moving.[11] If a person fixes his gaze on a mental image, it likewise tends to disappear. Whereas if a person scans a mental image as if it were a perception, he will find the image tends to be clearer and more stable.

Another characteristic of normal seeing involves depth perception. Just like a camera, a person perceives an external image as sharp and clear only when his eyes are properly focused. Unlike a camera, a person's eye has a very narrow depth of field. For instance, a person can only see the foreground or the distance clearly—never both at once. People generally perceive external reality as being constantly in focus because they automatically re-focus as their gaze shifts from near to far. If a person holds his finger twelve inches or so in front of his eyes and focuses on it, but tries to "see" an object across the room, he will find the object is not in focus. Likewise, if he focuses on the object across the room, his finger will be out of focus. Visualization seems much like perception in this respect. If a person closes his eyes and tries to visualize a ball as it would appear two feet in front of him, but "mentally" focuses as if the ball were across the room, his mental image will be fuzzy and unclear.

The pathways of visualization and perception are so similar that the two sometimes occur at the same time. People have reported that they can easily visualize with their eyes open. Perhaps everyone can do this naturally, although some people may be able to do so more vividly or predictably than others. Sometimes a person whose eyes are open can see a memory image superimposed upon their image of the external environment so clearly that the inner image blots out, distorts, or takes over the external one (see pages 5 and 6). Looking at visualization and perception from this viewpoint, the line between internal and external reality is thin indeed.

Just as psychologists have been studying perception, they have also been studying how specific areas of the brain deal with different thought processes. Psychologists believe that the brain's two hemispheres function in specialized, distinct ways. The left hemisphere, which controls the right side of the body, "is predominantly involved with analytic, logical thinking, especially in verbal and mathematical

Two photographs of a small puddle showing leaves floating in the water and trees reflected on the water's surface. One photograph is focused on the leaves, and the reflection of the trees is out of focus. The other photograph is focused on the reflection of the trees, and the leaves in the puddle are out of focus. A person sees and visualizes what he focuses on. *Leaves, Reflection–Depth of Field Study*. Photographs by Michael Samuels.

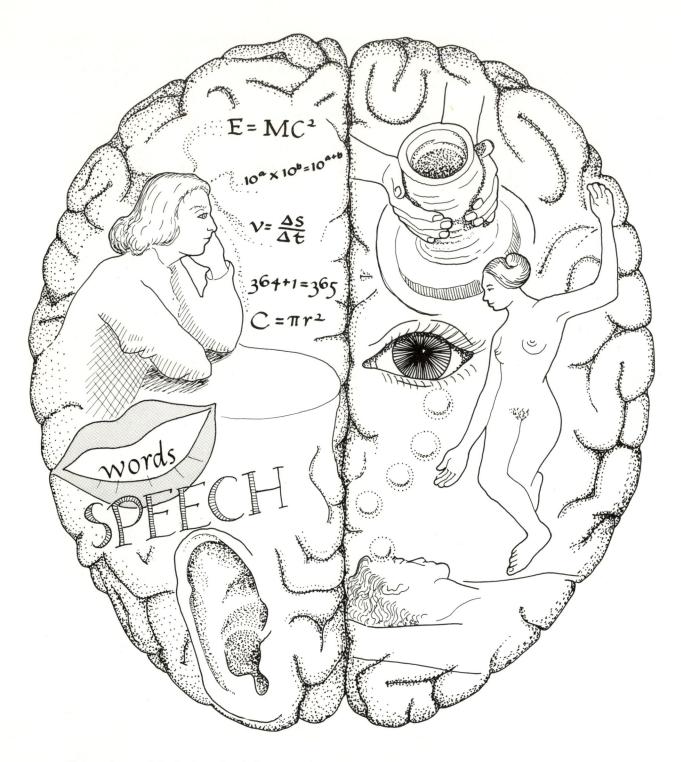

The cerebrum of the brain is divided into two hemispheres, each of which has specialized functions. The left hemisphere is basically concerned with verbal analytic information, while the right hemisphere is basically concerned with visual/intuitive information. Psychologists now believe that strengthening the right hemisphere helps visualization. Illustration by Susan Ida Smith.

functions."[12] The right hemisphere, which controls the left side of the body "is primarily responsible for orientation in space, artistic endeavor, crafts, body image, recognition of faces."[13] The right hemisphere then is the one that deals with visual, intuitive nonlinear thought. It also appears to be involved in dreaming. Robert Ornstein, a research psychologist at the University of California, comments on the fact that various types of thought, including seeing with the mind's eye, produce "active restriction of awareness to one single, unchanging process, and the withdrawal of attention from ordinary thought."[14] He also believes that this experience de-automatizes ordinary thinking. "The 'mystic' experience, brought about by concentrative meditation, de-automatization exercises, and other techniques intended to alter ordinary, linear consciousness is, then, a shift from that normal, analytical world containing separate, discrete objects and persons to a second mode, and experience of 'unity,' a mode of intuition. This experience is outside the province of language and rationality."[15]

Dr. Ornstein believes that people can train the right hemisphere in order to build up the intuitive side of themselves by viewing geometric forms. Visualization enables a person to concentrate on internalized geometric forms, thus strengthening the brain's right hemisphere. Other methods Ornstein lists for developing intuitive functions are learning crafts and paying attention to dreams. He believes that when the right hemisphere or intuitive mode is developed, "de-automization," freeing of body energies, physiological self-control and lack of attachment are the result.

FOOTNOTES

1. Roffwarg, H. P., *et al.* "Dream Imagery: Relationship to Rapid Eye Movements of Sleep," *The Archives of General Psychiatry,* 7:235–258, 1962.
2. Richardson, A. *Mental Imagery,* New York, Springer Publishing Co., 1969, p. 31.
3. _____ *Perception, Mechanism and Models;* San Francisco, Cal.; W. H. Freeman & Co.; 1972; from V. Neisser, "The Processes of Vision."
4. Horowitz, M. *Image Formation and Cognition,* New York, Appleton-Century-Crofts, 1970, p. 202.
5. Gatz, A. *Manter's Essentials of Clinical Neuroanatomy and Neurophysiology;* Philadelphia, Pa.; F. A. Davis Co.; 1970; p. 112.
6. _____ *Altered States of Awareness;* San Francisco, Ca.; W. H. Freeman & Co.; 1972; p. 37, from J. Eccles, "The Physiology of Imagination."
7. _____ *Altered States of Awareness;* p. 37.
8. _____ *Altered States of Awareness,* p. 38.
9. Horowitz, M. p. 229.

10. Hebb, D. *The Organization of Behavior,* New York, Wiley, 1949.
11. Yarbus, A. *Eye Movements and Vision,* New York, Plenum Press, 1967.
12. Ornstein, R. *The Psychology of Consciousness;* San Francisco, Cal.; W. H. Freeman & Co.; 1972; p. 52.
13. Ornstein, R. p. 52.
14. Ornstein, R. p. 122.
15. Ornstein, R. p. 138.
16. Ornstein, R. p. 163.

OTHER READING

1. Gregory, R. L. *Eye and Brain: The Psychology of Seeing,* New York, McGraw Hill, 1973.

Visualization is experience. When people visualize they become totally absorbed, participating in the experience with their whole being. It is said that when Henri Rousseau painted the strange and terrifying beasts that stare at us from his canvases, his heart would pound with terror and he would rush to a window for air. In looking at Rousseau's *The Dream* the viewer is taken beyond words, into a world of pure experience. 1910. Oil on canvas, 6' 8½ inches × 9' 9½ inches. Collection, The Museum of Modern Art, New York. Gift of Nelson A. Rockefeller.

Chapter 6

THE EFFECTS OF VISUALIZATION

By its very nature, visualization is experienced, not deduced. A thousand words or thoughts about visualization do not substitute for the experience itself. Visualization involves participation, involves a feeling of union between the person and the object being visualized. It calls up an emotional-physiological response that involves a person's whole being. Theories about what visualization is or is not are simply efforts by people to fit a particular kind of experience into a logical framework. While the logical-intellectual explanations of visualization are interesting, they do not have to be known in order to experience visual effects.

Psychologists have dealt in some detail with the types of visualization images and with the relationship between visualization and perception, but they have just begun to study the effects visualization has on the visualizer. Some psychologists have theorized that visualization affects a person's state of mind. Most people in their daily activities are not aware of their inner state. They become aware of it only in the extreme—when they are very happy or very unhappy. And they often feel that those extreme states of happiness and unhappiness are produced by things outside themselves—by events that befall them or by the way people act toward them. Similarly, most people do not realize how little control they have over their own thoughts. This lack of control is readily demonstrated if a person tries to concentrate only on counting his breaths for a few minutes (see page 112). Most people immediately find other thoughts going through their mind.

When a person consciously visualizes he gains the ability to hold his mind on one object, to concentrate. This *one-pointedness of mind* is a state that has special properties: alertness, clarity of thought, identification with the object, and a feeling of participation in the visualization. The feeling of identification-participation causes a person to be less involved with himself as an entity separate from the world around him. He goes beyond the boundaries, the limitations of his physical body, beyond the awareness of his personality. The image that he holds becomes the only thing in his awareness. And his awareness of it expands. The only goal he has in relation to the image is to hold it in his mind. So his awareness of it becomes multifaceted; he becomes open to all its potentialities. He no longer sees the image in terms of categories or labels, functions or expectations. Desire and attachment disappear, and, in that sense, he sees the image for itself, not as it relates to him. Perhaps for the first time since childhood he sees the image free of learned habits, cultural biases, secondary gain. He is aware of the whole and all its parts, the inside and the outside, the generalities and the particulars. Time and space disappear. At that point there is no separation between him and the image; there is just the pure experience of his psychic awareness.

As a person approaches this experience, certain unusual things happen to him. He receives new information in the form of images, ideas, feelings and sensations. This information is different from the information of learned habits and biases. This new knowledge and understanding may appear to come from outside of him, in much the same way that dreams and visions seem to come from outside. A person does not so much summon the information as it comes to him and he receives it. A person who has this experience feels it unites him with the universe. He feels he is a part of creation, rather than an observer of it. And the information he receives is pure, tied to the most universal of rhythms.

This purity of vision, this one-pointedness of mind, is associated with tremendous energy surrounding both the visualizer and the image, and the unity of the two. Such energy cannot help but affect the world around it. Each image a person chooses to concentrate upon has a specific effect that is inseparable from the pure nature of the object-image. These specific effects of the image will affect a person's body, his state of mind and his environment.

Our bodies react to mental images in ways similar to how they react to images from the external world. The American physiologist, Edmund Jacobson, has done studies which show that when a person imagines running, small but measurable amounts of contraction actually take place in the muscles associated with running.[1] The same neurological pathways are excited by imagined running as by actual running. This study concerned skeletal muscles, which are under voluntary or conscious control. But anatomists have also long been aware of pathways between the cerebral cortex, where images are stored, and the autonomic nervous system which controls the so-called involuntary muscles. The autonomic nervous system controls sweating, blood vessel expansion and contraction, blood pressure, blushing and goosepimpling, the rate and force of heart contraction, respiratory rate, dryness of mouth, bowel motility and smooth muscle tension. There are also pathways between the autonomic nervous system and the pituitary and adrenal cortex. The pituitary gland secretes hormones which regulate the rate of secretion of other glands: especially the thyroid, sex and adrenal glands. The adrenal glands secrete steroids, which regulate metabolic processes, and epinephrine , which causes the "fight or flight" reaction (see page 219). Through these pathways, an image held in the mind can literally affect every cell in the body.

The nervous innervation of voluntary and "involuntary" muscles is also associated with the physical expression of emotion. When an image or thought is held in the mind, there is neuronal activity in both hemispheres of the brain. Nerve fibers lead from the cerebral hemisphere to the hypothalmus, which has connections with the autonomic nervous system and the pituitary gland. When a person holds a strong fearful image in his mind's eye, his body responds, via the autonomic nervous system, with a feeling of "butterflies in the stomach," a quickened pulse, elevated blood pressure, sweating, goosebumps, and dryness of the mouth. Likewise, when a person holds a strong relaxing image in his mind, his body responds with a lowered heart rate, decreased blood pressure, and, obviously, all his muscles tend to relax.

Recently it has been found that people can have extraordinary control over their body, in-

66

Visualization produces one-pointedness of mind. The visualizer's attention is drawn out of himself, into the object. And the visualizer sees the image for itself. *Untitled*. Photograph by Michael Samuels.

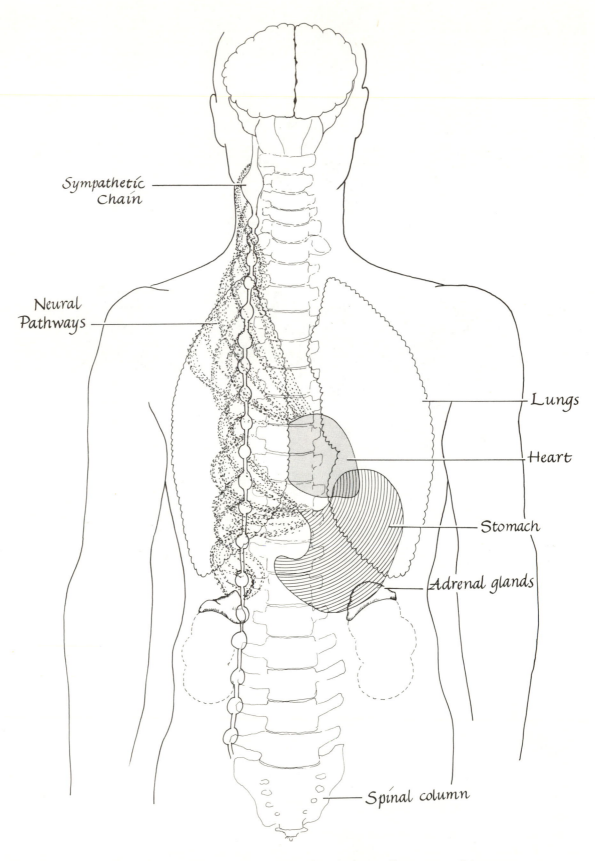

Sympathetic
Chain

Neural
Pathways

Lungs

Heart

Stomach

Adrenal glands

Spinal column

Through the autonomic nervous system images held in the mind can affect every cell in
the body. Illustration by Susan Ida Smith.

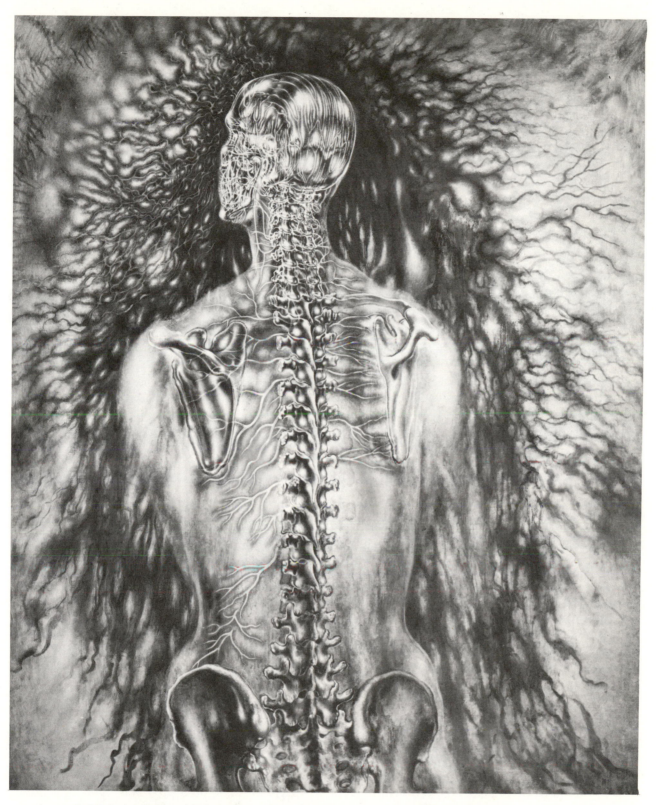

Anatomical Painting by Pavel Tchelitchew shows the figure of a person radiating energy. For centuries yogins have believed that subtle body energies travel along the spine and can be moved through visualization. No date. Oil on canvas. 56 × 46 inches. Collection of Whitney Museum of American Art. Gift of Lincoln Kirstein.

Relaxing images actually produce physiological changes in the body. A person can deliberately call to mind an image such as this in order to produce mental and physical relaxation. Claude Monet. *The Beach at Sainte-Adresse.* 1867. Oil on canvas. 28½ × 41¼ inches. Courtesy of The Art Institute of Chicago.

cluding those functions previously thought to be under involuntary control. Yoga masters have been found to be able to raise their heartrate from 80 to 300 beats per minute,[2] as well as raise their body temperature sufficiently to melt snow.[3] The techniques by which they were able to do these things were found to be made up of detailed visualizations. We will go into this subject in much greater depth in the chapters *Medicine and Healing and Spiritual Life.*

Going one step further, physicists have also begun to study subtle body energies and their effects on the world outside the body. Throughout history, philosophers have recognized this energy and given it many names. The Chinese called it *chi,* and the Indians *prana* or *kundalini,* the Japanese *ki;* 20th century parapsychologists have referred to it as *bio-plasmic energy.* Some parapsychologists have actually measured what they feel is bio-plasmic energy, others have photographed it through *kirlian photography.* Russian and Czechoslovakian scientists have studied bio-plasmic energy in association with healing, telepathy and psychokinesis. They have found that through visualization a woman named Nelya Mikhailova can change her bio-plasmic energy fields, causing needles under glass to rotate on a pivot and causing ordinary objects such as a writing pen to move across a table.[5] Studies like this tend to confirm occult belief in such concepts as auras and astral bodies. These experiments demonstrate how a visualization can produce energy which directly affects objects in the external world. We will say more about this in the chapter *Parapsychology*.

Everyone has had some awareness of how the images and thoughts he holds in his mind can affect the world around him. Probably everyone has noticed that if he awakens cheerfully, with a positive image of himself and the coming day, that image will manifest itself in the external world. People he meets will also tend to be cheerful and happy, or will become so in the presence of his positive attitude.

Events that draw his attention are likely to be positive, or he will tend to see something positive in them. A person who notices this kind of causality feels that the images he holds in his mind become his reality. This effect may extend beyond day-to-day events into the future. For example a person who has always dreamed of living in the country may find, through no conscious effort of his, that such an opportunity arises. And that same person may find that many of the characteristics of his new environment seem to correspond to images he had held in the past.

Mental images influence people's moods and the events in their life. Holding positive images tends to transform people's lives positively. Auguste Renoir. *Rower's Luncheon.* 1879-1880. Oil on canvas. 21½ × 25½ inches. Courtesy of The Art Institute of Chicago.

Many of the daily choices a person makes are based on inner images that he is unaware of. These unconscious images often surface first in dreams and fantasy, and only later manifest themselves in the world around him. Carl Jung has constructed a theory of the psyche which depicts the ego as a small illuminated area in the larger, dark sphere of the psyche. The illuminated ego is a person's conscious awareness —the "eye" that sees images—but the images themselves can come from all parts of the psyche. Jung believes that the center of the psyche is the "self" or soul. This "self" is the "inventor, organizer, and source of dream images."[6] Jung theorizes that the self sends images to the ego and that images sent by the self are those most necessary to a person's inner growth and development. This idea suggests that a person can look at his images as being self-regulatory, that is, they may help to keep him on the path of his own development, at the proper rate. They can be guiding images that function to give a person the help that he needs at any point in his growth. Even more profoundly, images center the universe. Jung suggests that a particular image will surface in many people when that image is needed to solve a common cultural problem or give inspiration.[7] One way to look at images is that they are the homeostatic mechanism of the universe.

If the image a person holds in his mind manifests itself in the outer world, then each person is a creator and visualizing is the mechanism of his creation. Thus visualization becomes reality, and reality, as a person generally thinks of it, is a reflection of his internal images. Science and metaphysics are beginning to agree—each person has the power to create and change the world. Through visualization, inner and out become one.

FOOTNOTES

1. Jacobson, E. *Progressive Relaxation*, Chicago, University of Chicago Press, 1942.
2. *Green, E. From a speech at De Anza College, Cupertino, Cal.; Oct. 30, 1971.*
3. Evans-Wentz, W. Y. *Tibetan Yoga and Secret Doctrines*, London, Oxford University Press, 1967, p. 203.
4. Ostrander, S. and Schroeder, L. *Psychic Discoveries Behind the Iron Curtain*, New York, Bantam Books, 1971, pp. 200–213.
5. Ostrander, S. and Schroeder, L. p. 70.
6. Jung, C. G. *Man and His Symbols*; Garden City, N.Y.; Doubleday and Co.; 1968; p. 161, from M.-L. von Franz, "The Process of Individuation."
7. Jung, C. G. *Modern Man in Search of a Soul*; New York; Harcourt, Brace & World; Inc.; 1933, p. 171.

OTHER READING

1. Humphreys, C. *Concentration and Meditation*; Baltimore, Md.; Penguin Books, Inc.; 1970.
2. Besant, A. and Leadbeater, C. W. *Thought-Forms*; Madras, India; The Theosophical Publishing House; 1961. Both of these authors have written a number of books on the energy, forms, and effects of thought.
3. Argüelles, J. A. *The Transformative Vision*, Berkeley and London, Shambhala, 1975.

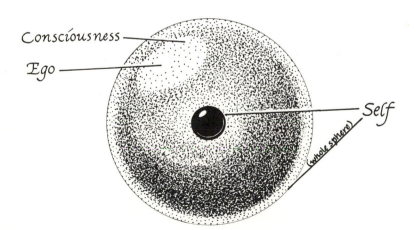

A diagram illustrating Carl Jung's concept of the self. By Susan Ida Smith.

In visualization opposites unite, and inner and outer become one. Rene Magritte. *The Thought Which Sees.* (1965). Graphite, 15¾ × 11⅝ inches. Collection The Museum of Modern Art, New York. Gift of Mr. and Mrs. Charles B. Benenson.

COLOR PLATES

COLOR PLATE CAPTIONS

Plate 1 (top).   *The False Mirror* by Rene Magritte. This image is a logos for visualization. The picture shows inner and outer worlds inseparably joined. One has the feeling of looking inward, of looking inside another person; at the same time one has the feeling of looking outward at the world. Suddenly one becomes the person in the picture, staring into and out of his own eye. The superimposition of the two views conveys the feeling of seeing with the mind's eye—a feeling of unity, insight, and understanding.

Plate 1 (bottom).   *Earth from Apollo 10.* This may well be the most important visualization image of the twentieth century. Space travel began as outward exploration and it has succeeded in this goal. Surprisingly it has, in addition, brought man a greater sense of himself in relationship to the earth and the universe. Images of traveling in space take man beyond everyday consciousness to a more universal consciousness.

Plate 2.   *Bedroom at Arles* by Vincent Van Gogh represents a door into visualization. The easiest way to experience visualization is to picture a familiar room. Anyone can visualize his bedroom —can count the windows, see pictures on the walls, and locate furniture. *Bedroom at Arles* evokes the feeling of this experience. In this painting Van Gogh has depicted his room with the supra-real clarity of a mental image. The chairs, table, and bed stand out directly with the intensity of a thought. These objects seem to vibrate, almost hover just above the floor. Other objects in the painting—the bottles on the table, the windows, the pictures hanging on the walls—present themselves with less definition. The subjects in the pictures appear hazy, but the wire and nails that hang the pictures are clearly defined. *Bedroom at Arles* goes beyond the reality of objectivity and expresses the reality of emotion and feeling. The square sturdiness of the objects and the lack of shadows in the painting convey a feeling of safety and grounding. As in a visualization experience the viewer of this painting is drawn into the room and participates in its being beyond the level of verbal thought.

Plate 3.   *Mother and Child* by Pablo Picasso. In this painting Picasso has portrayed a classic image of family relationships. The figures are shown in a moment of personal warmth and relaxation. The baby looks on with the wondrous rapt attention of infancy, while the mother gazes at him with serene intensity. Through distortion Picasso takes the figures beyond learned concepts of beauty so that people can identify with the common humanity that the figures express. The simple, monumental forms transcend the particular and evoke a timeless, universal moment. In everyday life people are positively effected by holding such images. The concentration, energy, and purity of vision embodied in this painting convey the feeling of a visualization.

Plate 4 and 5.   *Water Lilies* by Claude Monet. In the last years of his life Monet painted many immense panels depicting water lilies. The panels were intended to go around the walls of a room, creating an "endless whole," a place of peaceful meditation. Monet's effort was successful—people who see the paintings often sit and meditate on them for hours and leave calmed and refreshed. Scenes of natural beauty that hold a viewer's attention are primary transforming visions for man. People often find a kind of spiritual fulfillment in natural scenes. Looking at such scenes in the external world or seeing them in the mind's eye gives man an elemental sense of union with the world around him.

76

Rene Magritte, *The False Mirror* (Le Faux Miroir).
1928. Oil on canvas, 21¼ × 31⅞ inches.
Collection, The Museum of Modern Art, New
York. Purchase.

Earth Showing Africa and the Far East from Apollo 10
Courtesy of NASA.

PLATE 1

Pablo Picasso, *Mother and Child.* 1921. Oil on canvas, 56½ × 64 inches. Courtesy, The Art Institute of Chicago.

PLATE 2

Vincent Van Gogh, *Bedroom At Arles*. 1888. Oil on canvas, 28¾ × 36 inches. Courtesy of the Art Institute of Chicago, Helen Birch Bartlett Memorial Collection.

PLATE 3

Claude Monet, *Water Lilies.* **(left panel)** c. 1920. Oil on canvas, triptych, each section 6 feet 6 inches × 14 feet. Collection, The Museum of Modern Art, New York. Mrs. Simon Guggenheim Fund.

PLATE 4

PLATE 5

Harrison Begay, *Navajo Boy Learning the Chant*. c. 1967. 15½ × 19 inches. Collection, Dr. I. Samuels.

PLATE 6

Petrus Christus, *The Nativity*. 1445–1446. Wood, 54¼ × 38¼ inches. National Gallery of Art, Washington. Andrew W. Mellon Collection.

PLATE 7

Paradise of Green Tara. 19th century Tibetan tanka. Colors on cotton, 28 × 19 inches. Collection of the Newark Museum.

PLATE 8

Plate 6. *Navajo Boy Learning the Chant* by Harrison Begay. This painting by a contemporary Navajo artist depicts a Navajo medicine man or *singer* teaching the Night Chant Ceremony to a young boy. Above the man and the boy is an image similar to ones used in the Night Chant sand paintings. In myth it is said that sandpaintings were given to the Navajo by the gods. Medicine men use the sandpaintings in ceremonies intended to heal sickness and restore harmony. The medicine man instructs assistants in the spreading of the colored sandstone and charcoal on the ground. For each chant there are specific sandpaintings which have been used without alteration for generations. The sandpainting is an altar on which a patient sits while he ritually identifies himself with the hero of the myth or chant. The sandpainting in this picture shows the Rainbow Goddess, her hands open to receive the medicine, surrounding four other gods and goddesses. The left figure, with plumed headdress and squirrel bag, is *Talking God.* The righthand figure with the humpback and the headdress of lightning is a sheep god. The humpback represents a sack of plenty. The gods are all shown wearing masks. The rectangular masks indicate females; the round masks represent males. The central figures either represent gods or the patient. The sandpainting is a visualization which helps the patient and everyone present at the ceremony to identify with mythic deities and absorb their powers. The ceremony serves to re-establish a relationship of harmony between the Navajo and his universe.

Plate 7. *The Nativity* by Petrus Christus. This painting portrays in one image a complex and momentous spiritual visualization—a visualization of a wholly different reality than everyday life. It portrays in symbolic form the Fall and Redemption of Mankind. This concept is at the heart of spiritual life. The scenes depicted around the arch through which the Nativity is viewed show the Biblical antecedents to Christ's birth. Adam and Eve are shown standing on columns borne by stooped figures which symbolize the story of how mankind came to be burdened by Original Sin. Around the top of the arch are scenes showing the expulsion from the Garden of Eden and other events from the Old Testament. At the two upper corners of the painting are two warring figures symbolizing worldly discord.

In the foreground Joseph and Mary are shown with four angels, worshipping the infant Christ who has been sent to redeem the world. Behind the worshippers peaceful countryside recedes into the distance. The whole scene has an extraordinary serenity and stillness, fixing this moment for all time. When people immerse themselves in such visualizations they share the spiritual reality of mystics and visionaries and experience a feeling of redemption and unity.

Plate 8. *Paradise of Green Tara.* This painting is a Tibetan tanka, a rolled scroll used in meditation. It portrays the goddess Green Tara holding a blue lotus in each of her hands. Tara is a personification of the divine Mother Force. She is the goddess of mercy, the savioress who carries her worshippers across troubled waters. She is believed to bestow charity, gifts, and protection. In this tanka Green Tara is shown in the center of an elaborate temple, surrounded by trees which bear jewels. Amitabha Buddha, her spiritual father, is seen above her head, near the top of temple. To her left and right are goddesses, attendants, and musicians. Below her is a pool with sacred emblems floating in it. At the bottom corners of the picture are fierce deities who guard her. At the top corners of the pictures the Eight Medical Buddhas are seen in two circles. At the top center sits Atisha and two disciples, surrounded by celestial beings who descend on clouds. Images portrayed in tankas are visualized in complete detail by worshippers. Through this visualization the duality of creation is unified.

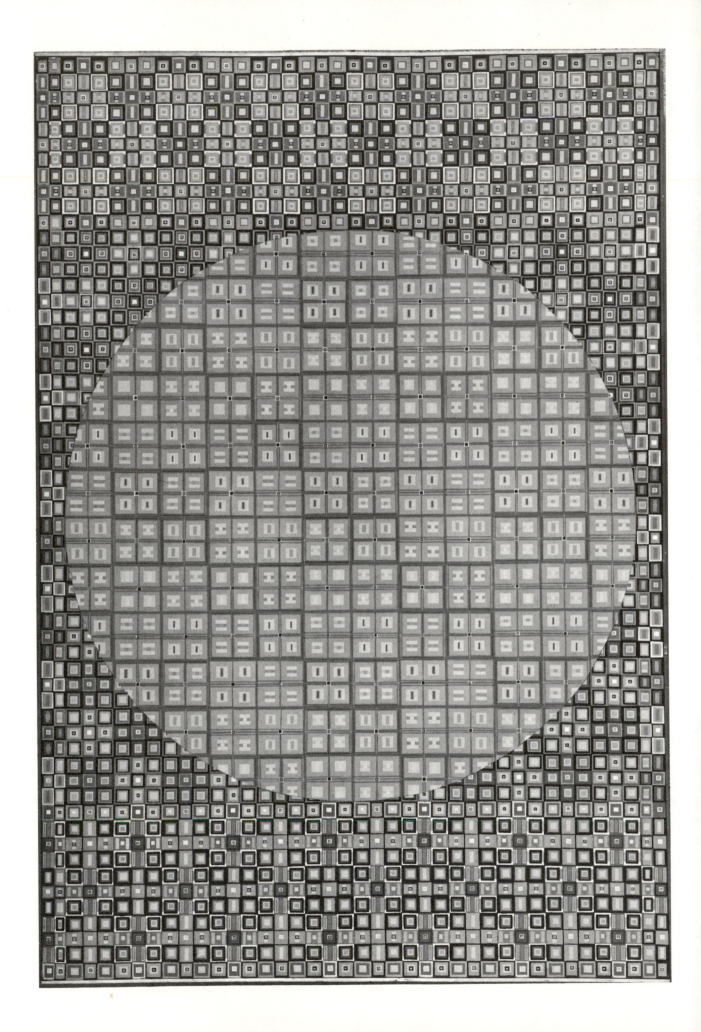

Pattern-recognition involves the mind as well as the eye. Each square in this painting is like a cell in the retina of the eye which is discharging or not discharging. The brain interprets on/off, discharging/not discharging information as a meaningful symbol, in this case a circle. *Painting A* (1961-62) by Toshinobu Onosato. Oil on canvas, 76¼ × 51⅜ inches. The Solomon R. Guggenheim Museum, New York.

Chapter 7

SYMBOL, FORM, AND COLOR

Symbols can be looked upon as the mechanism by which the brain makes meaning out of discrete pieces of information. For example, when the eye registers an image on the retina, messages are relayed from the rod and cone cells of the retina to the visual areas of the brain. These messages do not form a picture; they are simply positive or negative (on or off) ion flows around nerves indicating whether or not a particular cell in the retina has been stimulated. The retinal cells respond to conditions such as color and vertical, horizontal and moving boundaries. So the brain receives "not a portrait of either the outside or the inside world . . . only a constellation of physical signs . . . Somewhere in the organism something turns these signals, these signs, into meaning . . . into symbols. This is the key process called 'symbolic transformation.' "[1]

Thus even the simplest recognition of some object in our outer environment involves the image as symbol. The basic symbolizing process has also been found to be a natural means the brain uses for solving other, more complex problems than pattern recognition. Frequently the answer to any problem comes as a symbolic visual image. Herbert Silberer, a German psychiatrist, called this characteristic of the brain *auto symbolizing*. In 1909, Silberer experimented with this process by putting himself in a hypnagogic state and trying to think through complicated problems he had been unable to solve in the normal awake state. He found that the complicated problem he was considering would disappear from awareness and would be replaced by meaningful symbolic imagery. Silberer wrote that, "In a state of drowsiness I contemplate an abstract topic such as the nature of transsubjectively (for all people) valid judgments. A struggle between active thinking and drowsiness sets in. The latter becomes strong enough to disrupt normal thinking and to allow—in the twilight-state so produced—the appearance of an auto symbolic phenomenon. The content of my thought presents itself to me immediately in the form of a perceptual (for an instant apparently real) picture: I see a big circle (or transparent sphere) in the air with people around it whose heads reach into the circle. This symbol expresses practically everything I was thinking of. The transsubjective judgment is valid for all people without exception: the circle includes all the heads. The validity must have its grounds in a commonality: the heads belong all in the same homogeneous sphere. Not all judgments are transsubjective: the body and limbs of the peo-

ple are outside (below) the sphere as they stand on the ground as independent individuals . . . What had happened? In my drowsiness my abstract ideas were, without my conscious interference, replaced by a perceptual picture—by a symbol."[2]

Silberer goes on to say that he found this "picture thinking" an easier form of thought than rational logic. Silberer conducted extensive experiments in a hypnagogic state, considering a complex, abstract thought and waiting attentively for symbolic images to appear. He found that his thoughts, in this state, always gave rise to images, thus demonstrating to him that the mind automatically transforms

An illustration of a conceptual visual image described by the German psychiatrist Herbert Silberer. The drawing shows the common validity of transsubjective judgements, represented by the heads within the sphere. Silberer referred to the mental faculty by which a person envisions a complex idea or concept in the form of a graphic image as *auto symbolizing*. Illustration by Susan Ida Smith.

disparate verbal data into unifying picture symbols. Another example Silberer gave is, "My thought is: I am to improve a halting passage in an essay. Symbol: I see myself planing a piece of wood."[3] In the terms of this book, Silberer put himself in a receptive place (the hypnagogic state), introduced a problem, and looked for the answer to appear as a visualization. The results of his experiments demonstrated that problem-solving visualizations are often symbolic.

Images that come to awareness spontaneously come from outside a person's ego consciousness—from one's inner center, from one's subconscious, from discharging cells in one's brain or from other worlds. These images usually manifest themselves in symbolic form. They do so in an attempt to join inner and outer worlds, spiritual and material, invisible and visible, microcosm and macrocosm.

Non-ordinary states of mind naturally produce symbolic images. From Biblical times dreams and visions have been regarded as symbolic in meaning. The symbolic nature of dreams has always been so striking that that itself lent importance to the images. Religious, occult, and alchemical traditions are rich with symbolic images—most obviously in traditions which are mystical, traditions in which the practitioner seeks to experience the non-visible

In Christianity the sacrament of baptism symbolizes purification and rebirth. The physical man dies and is spiritually reborn. This painting, *The Baptism of Christ* by the Master of the St. Bartholomew Altar, shows Christ and John the Baptist surrounded by fourteen saints. When fourteen saints are pictured together they symbolize the Holy Helpers whose aid can be invoked in extreme situations. The painting is rich with symbolism such as the lamb in St. Agnes' arms at the top of the painting and the columbine growing in the foreground. The lamb symbolizes purity and sacrifice: in the Old Testament the blood of the lamp is associated with Passover; in the New Testament Christ becomes associated with the lamb after his Crucifixion. The purple columbine symbolizes the Passion of Christ and the suffering of the martyrs. Late 15th century, wood. 41¾ × 67⅛ inches. The National Gallery, Washington. Samuel H. Kress Collection.

A symbolic representation of the alchemical process which endeavors to transmute base matter into gold. The alchemic process itself is symbolic of spiritual illumination. The first stage in the process, *calcination*, stands for the death of the worldly man; in the second stage, *putrefaction*, the destroyed remains are separated; the third stage, *solution*, involves purification; in the fourth stage, *distillation*, the purified material recondenses and "rains" down; the fifth stage, *conjunction*, involves the joining of opposites; the sixth stage, *sublimation*, symbolizes the pain of detachment from the material world; the final stage, *congelation*, symbolizes inseparable union. From Andreas Libavius's *Alchymia*, 1606.

world. Primitive religions and shamanistic traditions are veritable symbolic cosmologies, wherein each object and act in the material world has significance beyond the physical.

Ananda Coomaraswamy, a twentieth century Indian philosopher, has defined symbolism as "the art of thinking in images."[4] Carl Jung has said that an image is symbolic when it has meaning beyond the obvious, beyond the grasp of reason. "Because there are innumerable things beyond the range of human understanding, we constantly use symbolic terms to represent concepts that we cannot define or fully comprehend."[5]

The symbol then is a mechanism for understanding. It is a bridge between the metaphysical world in which the Absolute knows All, and the physical world of the senses in which All can never be perfectly known. In the physical world, no matter how powerful a telescope or microscope man builds, there always remains matter that cannot be seen with even the aided eye. Man's physical senses, as complex and marvelous as they are, are limited by nature in what they can perceive. Therefore, man's knowledge gained through his physical senses can never be more than imperfect.

The symbol transcends the limits of the physical senses. Goethe, the German poet and philosopher, has said, "In the symbol, the particular represents the general . . . as a living and momentary revelation of the inscrutable."[6] J. E. Cirlot, a contemporary Spanish philosopher, poet, and art critic, says that symbols reveal transcendant truths and can express in antithetical ways the essence of an idea —beyond time, beyond space. Symbols by their nature can resolve paradoxes and create order from disorder. They link the disorder of nature with the cosmic order of the supernatural. They provide in flashes of insight knowledge which joins dispersed, disparate fragments in a unitary vision.

Thus symbols, in their function, change man. When people become aware of a symbol as an image, they become whole; they see, if only for a moment, the great scheme of things, the unity of the universe and their place in it. And they see that unity in terms of concrete images from the world around them—the only things that are "seeable"—but they see these concrete images in a novel, non-ordinary light.

Tibetan mandalas are rich with symbolism. The mandala itself symbolizes the cosmos, and the center of the mandala represents the axis of the universe. The deities on the periphery of this mandala symbolize the chaos of the world. The outermost circle shows the Eight Cemeteries, which represent the eight mental states to overcome. The second circle, showing flames in five sacred colors, symbolizes the burning of ignorance. The third circle, the Girdle of Diamonds, represents spiritual illumination. The innermost circle, made up of lotuses, symbolizes spiritual rebirth. Within the circles are triangles: the downward pointing triangles represent the female principle; the upward triangles represent the male principle. The overlapping of the triangles signifies the union of the two principles. *The Vajravarahi Mandala.* 18th century Tibetan tanka. Asian Art Museum of San Francisco, The Avery Brundage Collection.

Goethe has said of symbols that the particular stands for the general, revealing momentarily the unknowable. In this picture, perspective, lighting and tone all combine to express the essence of the pears. In a similar way, the essence can be glimpsed in visualization. Peter Dechar. *Pears.* 1966. Oil on canvas. 54 × 72 inches. Collection of Whitney Museum of American Art. Larry Aldrich Foundation Fund.

From primordial times, certain events or objects from the material world have served particularly well as translators between the physical outer world and the cosmic inner world that underlies and explains what we see. These objects have appeared again and again throughout history, across all cultures, in dreams and visions. They have manifested in myths, legends, religions, and works of art. Jung called these basic universal symbols archetypes from the collective unconscious. He believed them to be inherent in the brain structure of man, part of man's primal experience. Jung believed that these symbols, these univer-

sal images, are the images that are the most valuable to man's growth processes. One way to look at archetypal images is that they contain the most energy: "The psychological mechanism that transforms energy is the symbol."[7]

Archetypal symbols appear and reappear throughout history always expressing a facet of a greater whole. People experience these images according to their culture and their unique personalities, but the images are part of a common theme. These universal images can be apprehended and understood on many different levels—mythological, psychological, philosophical, spiritual—but the symbol stands

Symbols express universal concepts which go beyond simple verbal explanations. Such multi-faceted concepts emerge at many psychic levels. This painting conveys a deep-seated feeling of longing. *Untitled*. Oil on canvas. Schuyler G. Harrison. Courtesy of the artist.

by itself, as a whole. In its wholeness it produces an understanding beyond verbal explanations.

Awareness of a symbol, even without interpretation, changes a person's universe. For the symbol always operates first on a non-verbal, non-rational level, exciting in a common way the very physiology of the people perceiving the symbol. Each universal symbol has a specific generalized effect on the perceivers. It's as if the energy in the original form is transmitted to the people who perceive the symbol.

A primary example of a mythic visualization is man's fall from grace: from at-oneness to sep-

aration, from God and sacred life to material objects and secular life, from soul or thought to body or matter. This visualization underlies man's view of himself in relationship to the world around him. Visions of the fall have manifested themselves throughout history in the creation myths of many cultures. These myths deal with the creation of man and earth from endless space, with man's violation of the Creator's intent, and man's subsequent fall from grace. The scientific theory of entropy parallels the idea of this fall: it holds that all systems tend to assume the most random molecular arrangement possible, that is they tend to progress from order to disorder. Similarly many people believe that human beings are born pure and lose this purity with age and the acquisition of worldliness. In graphic terms the creation is symbolized by the progression from grayness (nothingness) to white (first) light; by an expanding circle of white light which evolves into a circle filled with geometric forms and eventually into the multiplicity of shapes in nature.

Inherent in the visualization of man's creation and fall from grace is the possibility of a return to grace: a return from separation to at-oneness; from worldliness to reunion of body and soul, reunion with God. More worldly versions of the redemption visualization are making body and mind whole—healing; fulfilling unsatisfied desire—succeeding; and manifesting the unmanifest—creating. The scientific parallel of the return is contained in the concept that although nature as a whole tends toward disorder, particular systems can, for a time, tend toward order. The sun, for example, is a vast fusion reactor, taking a simple hydrogen atom and creating the more complicated atom, helium. Helium is more highly ordered and contains more energy than hydrogen. Similarly the human body combines atoms into incredibly complex systems.

The Tantric visualization of the fall and return sees the Universal Creator or Cause as being beyond space and time. According to Tantric thought the world is created as energy which evolves into sound, then light, then matter—each form increasingly complex—then man. Man has the ability to think, to visualize the creation. Through visualization man can transcend the physical limitations of the body, the limitations of space and time, and become one with the Creator, returning to the source.

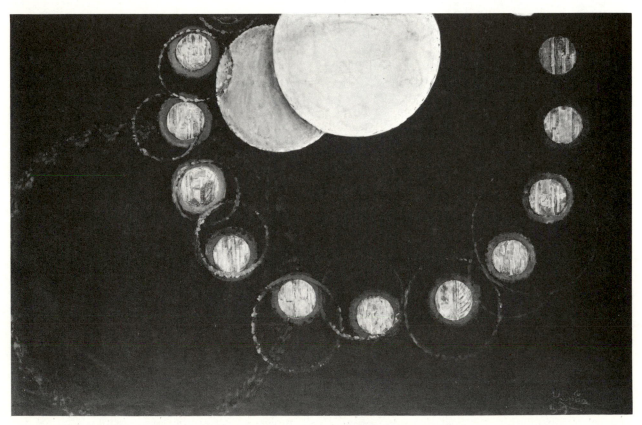

Frantisek Kupka's *The First Step* (1909) conveys the feeling of the universe evolving from one circle of white light into multiplicity. Oil on canvas. 32¾ × 51 inches. Collection, The Museum of Modern Art, New York. Hillman Periodicals Fund.

According to the Old Testament God created Adam and Eve in the Garden of Eden. The eating of the forbidden apple by Adam and Eve symbolized their fall from grace. For the first time they saw themselves as naked and separate, and God expelled them from Paradise. *Creation of Eve* by Veronese, (Pablo Caliari). 1570. 31⅞ × 40½ inches. Courtesy of The Art Institute of Chicago.

The Christian concept of redemption involves rebirth. Only those that have been spiritually reborn in Christ will join him in heaven. In this 15th century painting, *The Last Judgment*, by a Tyrolean master, Christ is shown blessing the faithful with his right hand and casting the damned into hell with his left hand. Beneath Christ, the Virgin and St. John pray for mercy on mankind. M. H. de Young Memorial Museum, San Francisco. Samuel H. Kress Collection.

This N'Tomo boy's initiation mask from Mali symbolizes the creation myth. Boys wear this mask in a ceremony in which they are admitted into N'tomo society. The horns on the back of the mask symbolize the primordial seeds from which God created the universe. The wearer of the mask acts out the part of God's first son, the creator of the Earth, who stole the seeds in an attempt to gain control of the universe. The figure in front of the horns symbolizes the female twin of the creator. The cowrie shells on the horns symbolize the reorganizer of the universe who defeated the creator and recaptured the seeds. Courtesy of The Museum of Primitive Art, New York.

Tantric Indian thought holds that each and every shape, color, object, and action in the world is a visible form of a vibrational level of a primal thought that exists beyond the sensate mind.[8] These visible forms of vibrational levels, like symbols, are capable of infinite combination and rearrangement, giving rise to the innumerable nuances of knowledge. If we view the world of our senses in this way, we become sensible of all similar or corresponding moments within our experience, and we transcend the limitations of the physical world, and, finally, enter the world of the Absolute. Rene Guénon, a contemporary French philosopher and author, says, "The true basis of symbolism is, as we have said, the correspondence linking together all orders of reality, binding them one to the other, and consequently extending from the natural order as a whole to the supernatural order. By virtue of this correspondence, the whole of nature is but a symbol, that is, its true significance becomes apparent only when it is seen as a pointer which can make us aware of supernatural or metaphysical truths."[9]

The effect of a particular symbol is different for each perceiver of that symbol; but there are generalizations that link most people's experiences. These generalizations can be looked upon as interpretations of the experience of holding that image in the mind's eye. Between the experience itself, verbal descriptions of it, and attempts to designate "meaning," much is lost; nevertheless, enough of the *gestalt* of the experience remains to make it identifiable by each of the perceivers. The more basic the form, the more difficult it is to interpret in a single verbal stroke.

Union is a primary visualization of mankind. *The Reunion of The Soul and The Body* by William Blake. An illustration from *The Grave Etching*, 1813. The Metropolitan Museum of Art, Harris Brisbane Dick Fund, 1917.

Natural forms can function as symbols of a reality greater than themselves. In doing so they do not lose their own essence, but they make men aware of the supernatural truths that lie behind them. Ogata Korin (1663-1743). Two-fold paper screen; wave design in colors on gold ground. The Metropolitan Museum of Art, Fletcher Fund, 1926.

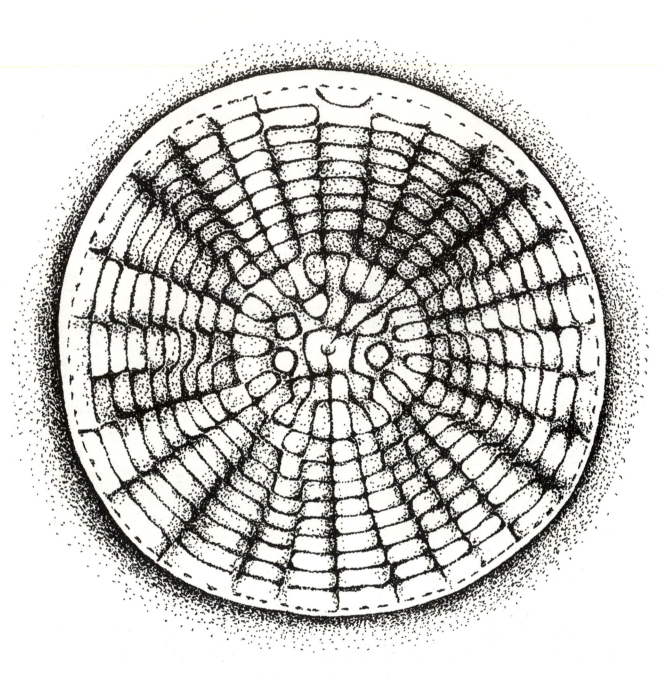

According to Tantric thought every sound has a particular form. *Pattern of sound waves produced by striking a steel disc.* Illustration by Susan Ida Smith for *Be Well*.

Having so said, let us take the circle as an example. The circle has been variously interpreted as a state of oneness, unity (as opposed to multiplicity), heaven (as opposed to earth), the sun, Yang (the masculine creative principle), the Self (the totality of the psyche), ultimate wholeness, enlightenment. The circle has manifested as the Chinese symbol of Yin and Yang, the mandala of India and Tibet, the lotus flower in Hindu and Buddhist religious art, the enlightenment symbol in Zen paintings, the halo around pictured Christian saints, the sun wheels on Neolithic rock engravings, the hub of activity in architecture and town planning. The circle is associated with the number zero (0), which is unity, and with the number ten (10), which symbolizes the return to multiplicity. The number zero both symbolizes nothingness and marks the boundary between real numbers (1, 2, 3, etc.) and imaginary numbers (+1, −1, etc.). So too, in the number ten, the zero marks a place without changing it (else it would be eleven or nine).[10,11]

Color, as well as being a property of objects, is one of the most universally recognized types of symbolism. Color had deep significance in all early cultures. In the cosmogony of Tibet, for example, the north was seen as yellow, the south as blue, the east as white, and the west as red.[12] The Chinese and the American Indian also thought of directions in terms of color. The elements—air, earth, fire, water—were likewise associated in early Greek and East Indian thought with colors. Color plays a fundamental part in Tantric visualization exercises: one color representing each of the chakras (the energy centers of the body) and also representing different forms of energy. In Jewish and Christian mystical thought, great importance is given to color symbolism. In Gnostic thought God the Father was symbolized blue, God the Son by yellow, and God the Holy Ghost by red.[13] Occult thought looked upon the aura (the field of energy and light surrounding a person which is visible to clairvoyants) as being a specific color for the visualizations held by each person: for instance, a dark clear blue aura indicates religious feeling.

Modern science thinks of color as different wavelengths of electromagnetic energy. The phenomenon we think of as "light" makes up one band of wave frequencies from red, at 1/33,000th's of an inch wavelength, to violet, at 1/67,000th's of an inch wavelength. Below red lie infrared and radio waves; above violet lie ultra-violet, x-rays, and gamma rays.

The human brain tends to interpret color in groups. Color theorists say that the brain interprets color as seven basic shades or hues: red, yellow, green, blue, white, black, and violet. Psychologists believe that color affects a person directly, below the level of rational thought. Whereas interpretation is necessary to the recognition of form, a person simply reacts spontaneously to color. The New York psychoanalyst Schachtel says, "Colors are not only and usually not even primarily 'recognized' but they are *felt* as exciting or soothing, dissonant or harmonious . . . joyous or somber, warm or cool, disturbing and distracting or conducive to concentration and tranquility."[14] He goes on to say that one's experience of color is passive, and is felt, in an almost primitive way, as pleasure or displeasure. Color not only affects mood or mind states, it affects the body directly. For his doctoral thesis, Robert Gerard, a Los Angeles psychologist, studied the effects of color on human physiology. He found that blood pressure, electrical conductance of the skin, respiration rate, eye blinks, and brain wave patterns increased over time when a person was exposed to red, and decreased when a person was exposed to blue. Gerard found that red caused people to become aroused or excited, while blue caused people to relax and feel more tranquil.[15] People have intuited these effects from ancient times and have applied them in color-healing, a treatment mode in which the sick person is bathed in particular colors of light in order to effect their cure.

Colors have long been associated with sounds. Ancient Tantric thought stated that "At the vibratory level, sound creates light, for light is sound at a particular frequency . . . Every colour has its life-sound and in turn every sound has its form-colour."[16] Psychologists have studied synesthesia, the phenomenon wherein a sensory impression in one modality arouses impressions in another sensory modality. For example, the Russian psychologist A. R. Luria found in the subject S. that the ringing

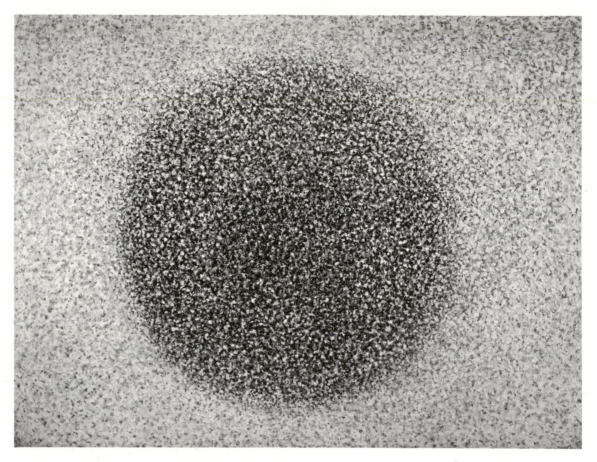

Radiance (1962-63). Richard Pousette-Dart. Oil and metallic paint on canvas, 6 feet ⅛ inches × 8 feet ¼ inches. Collection, The Museum of Modern Art, New York. Gift of Susan Morse Hilles.

Suprematist Element: Circle. (1913). Kasimir Malevich. Pencil, 18½ × 14⅜ inches. Collection, The Museum of Modern Art, New York.

Mandala of Vasudhara. 19th century. Tibetan painting. Collection of The Newark Museum.

SHAPES: SYMBOLISM AND ASSOCIATIONS

Circle	Heaven, ether, intellect, thought, sun, the number ten, unity, perfection, eternity, oneness, the masculine-active principle, celestial realm, hearing, sound
Triangle	Communication, between heaven and earth, fire, the number three, trinity, aspiration, movement upward, return to origins, gas, sight, light
Square	Pluralism, earth, feminine-receptive principle, firmness, stability, construction, material, solidity, the number four
Rectangle	Most rational, most secure, used in grounding objects such as houses and desks
Spiral	Evolution of the universe, orbit, growth, deepening, cosmic motion, relationship between unity and multiplicity, macroscom, breath, spirit, water

COLOR SYMBOLISM, ASSOCIATION, AND EFFECTS

Red	Sunrise, birth, blood, fire, emotion, wounds, death, passion, sentiment, mother, the planet Mars, the note "C," anger, chakra #1, excitement, heat, physical stimulation and strengthening the blood, iron, alcohol, oxygen, treatment of paralysis and exhaustion
Orange	Fire, pride, ambition, egoism, the planet Venus, the note "D," chakra #2, stimulation of the nervous system, treatment as emetic and laxative
Yellow	Sun, light, intuition, illumination, air, intellect, royalty, the planet Mercury, the note "E," luminosity
Green	Earth, fertility, sensation, vegetation, death, water, nature, sympathy, adaptability, growth, the planets Jupiter and Venus, the note "G"
Blue	Clear sky, thinking, the day, the sea, height, depth, heaven, religious feeling, devotion, innocence, truth, psychic ability, spirituality, the planet Jupiter, the note "F," the chakra #5, physical soothing and cooling, treatment as a sedative, anti-inflammatory, cure for headache
Violet	Water, nostalgia, memory, advanced spirituality, the planet Neptune, the note "B," a treatment for madness

COMMON SYMBOLS

Air	Activity, male principle, primary element, creativity, breath, light, freedom, liberty, movement
Fire	Ability to transform, love, life, health, control, spiritual energy, regeneration, sun, God, passion
Water	Passive, feminine, abysmal, liquid
Earth	Passive, feminine, receptive, solid
Ascent	Height, transcedance, inward journey, increasing intensity
Descent	Unconscious, potentialities of being, animal nature
Duality	Opposites, complements, pairing, away from unity, male-female, life-death, positive-negative, is-is not
Unity	Spirit, oneness, wholeness, centering, transcedance, the source, harmony, revelation, active principle, a point, a dot, supreme power, completeness in itself, light, the divinity
Center	Thought, unity, timelessness, spacelessness, paradise, creator, infinity, neutralizing opposites
Cross	Tree of life, axis of the world, ladder, struggle, martyrdom, orientation in space
Dark	Matter, germ, before existence, chaos
Light	Spirit, morality, All, creative force, the direction East, spiritual thought
Mountain	Height, mass, loftiness, center of the world, ambition, goals
Lake	Mystery, depth, unconscious
Moon	Master of women, vegetation, fecundity
Eye	Understanding, intelligence, sacred fire, creative
Image	Highest form of knowing, thought as a form
Sun	Hero, son of heaven, knowledge, the Divine eye, fire, life force, creative-guiding force, brightness, splendor, active principle, awakening, healing, resurrection, ultimate wholeness

The Voice of Space, 1928, by Rene Magritte, conveys the feeling of synesthesia. At one level of the mind sense impressions registered in one modality are felt in all sensory modalities. Thus sounds have shape, color and taste, and sights have sounds and feelings. Oil on canvas, 25½ × 19⅝ inches. Collection, The Museum of Modern Art, New York. Purchase.

of a bell triggered the visualization of a round object in front of his (S.'s) eyes, a rough feeling on his fingers, a taste of salt water, and the color white.[17] A number of composers have said that they see colors with their music, and many painters have described hearing musical tones when they look at the colors in their paintings. Occult tradition likewise has long accredited a color to each of the notes in the harmonic scale.

Like visualization of form, visualization of color has specific effects on the visualizer. The visualizer is changed by the energy of the color and, in a sense, becomes one with the color. As in the visualization of form, each person reacts individually to the visualization of color, but certain generalizations can be made. For example, red is exciting, arousing, stimulating. It is the color of blood and fire, surging emotions, wounds, warning and danger.

In all visualizations form and color play a part—not only in making the visualizations palpable, but also in giving them meaning. Basic forms and colors are often used to help people learn visualization. They are also used as visualizations for people to hold to achieve specific effects, in psychology, medicine, and spiritual life.

FOOTNOTES

1. Rugg, H. *Imagination*, New York, Harper & Row, 1963, p. 103.
2. Rapaport, D. *The Organization and Pathology of Thought*, New York, Columbia University Press, 1951, p. 198, from H. Silberer, "Report of a Method of Eliciting and Observing Certain Symbolic Hallucination Phenomena."
3. Rapaport, D. p. 202.
4. Cirlot, J. *A Dictionary of Symbols*, New York, Philosophical Library, 1962, p. xxix.
5. Jung, C. G. *Man and His Symbols*; Garden City, N.Y.; Doubleday & Co., Inc.; 1964; p. 21.
6. Cirlot, J. p. xxix.
7. Cirlot, J. p. xxxiv.
8. Mookerjee, A. *Tantra Art*, Paris, Ravi Kumar, 1971, p. 19.
9. Cirlot, J. p. xxxi.
10. Cirlot, J. p. 44.
11. Jung, C. G. pp. 240–249.
12. Birren, F. *Color*; New Hyde Park, N.Y.; University Books; 1963.
13. Birren, F.

14. Schachtel, E. *Metamorphosis*, New York; Basic Books, Inc.; 1959; p. 109.
15. Gerard, R. "Differential Effects of Colored Lights on Psychophysiological Functions," *American Psychology*, 13:340.
16. Mookerjee, A. p. 19.
17. Luria, A. *The Mind of a Mnemonist*; New York; Basic Books, Inc.; 1968.

OTHER READING

1. Gardner, E. *The Web of the Universe*, London, The Theosophical Publishing House, 1960.
2. Murchie, G. *The Music of the Spheres*, New York, Dover Publishing Co., 1961.
3. _____ *The Rainbow Book*; San Francisco, Cal.; The Fine Arts Museums of San Francisco/Shambhala; 1975.

SECTION II
OPENING THE MIND'S EYE

The eye has long been a symbol of sight—both outward and inward. People visualize when they open the mind's eye. *The Eye Like A Strange Balloon Mounts Toward Infinity*. 1882. Odilon Redon. Charcoal, 16⅝ × 13⅛ inches. Collection, The Museum of Modern Art, New York. Gift of Larry Aldrich.

INTRODUCTION

We have already said that visualization is a natural skill that people use all the time. Moreover, we believe that people can learn to improve their ability to visualize. In this section we will deal with how people visualize, that is, with methods people use to increase, control, and direct visualization in order to make it more effective. There is information about how people's minds work, and how they perceive images, that can assist people in visualizing.

Since the late 1800's, psychologists have written extensively about people's differing abilities to visualize. Some people have great detail, while others have felt they only receive thoughts in the form of words. In 1883, Sir Francis Galton, the English psychologist, formulated a theory that people have characteristic modes of thought, such as visualization (thinking in images) and verbalization (thinking in words). At that time, psychologists felt that people were either one or the other—verbalizer or visualizer. Since then several tests have been developed to measure personal differences in the ability to visualize, and even to measure the degree of vividness and controllability of a person's images. A number of psychologists have come to the conclusion that people cannot be categorized as either visualizers or verbalizers. They believe that people generally use both modes of thought, although one person may use images (or words) more than another person. The extent to which a person uses imagery depends a great deal upon cultural factors such as education and experience.

This section describes ways that people can build on their present visualization abilities and become stronger visualizers. The exercises in this section make people aware of visualization in a concrete way. Once people are aware of the different aspects of visualization they often discover that they notice situations in which they naturally visualize all around them and so they tend to consciously visualize more.

A serene setting, indoors or outside, quiets the mind and makes visualization easier. Arthur Okamura, *Rock Garden*, silk screen print, 19 × 26 inches. Courtesy of the Artist. Japanese rock gardens have traditionally been places for relaxation, contemplation, and meditation.

Chapter 8

PRELIMINARIES

Certain things that people naturally tend to do, but may not be aware of, greatly increase their ability to hold an image in their mind. In this chapter we will discuss techniques people have used to develop the natural skills of relaxing, concentrating, and seeing. Some of these techniques stem from yogic practices that are thousands of years old, and some are the result of research by contemporary psychologists and physiologists.

Visualization is an inner state of mind. In order to visualize effectively people have to put themselves in a state in which they can be aware of inner processes. For most people, at least initially, it is helpful to separate them-

selves from distracting or chaotic external stimuli. This means finding a quiet, tranquil place, in or out of doors, for visualizing. Eventually, it becomes possible to focus so clearly on internal stimuli that even strong external stimuli recede from consciousness. But it is much easier to visualize in the beginning if external stimuli are at a minimum.

In addition to finding a quiet physical space, it is helpful to find a quiet mental space. This means putting aside, as far as possible, ordinary concerns. People must make a choice to temporarily put aside matters that are not directly pertinent to their visualizing.

Relaxation

Body relaxation is the first step in learning how to improve the ability to visualize. As soon as a person picks a quiet time and place he will find himself beginning to relax. Conscious relaxation further removes extraneous stimuli, thereby allowing a person to concentrate more intensely on his inner state. Body relaxation has also been found by several researchers to facilitate the flow of internal images.[1]

In order to relax it's important to know how tension and relaxation feel. Most people know when their muscles are really tense, but they usually cannot distinguish low levels of tension and they do not feel they are able to relax their muscles at will. In the 1920's, Dr. Edmund Jacobson, an American physician, conducted research in muscle physiology, with emphasis on relaxation. Jacobson proved that people can become aware of tension and learn to relax. From his research Jacobson developed a technique called *progressive relaxation.*[2] Jacobson's studies were the first major scientific work on relaxation and provided the groundwork for some psychotherapeutic techniques, a natural childbirth technique, and techniques for treating tension-related diseases such as high blood pressure.

People can become aware of the difference between tension and relaxation in their bodies by tensing a muscle and then letting it go. Here is an exercise for becoming aware of tension and relaxation similar to ones used in Jacobson's progressive relaxation technique. With your arm resting on a flat surface, raise your hand by bending it up at the wrist. When your hand is raised, the muscles on top of your forearm, below the elbow, will be contracted, tense. If you let your hand go limp, those muscles will be relaxed and your hand will drop. The feeling of tension, of contraction, when you raise your hand is subtle. If you raise your hand back too far you may be confused by a feeling of strain in the opposing muscles of your lower forearm. If you don't feel the upper forearm tension at first, alternately raise your hand in a slow, even motion and then let it go limp. You might even rest the fingers of your other hand lightly on top of your forearm in order to feel the muscle contract under your fingers.

People can use exercises similar to the one above to become aware of tension and relaxation in any muscle in their body. In progressive relaxation Jacobson has people work on different areas of their body, one by one, contracting muscles, letting them go, and then letting their whole body relax, for about an hour.[3] For most people the muscles with the greatest residual tension are those of the face and neck, especially those around the eyes and jaw. These are the muscles associated with speech and vision. Jacobson found that when people see something in their mind's eye, there is measurable tension in their eye muscles. In fact, if people imagine a dog running from right to left, their eyes will shift from right to left. Likewise, Jacobson found that when people think in words (inner speech) there is measurable tension in the muscles of speech, especially in the tongue and the muscles of the jaw. When people are totally relaxed their jaw actually drops loosely and their eyes become motionless. Jacobson believes that when the body is totally relaxed, there are no images in the mind; at that moment the mind is essentially clear. He believes that the mind becomes relaxed and clear naturally as the body becomes more deeply relaxed.

It's not doing the exercises which is most important in the Jacobson method; it's allowing oneself to relax and remain relaxed. This concept of *allowing* relaxation to take place is an important one. Emil Coué, a famous French pharmacist who wrote on the power of suggestion in the 19th century, pointed out what he called the law of reversed effort: "To make good suggestions it is absolutely necessary to do it without effort . . . the use of the will . . . must be entirely put aside. One must have recourse exclusively to the imagination."[4] This is similar to the effect that Zen philosophers have referred to as "letting go."

Another commonly used technique for achieving body relaxation involves autosuggestion. Doctors and psychologists have been using this technique for a hundred years.

Body relaxation facilitates the flow of internal images. Relaxation has been described variously as a sense of heaviness or a sense of floating. Picturing this logos in the mind's eye signals the body's muscles to relax. Illustration by Susan Ida Smith.

It consists basically of a set of verbal instructions. People mentally repeat the instructions and *allow* the suggestions to work by themselves. The basic principle of auto-suggestion is that people's bodies respond to ideas held in their mind. Repeated inner speech is a simple way for people to hold an idea in their mind. The concept of people giving themselves a set of instructions through inner speech if fundamental to directing inner processes. The instructions don't have to be memorized, but people need to have a sense of their meaning in words best suited to themselves, which they can repeat internally. In John Lilly's terms, what people are doing is programming their own bio-computers. They are giving themselves a set of instructions in order to accomplish a particular goal.

People frequently give themselves mental instructions in reference to actions in the outer world. For example, in following a recipe from a book, a person might say to himself, "First I have to beat the egg whites until stiff." If he is unfamiliar with the process, he will tend to give himself more complete mental instructions almost as if someone were reading the recipe to him (in fact, he might have someone read the instructions). As he comes to know the recipe

From ancient times, the spiral has been used in art and the dance to induce a state of ecstasy, helping man to journey past the material world into the beyond. We use the spiral here as a symbolic image for deepening relaxation and going to a deeper level of mind. Illustration by Susan Ida Smith.

"by heart," he may simply say to himself, by way of instruction, "Eggwhites." Finally he may not even "hear" any instruction in inner speech, he may simply have a mental image of beaten eggwhites, or a sense of beating in his hand, or even a space of silence in which he just knows what to do. Similarly, when people first begin to cook they follow recipes closely. As they become more experienced, they may alter the ingredients or their amounts as they get ideas for making recipes better. Learning a recipe is a process that takes place in the outer

world, but the same sequence is followed in learning a process in the inner world.

Here is an example of a relaxation exercise that uses autosuggestion: Find a tranquil place where you won't be disturbed. Lie down with your legs uncrossed and your arms at your sides. Close your eyes, inhale slowly and deeply. Pause a moment. Then exhale slowly and completely. Allow your abdomen to rise and fall as you breathe. Do this several times. You now feel calm, comfortable, and more relaxed. As you relax, your breathing will

The sun in this drawing provides a logos for awakening or returning to ordinary consciousness. The sun has always been associated with the active principle, here meaning going from the inner to the outer world. Visualizing the image helps a person return to ordinary consciousness refreshed and full of energy. Illustration by Susan Ida Smith.

become slow and even. Mentally say to yourself, "My feet are relaxing. They are becoming more and more relaxed. My feet feel heavy." Rest for a moment. Repeat the same suggestions for your ankles. Rest again. In the same way, relax your lower legs, then your thighs, pausing to feel the sensations of relaxation in your muscles. Relax your pelvis. Rest. Relax your abdomen. Rest. Relax the muscles of your back. Rest. Relax your chest. Rest. Relax your fingers. Relax your hands. Rest. Relax your forearms, your upper arms, your shoulders. Rest. Relax your neck. Rest. Relax your jaw, allowing it to drop. Relax your tongue. Relax your cheeks. Relax your eyes. Rest. Relax your forehead and the top of your head. Now just rest. Allow your whole body to relax.

You are now in a calm, relaxed state of being. You can deepen this state by counting backwards. Breathe in; as you exhale slowly, say to yourself, "Ten. I am feeling very relaxed . . ." Inhale again, and as you exhale, repeat mentally, "Nine. I am feeling more relaxed

. . ." Breathe. "Eight. I am feeling even more relaxed . . ." Seven. "Deeper and more relaxed . . ." Six. "Even more . . ." Five (pause). Four (pause). Three (pause). Two (pause). One (pause). Zero (pause).

You are now at a deeper and more relaxed level of awareness, a level at which your body feels healthy, your mind feels peaceful and open. It is a level at which you can experience images in your mind more clearly and vividly than ever before. You can stay in this relaxed state as long as you like. To return to your ordinary consciousness, mentally say, "I am now going to move. When I count to three, I will raise my left hand and stretch my fingers. I will then feel relaxed, happy and strong, ready to continue my everyday activities."

Each time people relax, by any method, they find it easier and they relax more deeply. People experience the sensation of relaxation as tingling, radiating, or pulsing. They feel warmth or coolness, heaviness or a floating sensation. When people have followed a method of relaxation several times they may be able to relax deeply just by breathing in and out and allowing themselves to let go.

Everyone has his own methods that he uses, consciously or unconsciously, to relax. In our society, with its external orientation, most people relax through their leisure-time activities. These activities are often physical. Swimming, bike riding, jogging, hiking and yoga are all activities which, when done in harmony with the body, leave people feeling energized, tingling and relaxed. Gardening, taking walks in the country, sailing, and crafts likewise produce in the people doing them a relaxed state of body and mind similar to that achieved by relaxation exercises such as we have described. Bathing, napping, taking long car rides, listening to music, and lying in the sun can also produce states of mental and physical relaxation.

Many people have discovered that hatha yoga (the yoga of phisical exercises and posture) is relaxing to both body and mind. This lithograph by Robert Moon evokes the feeling of relaxation and tranquility that accompany hatha yoga. *Swami Vishnu No. 5,* 20½ × 26⁵/₁₆ inches. Collection, The Museum of Modern Art, New York. John B. Turner Fund.

Concentration

We've said that one useful preliminary step before actually visualizing is relaxation. Deep relaxation serves to clear people's minds and to remove muscular tension which can be distracting. In order to visualize effectively people must also be able to concentrate, to fix their mind on one thought or image and to hold it there. The counting breaths exercise we mentioned on page 65 demonstrates that thoughts constantly enter people's minds, one after another, and that people seem to have little control over the occurrence or nature of such thoughts. Indeed, everyone has had an experience like starting to think about dinner, only to find himself thinking about what he likes to eat, then about college friends he has eaten with, and then about life at college. Ob-

viously, if people are trying to fix their mind on one image, this lack of thought control is not helpful.

Yoga students are taught some simple exercises to help them concentrate.[5,6] In addition to helping people to concentrate, these exercises also help people understand the nature of their thinking. The first of these yoga exercises involves concentration on a small external object. The object may be of any shape or substance, but it should be fairly simple and small enough so that its whole image can be taken in at a glance. Such an object might be an orange, a pencil, a light bulb, or a rock.

Here is an exercise for concentrating on a small object. Place the object several feet from you, so that you can easily see all of it. Look di-

This X-XIth century Indian statue of Brahma conveys the feeling of meditation. Brahma, the Universal Spirit, the Creator, abides beyond the earthly cares of man and is in full control of himself and the universe. There are many yogic meditational exercises for concentrating the mind. When the mind is concentrated visualization can be controlled. The Metropolitan Museum of Art, Eggleston Fund, 1927.

Counting breaths is one of the most basic yogic concentration exercises. One technique involves counting "One," on inhale and "Two," on exhale. If a person notices an outside thought he should return to the count. Illustration by Susan Ida Smith.

rectly at the object. Keep your eyes open and think *only* of the object. You may notice the size, the shape, the color, the texture, or the parts of the object. Beyond such analysis, you may think only of the object as a whole. The goal of this exercise is to keep your attention fixed only on the object. Try to do this for at least a minute. Each time another thought comes to mind, simply go back to the object on which you're concentrating. Practice in going back each time thoughts intrude will strengthen your ability to concentrate.

In doing this exercise most people are surprised to find that their mind wanders. They find themselves thinking about how well they're concentrating. The next moment they find themselves wondering if it hasn't been a minute yet. Then they wonder why they're doing this exercise at all. Then they hear a noise outside and wonder what's causing the noise. The point is, they are trying their best to concentrate on the object, but they find their minds are darting about—as the yogins say—"like a mischievous monkey."

Another yoga concentration exercise is based on counting breaths. People who count their breaths, as in the exercise on page 65, also notice that thoughts come into their mind, which make them lose track of counting. To use the breath-counting exercise to build concen-

112

tration, people just return to the count each time intrusive thoughts enter their mind. After people have become used to noticing their thoughts and returning to the breath count, there are several other things they can do to sharpen their ability to concentrate. One is simply to stop the thought as quickly as possible, to "cut it off in mid-sentence," as it were. The natural desire is to follow the thought through. Practice in chopping the thought off at the roots frees people from having to follow thoughts through and prevents them from becoming enmeshed in a train of thoughts that does not pertain to the count. In fact it makes people more aware that thoughts constantly arise in their consciousness.

A second way of dealing with arising thoughts is simply to let them pass. In this approach, people maintain an impersonal attitude toward their thoughts, as if they were someone else's. They neither grab hold of the thoughts nor chop them down. They neither stop them nor pursue them. There is a Zen metaphor that thoughts are like birds flying across the sky of one's mind, and one simply watches them come into view and then disappear.

This exercise in time brings people to a state of heightened awareness, one in which they are relaxed yet alert. People practicing this exercise find that the quiet periods when they are only aware of counting their breaths lengthen and increase. As people become better able to concentrate on counting their breaths, they find themselves better able to concentrate on a single image. People find that they are able to hold an image for longer periods of time and are less bothered by intruding thoughts. People who've practiced any method of meditation have already developed some skills in concentration and relaxation that are useful in visualization.

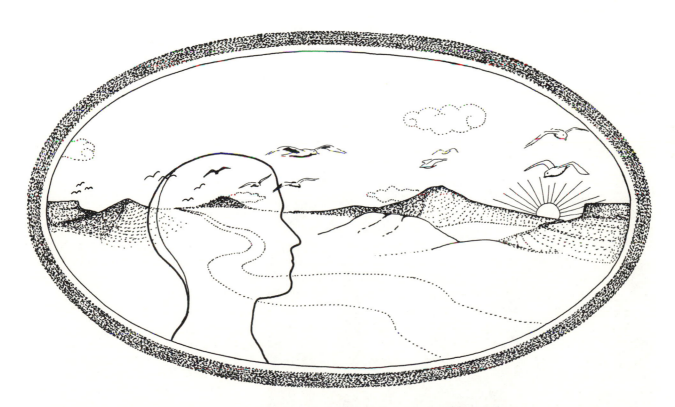

An ancient yogic saying holds that thoughts are like birds flying across the sky of the mind. In meditation a person simply watches thoughts come into mind and go.
Illustration by Susan Ida Smith.

Seeing

Active, alert seeing is another preliminary that is helpful in strengthening the ability to visualize. Seeing, as we usually speak of it, involves much more than exciting the cells of the retina. It involves more than the eye, it involves the mind. We have already discussed how seeing requires thinking in three parts of the brain. Seeing is not like pointing a camera at a scene; it is a learned ability which can always be further developed. The better people train their minds to perceive external images, the easier it becomes for them to imagine internal images as well.

Many psychologists believe that congenitally blind people do not have visual images.[7] In the same way, people who see blindly will find it difficult to picture visual images in their mind. And people can see blindly. For example, a man who is deep in thought might walk right by a friend on the street. If that fact is pointed out to him he might truthfully say, "I didn't even 'see' her," although she was directly in his field of vision. In fact he did see her, but his brain was concentrated on another thought and did not bring to consciousness the image of his friend.

Another, somewhat different, example of blind seeing may take place when people view an object only with regard to a specific function. For instance, if a person is at a party and wishes to sit down, he may notice an empty chair and "see" it only as a place to sit and rest. If someone were to ask him the next day to describe the chair in which he sat, he might not even be able to remember the color or shape of the chair. But he did see the chair and his brain recorded information about it even if he cannot consciously recall it.

We've talked before about the fact that most formal education does not promote visual imagery. Its main focus lies in goal-oriented verbal thought. In most elementary and high schools, for instance, art is considered a minor, even a recreational subject. Prestige is accorded only to those courses, such as physics and mathematics, which require a high degree of abstract thought. Likewise, success in the latter courses is considered a mark of intelligence. In fact, at the highest levels, such fields of abstract interest demand a high degree of visual imagery.

The first step for people to take in developing their ability to see is to look with awareness and alertness at whatever is in their visual field. This is similar to what people did in the

Letting your eyes explore an object, noticing highlights, textures, and gradation of tones and colors helps to strengthen and awaken the visual sense. *Beach Metal*. Photograph by Michael Samuels.

114

exercise for concentrating on an external object. But in this case the goal is to go beyond the everyday labels associated with the things seen and to concentrate purely on the visual images. Here is a series of exercises on seeing similar to those used in college courses on visual thinking.[8]

There is much more in what people see than they usually notice. One way to become aware of this is to look at one characteristic of an object after another. This is the substance of the first exercise. Notice the way light strikes objects: the highlights and shadows, reflections, radiolucent quality, and the range of tones it creates. With your body completely relaxed, let your eyes wander over the outline of each object. Notice sharp lines, soft lines, the total shape of the object and the smaller shapes which comprise it. Notice the texture and finish of the object: is it rough, smooth, dull, or shiney? Look for the grain in the surface. Look at the color of the object; the subtle gradations of tone. Is the color bright or dull, faint or dark, uniform or varying? Be aware of the depth and perspective inherent in what you are looking at.

Another way of looking at objects is to simply stare at an object and experience it. Here is an exercise for experiencing objects. Allow thoughts to arise freely as you fix your eyes on different aspects of an object. Try not to react verbally to, or to label, what you see. Just try to experience the images, and the feelings that surround those images. If you do this for a long time, say fifteen to thirty minutes, you will discover a great deal about the object beyond its labelled aspects.

One of the goals of these exercises is for people to allow the object they're looking at to fill their whole consciousness. This is similar to the concentration exercises discussed earlier in that the goal is for people to let no other thoughts enter their mind. Here is an exercise which people can use to allow an object to fill their consciousness. Move quite close to the object so that it fills your visual field. Then move even closer in order to concentrate on a single part of the object. In doing this, you will probably realize that what your eye focuses on, and takes in the details of, begins to fill your whole consciousness as well as your visual field. Once

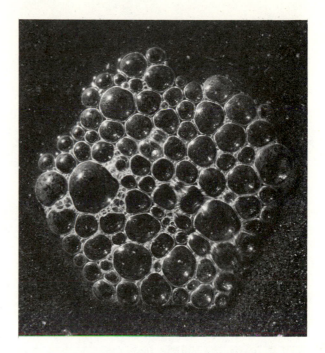

Moving in very close to view an object allows a detailed area to fill a person's whole consciousness. A person can also imagine moving in, like a zoom lens on a camera. *Bubbles.* Photograph by Michael Samuels.

you become experienced at moving in until an object fills your consciousness, you will be able to accomplish the same thing without changing your position, by mentally "moving in," like a zoom lens on a camera. Or, you can imagine the object actually becoming larger and larger. Also, you can practice mentally "zooming out," so that the object becomes smaller, and your field of vision takes in the entire side of the room in which the object is located. As you zoom in or out you will notice new details in the object. When you zoom in you will be more aware of surface texture, small cracks, specks of dust, hair, etc. As you zoom out, you'll be more aware of shape, depth and perspective and the relationship of size between objects.

Another way for people to develop their ability to see is to look at an object from different mental points of view, as well as from different physical vantage points. Here is an exercise which involves rapidly shifting viewpoints. Look at an apple. First, look at it as something to be eaten. You might imagine how the apple tastes, whether it is a variety you especially like, whether it is fresh or not. Just as you become a hungry person ready to bite into the apple, shift your viewpoint to that of an artist painting a picture of the apple. Become aware of the color of the apple, the texture, the light that is striking the apple, how difficult or easy it will be to paint it. As you become ready to pick up your brush, shift rapidly to the point of view of a worm eating his way through the apple. Then shift again, to the point of view of a migrant worker picking the apple . . . Shift once again to the viewpoint of a small child bobbing for the apple in a tub of water.

Each time people's viewpoints change, they will be aware of different aspects of the apple. Experiencing this and understanding it helps people to break free of their habitualized ways of seeing familiar objects. It makes the objects appear fresh and new and gives people greater control over the labels and associations they unconsciously use in ordinary seeing.

Another useful exercise involves *here and now* seeing. Walk down a street and concentrate only on what is immediately in your field of vision. If you begin to think of problems you have or what you'll be doing after this exercise, bring your attention back to your seeing. In doing this, you'll realize that seeing is a here and now experience. As you move, the images change. All there is at any one moment is the present image. You may also notice that qualities such as the intensity of color increase. You may find this to be a beautiful, exhilarating experience which leaves you with the kind of relaxed alertness we discussed earlier in the concentration exercises. You may even notice that you experience certain blank periods in which you cannot recall anything happening—thinking, seeing or moving. If that happens, simply return to seeing the here and now. The blank periods are examples of what the Russian mystic/philosopher Gurdjieff calls not remembering yourself.[9] In terms of this particular exercise, these periods are simply breaks in concentration. You can do the same exercise, walking down a street, from a slightly different point of view—that of remembering everything that you see. After you've walked a short distance, stop, close your eyes, and try to recall as many of the things that you saw as you can.

Another example of here and now seeing involves staring at a table with a number of objects on it. Put a number of diverse objects on your dining room table. Stare at the table for a minute, then close your eyes and see how many of the objects on the table you can see in your mind's eye. Do not list the objects verbally in your mind as you do this. Then look at the table again and see how closely what you remembered matched the things on the table. If you try this exercise several times you will probably find that you remember more objects each time.

Another exercise designed to improve visual awareness is called *daVinci's Device*.[10] Leonardo daVinci noted that when he looked at a wall that had cracks, chips, and paint stains, and let his imagination wander, he noticed resemblances to animal shapes, figures, even whole landscapes in these random defects. DaVinci felt that looking at such amorphous patterns and allowing the mind to play upon them, inventing one object after another, helped to stimulate imaginative seeing. Everyone has had similar experiences as a child when he lay on his back and stared at fluffy cumulus clouds, finding in them ships and faces, seeing new patterns as the wind continually changed the billowy white masses. A somewhat different exercise is to find basic shapes and patterns within recognizable objects. For example, a person can look at a bicycle and notice that the hub of the wheel and the spokes make a circle with lines radiating out, while the reflector on the rear fender makes a circle on a wide line.

Artists and craftsmen have developed their ability to see through the study and practice of their art. Drawing, photographing, sculpting, throwing pots, all teach people how to see. People who have done any of these things have learned skills that will carry over to the practice of visualization. Other people, who haven't done anything like drawing or painting since elementary school, might enjoy trying some of these things anew, purely from the point of view of developing their ability to see. The process is what is important here, not the art produced. Learning to see directly affects the ability to visualize. In seeing the images are external; in visualizing the images are internal. But the process and the effects are similar.

Apples by Henri Matisse, a French painter. Oil on canvas, 1916. In this picture Matisse has depicted a bowl of apples against a stark background, removing almost all external referents, thereby eliminating distractions and concentrating attention on the apples. The apples become a generalized symbol which is not tied to any particular time or place. Both the lack of detail and the perspective serve to heighten this symbolic quality. Looking at this picture a viewer can shift his viewpoint, seeing the apples as a painter or as a person who wants to eat an apple. Courtesy of The Art Institute of Chicago, Gift of Samuel A. Marx.

Simply staring at an object, without trying to identify it or label its aspects, opens up a new experience. *Untitles*. Photograph by Michael Samuels.

The visual imagination sees meaningful patterns within amorphous shapes. Photograph by Michael Samuels.

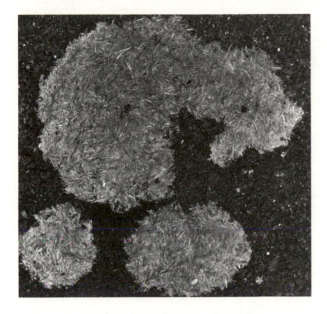

The ability to visualize is strengthened by visual experiences, especially arts and crafts. *Nancy Taking Pictures at the Beach, Summer 1969*. Photograph by Michael Samuels.

FOOTNOTES

1. Richardson, A. *Mental Imagery*, New York, Springer Publishing Co., 1969, p. 88.
2. Jacobson, E. *Progressive Relaxation*, Chicago, University of Chicago Press, 1942. A landmark in the physiology of relaxation, highly technical.
3. Jacobson, E. *How to Relax and Have Your Baby*, New York, McGraw-Hill Book Co., 1965. This book contains complete instructions for doing progressive relaxation, with photographs.
4. Coué, E. *Self-Mastery Through Conscious Auto-Suggestion*, London, Allen & Unwin Ltd., 1922.
5. Humphreys, C. *Concentration and Meditation*; Baltimore, Md.; Penguin Books, Ind.; 1970; pp. 30–71.
6. Most available yoga books have a section on concentration, with specific exercises.
7. Horowitz, M. *Image Formation and Cognition*, New York, Appleton-Century-Crofts, 1970, p. 35.
8. McKim, R. *Experiences in Visual Thinking*; Belmont, Ca.; Wadsworth Publishing Co., Inc.; 1972. A fine book that came out of a visual thinking course at Stanford.
9. Ouspensky, P. D. *In Search of the Miraculous*; New York; Harcourt, Brace & World, Inc.; 1949; p. 120.
10. McKim, R. p. 57.

OTHER READING

1. Swananda, S. *Practice of Yoga*, Himalayas, The Divine Life Society, 1970.
2. Sadhu, M. *Meditation*, Hollwood, Cal.; Wilshire Book Co., 1971.
3. Wilhelm, R., trans. *The Secret of the Golden Flower*, London, Routledge & Kegan Paul, 1969.
4. Evans-Wentz, W. Y. *Tibetan Yoga and Secret Doctrines*, London, Oxford University Press, 1967.
5. Kapleau, P. *Three Pillars of Zen*, New York, Harper & Row, 1961.
6. Eliade, M. *Yoga: Immortality and Freedom*, New York, Pantheon, 1954.
7. Mishra, R. *Fundamentals of Yoga*, New York, The Julien Press.
8. White, M. *Zone System Manual*; Hastings-on-Hudson, N.Y.; Morgan & Morgan, Inc.; 1970. This is a book which teaches photographers how to previsualize pictures before they shoot them, but the section "Previsualization and the Development of Intuition" is useful for anyone interested in visualization.
9. Huxley, A. *The Doors of Perception*, New York, Harper & Row, 1963.
10. Huxley, A. *The Art of Seeing*, New York, Harper & Row.

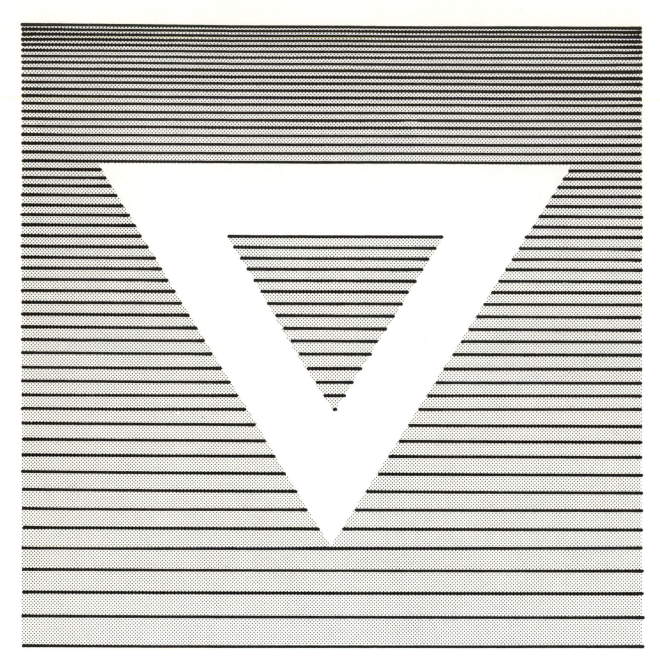

The triangle is a simple geometric shape that is often used for a first visualization exercise. The neutral gray background corresponds to what most people see when they close their eyes. The wide white line stands out in sharp contrast. Illustration by Susan Ida Smith.

Chapter 9

VISUALIZATION TECHNIQUES

We've said that visualization is creating a mental image, creating a picture in the mind, seeing with the mind's eye. Especially when people first begin to consciously visualize, the images in their mind's eye are different from the images that they see with the aid of their retinas. Indeed, these mental images more resemble thoughts and ideas than sights. Many people feel as if they are "making up" the images rather than seeing them. This is natural. The feeling of making it up is the way beginning visualization feels. Early mental images appear less vivid than external images. In fact, some people feel that they sense their inner images rather than see them. This may be because they are consciously appraising their inner images for the first time. For the first time they are questioning the reality of their inner images with the analytical sphere of their mind.

This chapter is made up of a series of exercises designed to help people improve their ability to visualize. The exercises are similar to those used by psychologists, doctors, artists, and yogins in teaching visualization.[1] The exercises help to improve people's natural ability to visualize, making it possible for them to use visualization to achieve specific goals. Each exercise in this chapter is intended to strengthen a particular aspect of visualization.

The first exercise consists of visualizing a small, uncomplicated, two-dimensional object such as a triangle. Here is the exercise. Take several deep breaths and relax. Look directly at the triangle on the page for about a minute, or until you feel you are quite familiar with it. Close your eyes. Imagine that you are still looking at the page. See the triangle. Allow your eyes to scan it just as you did when you were looking at the page. See the whiteness of the triangle and the grayness of the area around and within the triangle. Now open your eyes and look at the triangle on the page again.

121

Compare the triangle on the page with the one that you visualized. Close your eyes once more and again visualize the triangle. Imagine that you see the image of the triangle on the page about 18 inches in front of your eyes. You are projecting your imagined triangular image outward. When you project outward in this way you will be able to scan the image with your eyes as if it were an external image.

Many people who do this exercise for the first time expect to see an inner image as sharp and clear as the image on the page. But actually people often see something different from their expectations. For example, the first time Nancy did this exercise she described it as follows: "I was aware of the triangle only fleetingly. At one moment I was aware of it, the next moment I was not. At times I was only aware of part of the image, like the point at the bottom. Then for a second I would see the whole image. The image was never as bright as the image on the page. In fact, I felt as if I was looking at the image in a darkened room."

Michael, who had done this exercise many times, gave this description of what he saw: "I see the image clearly. However, it is a different experience than looking at the image on the page. The image fills my whole consciousness. I don't see the page in a room with other objects around it. I constantly look around the triangle and I basically see just the area that I'm looking at. I'm aware of the details: the sharpness of the white compared to the gray; the texture of the paper. If I stare directly at the center of the triangle, I then see a bright, ill-defined triangle flashing at me. It's almost like a neon light. It's easier for me to move my eyes around to different areas than to stare fixedly at the triangle, which requires more concentration. The image has a reality about it which is as real as an external triangle, but I would not confuse it with one. Sometimes the triangle drifts away or one even disappears if my interest wanes. Then I concentrate on the mental image of the triangle again and it comes back."

The important thing for people is to accept whatever they see as the right visualization experience for them. If people have fixed expectations of what they think they *ought* to see, they are apt to feel discouraged, to feel that they aren't doing the exercise correctly or that they can't visualize. These feelings virtually extinguish any image that they do see. For one thing, negative feelings break people's concentration on the image. They also program people's minds against any improvement. When people's egos enter into their visualizations—for whatever reason—the visualization experience changes. We call this *ego static*. Often the visualization will disappear and there will be a black period (similar to the one discussed in here-and-now seeing, page 116) when people suddenly realize that they have stopped visualizing. Then they may become aware that they're having thoughts such as, "I'm really good (or bad) at this visualization." At this point, it is helpful if they simply turn their attention to the visualization again (just as they returned to observing in the here-and-now seeing exercise) or if they re-do the relaxation technique. It's been our experience that the more people visualize, the more understanding they have of the whole experience and the more real their images become to them.

We will present many exercises for visualizing in this book. In most techniques a two-dimensional shape is usually given as the first visualization exercise because of its simplicity. However, the fact that the shape is simple, abstract, and, in a sense, not a part of everyday experience may make it more difficult for some people to visualize. Motivation plays a tremendous part in visualization, and some people may feel little involvement with the triangle and little motivation to visualize it. For that reason some people will find it easier to visualize a more familiar object such as an apple or a pencil. People sometimes do an exercise involving a simple two-dimensional shape, and are disappointed in their experience and decide that they are poor visualizers. Whereas the same people may find it easy for instance to visualize a naked person of the opposite sex, and may have done so for years, not realizing that they were visualizing.

The second exercise involves visualizing a simple, familiar three-dimensional object such as an apple, a flower, or a cup. Place an apple about two feet in front of you. You will probably find it easier if the apple is at eye level. Set the apple by itself, with no other objects around it to confuse or distract you. Take

The picture shows specific characteristics of this apple—a linear bruise to the right of the stem and the shadow to the left of the stem—as well as general characteristics such as shape, highlighting, and flecking. In visualizing an apple a person may be aware of any or all of these characteristics. Photograph by Mike Samuels.

several deep breaths and relax. Now look directly at the apple until you feel you are familiar with it. Close your eyes. Imagine that you still see the apple about two feet in front of you. See the apple in your mind's eye. Scan the image just as you did when you were looking at the apple with your eyes open. As you look at the image, notice the shape of the apple, the shadings of color, any irregularities, the tilt of the apple, the angle of the stem. Open your eyes. Compare your inner image with the outer one. Notice any aspects you were not aware of while visualizing. Close your eyes again and repeat the exercise.

Another memory image exercise that people can do involves visualization of a room that they remember from childhood. We've already described a form of this exercise on page 39. Some psychologists believe that most people find this the easiest visualization exercise to do. Here is another form of the childhood room visualization. Close your eyes. Take several deep breaths and relax. Picture yourself in a room from your childhood. Look at the wall in front of you. Scan it with your eyes just as if you were there. Notice the furniture in front of

you and any pictures on the walls. Let your gaze travel downward. Notice if you are standing on a rug. Notice what the floor is made of. Now look at the wall to your right . . . to your left . . . and finally turn around and look at the wall behind you. Notice doors, closets. Look at the windows, notice the color and texture of the curtains.

These visualizations are arranged more or less in a graded series. Each one introduces new aspects of the visualization process. The exercise with the triangle is an introduction to visualizing shape and black and white tone. The apple exercise introduces color, texture, and three-dimensionality. Both of these exercises consist of very recent memory images formed from objects immediately present in the outside world. The childhood room visualization is a distant memory image, of a place and objects most likely not present. In that exercise visualizers mentally move about for the first time and locate themselves spatially within a visualized place.

The next exercise also concerns moving about. But in this exercise, visualizers will move around an object, rather than within it.

A house is a good large object to visualize. Most people can easily imagine mentally walking around a familiar house, seeing the doors and windows on each side. The levels and tones in this picture evoke the feeling of walking around a house in imagination. Charles Sheeler. *Architectural Cadences.* 1954. Oil on canvas. 25 × 35 inches. Collection of Whitney Museum of American Art.

Relax. Close your eyes. Visualize a large object that you know well, such as a house. Imagine that you are standing, facing the front of the house, which fills your visual field. Look at the door, the windows, the angle of the roof. Notice the material of which the house is constructed—the color and texture of it. Walk up to the house and look closely at the siding.. Notice fine details of the texture. Look at other details as well, from this close vantage. Now walk slowly around the house, pausing to look at each side. Notice windows, doors, shutters, etc. Walk completely around the house and come back to the front.

The process of visualization seems to bypass many of the laws of the physical world. Some people may have noticed, while doing the last exercise, that when they wanted to observe something more closely they could walk up to it

or they could just move their consciousness up to the object without thinking about moving their body.

The next exercise involves more practice with mental moving. Look carefully at a chair. Notice the seat, the back, the sides, and if it has arms, the arms. Now relax. Close your eyes. Imagine that you are facing the front of the chair. Look at it, notice details of color, texture, and shape. Now look at the side of the chair; notice the profile. Then look at the back of the chair; notice its silhouette. Now look at the other side. Then come back to the front. Look down on the chair as if you were standing above it. Then look at the bottom as if you were below the chair. In doing this exercise people learn that they can move their consciousness at will, without moving their bodies. When the instructions say, "Look at the side of the chair,"

A view of a teakettle from above. Because of its protuberances a teakettle is an excellent small, three-dimensional object to visualize. Photograph by Mike Samuels.

125

they just seem to be at the side of the chair and no longer in front of it. Other people feel a sense of disembodied movement.

The next exercise continues to explore mental moving and introduces another kind of movement. Get a small three-dimensional object with protruberances, such as a teakettle. Look at all sides of the object. Notice the overall shape, the handle, the spout, the lid, and any dents or chips in the kettle. Relax deeply and close your eyes. Picture the teakettle in front of you. Orient yourself so that you are looking at one side of the kettle. Now imagine that you are moving slowly around the kettle, observing how its shape changes. Notice how the spout goes out of sight when you are looking directly at the back of the kettle. Float slowly up above the kettle and look down on it: look at the handle of the cover and the opening of the spout. Float back down until the kettle is at your eye level. Now imagine that the teakettle is rotating slowly in front of you, while you remain stationary. Again notice how shapes change as the kettle turns.

The teakettle exercise is the first exercise to introduce an imagination image. People imagine that the kettle is turning, although they had not observed that in their outer-world perception of the kettle.

The next exercise mixes memory and imagination images. Lie down. Relax deeply and close your eyes. Go back in your mind to the childhood room you visualized earlier. Reorient yourself in the room. Picture the walls in front of you and scan them until you come to a light switch. Turn it on. Look at the light. Notice how the bulb glows. Turn the switch on and off several times, watching the bulb brighten and dim as you do so. Mentally move to a desk or table top. Pick up an object from the surface, such as a book or a pencil. Turn it around; look at it. Put it back down on the table. Now imagine that the same object starts to float up in front of you, as if it were weightless. Watch it float up past your eyes and bump gently on the ceiling. Watch it float back down and land gently on the table surface. Now turn until you face the window. Imagine yourself floating slowly toward the window and passing out through it. Let yourself hover a few feet outside the window. Look at the scene in front of you. Notice other houses, roads, trees, the sky. Still floating, look at the ground below you. Notice grass, sidewalks, shrubs, and other objects. Now float gently down until your feet touch the ground.

In this exercise people experience control over their visual images. Not only that, they are able to do things beyond the laws of physical space. For example, they are able to float through a window themselves and make objects float in front of them. They are also able to make an object's appearance change when they switch the light on and off. The image of the light bulb changes from luminous to dark and back.

The next exercise is designed to extend people's ability to transform images through visualization. This exercise has people play with objects and their characteristics. Picture an uninflated red balloon. Mentally blow it up until it is half full, but distinctly round. Knot it. Throw the balloon up in the air. When it gets near the ceiling, stop it there. Make the balloon rotate . . . faster and faster . . . then stop it. Make it bounce along the ceiling. Stop it. Bring it down until it's hovering just above eye level. Then change the color of the balloon to yellow. Look at it. Change the color to blue. Now make the blue balloon bounce along the floor. Stop it. Make the balloon bigger, until it's almost doubled in size. Now make the balloon very small, and let it come to rest on the floor.

In doing the balloon exercise and others before, people may have been surprised to find themselves visualizing things not specifically mentioned in the exercise. For example, when people watched the balloon float up to the ceiling, it may have been a familiar ceiling that they saw. Or it may have been an unfamiliar ceiling which had particular details that they noticed. In this exercise people also experimented further with control over their images. As a result of verbal instructions, they were able to change their visualizations in color and size.

So far, these visualization exercises have dealt with objects. The next exercise deals with practicing visualization of a person. It is helpful if people choose someone who they know and see frequently—a close friend, a spouse, a child, or a business associate. Relax. Close your

The darkness of the room and the light outside seem to mentally draw the viewer's consciousness out of the window in this lithograph by Odilon Redon. *The Day,* from *Dreams.* Plate VI. 1891. 8¼ × 6⅛ inches. Collection, The Museum of Modern Art, New York. Lillie P. Bliss Collection.

eyes. Imagine that you see the person standing a few feet away from you. Look at his or her face. Allow your eyes to scan the person's face as if he or she were standing in front of you. Notice the color of the person's eyes, skin and hair. Look closely at the shape of the person's mouth, nose, and chin. Look at the rest of the person's body, noticing the person's clothes and how he or she is standing. Now imagine the person doing something you've frequently watched. Notice the way the peson's arms move, the way the person's body is held. Imagine that the person is talking on the phone. Watch the person's facial expressions. Listen to the person's voice; hear what he or she is saying. Listen to the tone, the inflection, the volume. Finally, watch the person as the conversation ends.

Many people find this exercise harder than some of the others. This may be because a familiar person evokes many images and it can be difficult to focus in on the specific images described in this exercise. But people often have vivid daydreams about other people. If people realize that their daydreams are visualizations they can use them as exercises for improving their image control.

The next exercise deals with people visualizing themselves. Interestingly enough, many people really do not have a clear image of what they look like. Some people find it useful to spend time looking at themselves in a mirror before doing this exercise. Looking at photographs and home movies is another way people can become familiar with the way they look. Relax. Close your eyes. Mentally see yourself. Look at your face. Notice your hair, eyes, nose, mouth. Look at your body: your hands and arms, your feet and legs, your torso. Watch yourself doing something you frequently do. Look at your movements, the way you hold your body. Imagine yourself answering the phone. Listen to your voice, to the inflections it has when you say something familiar.

Many people find visualizing themselves more difficult than visualizing an object such as an apple. More thoughts seem to intrude. For example, a person may think, ''Do I really look like that?'' or ''That's not how I look!'' Because the object of a person's visualization is himself, his ego, with its fears, doubts, and wishes, is much more likely to make itself heard and thereby enter into the visualization process. Actually, people are present as observers in all of the exercises that have been described up until this one. The attitude of observing objects and other people is much closer to ordinary consciousness than is the attitude of observing oneself. So far in the visualization exercises even when people are active (and doing phenomenal things such as floating out a window) they do so from within themselves. But in this last exercise people visualized themselves, which, in a sense, requires them to step outside of themselves. In other words, they have to separate their consciousness from their body. Many people find this disturbing the first time that they try it. Often they find the process easier if they visualize themselves in a real or imaginary situation with people and objects around them.

In the two previous exercises people imagine hearing a voice, as well as seeing visual imagery. Mental imagery is not restricted to the visual alone, but involves other sensory modalities. Becoming aware of, and using, all the sensory modalities deepens and enriches the visualization process and its effectiveness. The next exercise will involve all of a person's senses. Close your eyes. Relax deeply. Visualize a tranquil scene from your past in which you felt strong, happy, and at ease. You may remember being in the mountains or at the seashore. Or you may remember a particularly warm, quiet time at home. In any case, the moment should be an especially fine one, one in which you felt as good as you ever have. Notice your surroundings—if you're at the beach, notice the sand, the waves, the sky. If you are at the mountains notice the trees, the ground and again the sky. Wherever you are, notice details in your surroundings, such as pebbles on the ground, light dancing on the water or coming through the trees, leaves on the ground. Notice the breeze, the way the air *feels* on your skin. Notice the warmth of the sand, the coolness of the ground. Notice the way the ground feels against your body. *Smell* the air: the salty odor from the sea, the live, humusy odor of the woods. *Hear* the sounds around you: the waves breaking on the shore, the leaves of the trees rustling in the wind, the

People often find it hard to visualize themselves. Spending time looking at themselves helps people visualize better and see themselves with less distortion. Photograph by Michael Samuels.

A visual image of the exercise in which a person *imagines* one hand becoming heavy and the other hand becoming light. This exercise is used in medicine to graphically demonstrate that what people mentally picture affects their body. Illustration by Susan Ida Smith.

cries of birds overhead, the chirp of nearby crickets. Remember how you felt—the warm heaviness in your arms and legs, the gentle rise and fall of your chest as you breathed. Enjoy these sensations.

In this exercise people experience how in using the mind's sense of hearing, touch and smell, their visualizations acquire richness, reality and presence. After doing this exercise most people feel very good. They are able to bring the pleasurable sensations of their visualization back into their ordinary consciousness. In fact, in doing this exercise they discover a quiet place in their mind that they can return to whenever they wish to feel those good sensations. In this exercise people primarily re-experience past sensations.

The next exercise involves having people *imagine* sensations and experience them in their body. Sit down. Close your eyes. Relax deeply. Hold your arms straight out in front of you. Imagine that your left hand is becoming heavy, very heavy. Imagine that it feels as if it were made of lead. Picture a heavy object such as a book resting on your left hand. Feel the weight of the object. Now imagine that your right hand feels very light. Imagine that there is a string around your right wrist that is attached to a helium balloon. Feel the buoyancy of the balloon. Now open your eyes.

Most people who do this exercise will find that their left hand has dropped considerably and that their right hand has drifted upward. Often poeople feel the tendency of their hands to move as they are doing the exercise. (And some people unconsciously act to keep their hands level.) This exercise gives people practice in visualizing situations which produce changes in their body. The sight of their hands in different positions when they open their eyes shows them that their body responds to the visual images that they hold. We will talk more about this in the chapter on medicine.

Until now, all the visualizations we have dealt with have involved the conscious programming of visual images. For example, a person has said to himself, "The balloon is red . . . yellow . . . blue," and he has seen the balloon correspondingly change in color. The next exercise involves people experiencing undirected visualizations that arise spontaneously. We've mentioned that people are sometimes surprised when they see details that were not mentioned in an exercise. This element is a kind of spontaneous visualization. Another difference in the next exercise is that it will focus on an imagination, not a memory, image. So objects that people will picture may be objects that they have never seen before. Earlier, we talked about the fact that some people may feel that they are "making it all up." This feeling is especially common in spontaneous imagination exercises. We call this type of exercise a receptive visualization.

Close your eyes. Relax deeply. In this exercise you will visualize a place or a room where you can go to work in your inner world. The room is as real as a studio or a shop, but it exists in inner space, in your mind. Begin to visualize yourself in this space. You may see the space all at once, or parts of it may appear gradually. Begin to look around. Notice where you are. Notice whether you are out of doors or in a room. If you are in a room, notice how the walls, doors and windows look, what they are made of. Look at the ceiling, the floor, the rugs, the furniture. If you are out of doors, notice the kind of place where you are. Is it a clearing in the woods, a meadow, a cave? Look closely at the trees, the plants, the rocks. Find a comfortable place to sit. It may be a chair, a rug, or the ground. You may be surprised to find that your inner space is filled with plants although it is a room, or that it has a comfortable chair although it is out of doors. Because you are visualizing this space, there

People can visualize a place which exists only in their mind. This place can serve as a quiet space, a mental workshop, or a place where a person can go to feel good. Most people are surprised to find that they can visualize such a space in detail. Illustration by Susan Ida Smith.

are no limits on what you may see in it. There may be objects made from materials you've never seen before, even objects that float in space. Explore the space, until you feel familiar with it. There are several things which people find useful in their inner space, and you can visualize them if you wish. You may already have noticed some of these things in looking around your inner space. The first object is a clock. The second is a viewing screen. You may also visualize a guide, someone who can help you answer questions. If you visualize a guide, notice what he or she looks like and how he or she is dressed. You can even ask the guide's name and talk to them now. Look around once more and visualize anything else you would like in your workshop. This is a space you can return to whenever you wish, to work, to think or just to feel good.

In this exercise people experience receiving a visualization, having a visualization come to them without pre-programming its contents. In the exercise we suggested objects, such as a room, with no details to define them. Most people are surprised when they do see a room. Often these locations are very detailed even though the person has never seen them before. A feeling similar to this is experienced by artists when they envision a new work and by writers when they visualize fictional characters as we will see in the chapter on creativity.

FOOTNOTES

1. Specific techniques are discussed in Section III.

OTHER READING

1. Assagioli, R. *Psychosynthesis;* New York; Hobbs, Dorman & Co.; 1965.
2. Luthe, W. *Autogenic Therapy,* New York, Grune & Stratton, 1969.
3. Samuels, M. and Bennett, H. *Spirit Guides,* New York, Random House/Bookworks, 1974. This is a book on visualizing a spirit helper.
4. Samuels, M. and Bennett, H. *The Well Body Book,* New York, Random House/Bookworks, 1973. This book has a lot of information about to visualize health.
5. Samuela, M. and Bennett, H. *Be Well,* New York, Random House/Bookworks, 1974. More information on visualizing health.
6. Casteneda, C. All of his books contain North American Indian methods of teaching visualization.
7. Masters, R. and Houston, J. *Mind Games,* New York, Dell Publishing Co., 1972.
8. Silva Mind Control, EST, and Mind Dynamics all teach visualization methods as part of their courses.

Henri Rousseau's paintings show that he was in contact with a coherent inner world which was as real to him as the external world. It is said that he used no specific exercises to get in touch with his visualizations, that he simply was convinced of the reality of his visions and drew no hard and fast line between inner and outer. *The Sleeping Gypsy*, 1897. Oil on canvas, 51 inches × 6 feet 7 inches. Collection, The Museum of Modern Art, New York. Gift of Mrs. Simon Guggenheim.

Chapter 10

A RECEPTIVE PLACE

In the last chapter we presented exercises which led people to experience specific kinds of visualizations. In this chapter we'll talk about things people can do and things they can be aware of which will encourage their visualizations. First it helps for people to be aware of what visualization is. Even though they have been experiencing visual images in a number of forms all through their lives, most people have probably never thought of their images as a special kind of experience until now. And they've probably never thought of images as events which they can control and use in a number of ways. When people know what different kinds of visualizations are, they are more likely to be aware of them as they occur. This awareness gives them the opportunity to devote their attention to the images and to learn to concentrate on them. Research has shown that almost everyone fantasizes or daydreams in visual images.[1] Here then is a rich and easily accessible area for becoming aware of one's visualizations.

Simply setting visualization as a goal makes it much more likely that people will visualize. We're not talking now about a person willing himself to visualize, but about acknowledging a desire to visualize. This acknowledgment is in itself a kind of visualization. It sets a scene, creates a climate wherein people are likely to do things that promote visualization. Another way to look at it is that people are programming their bio-computer to be in readiness to accept a visualization experience.

We've already talked about how body relaxation makes it more likely that people will visualize. There are many other things people can do to promote visualization, whether or not they actually do specific exercises like the ones in the last chapter. People can simply put themselves in a receptive place. Visualization is an inner process and it requires that people put themselves in a place where inner processes can be heard. For most people this means, physically, a place in which they can be quiet and undisturbed. Each person has, or can create, his own places that fulfill these requirements. One person may go into a room and close the door. Another person may go for long walks. Another might lie in bed. Some people prefer a particular time of day, when it is dark or light outside. In any case, it helps to eliminate annoying external stimuli and interruptions. It is also helpful to set aside situations of heavy personal responsibility, situations that cause a person to worry, and (usually) situations involving direct problem-solving activity. One common reason why people don't

visualize more is that *they don't give themselves time to visualize.* The California psychologist and imagery researcher Dr. Mardi Horowitz says that visualization increases "when planfulness decreases and persons enter a state of directionless thought."[2]

To achieve directionless thought people can meditate, or they can just let their minds wander. Scientists and artists often take advantage of this when they put a difficult problem aside, rest, and let the answer "come" to them (see *Creativity*). Some people find that "sensory cues" stimulate visualizations and they learn how to make use of those cues. For example, the poet Schiller was stimulated to visualize by the smell of decomposing apples

Mortlake Terrace by the British painter William Turner shows an almost deserted walk along a river. Many people have found that they visualize best on long leisurely walks when they have put aside responsibilities and just let their mind wander. National Gallery of Art, Washington. Andrew Mellon Collection, 1937.

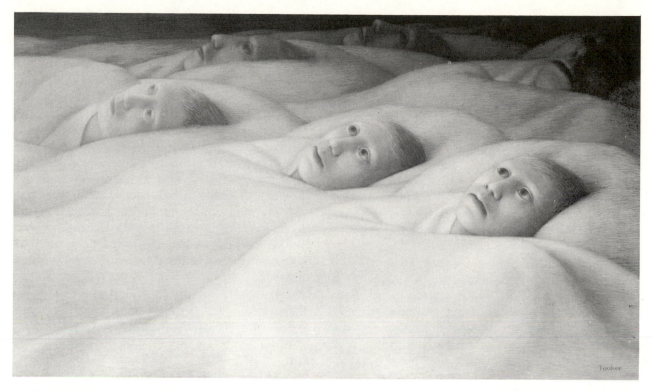

The state between wakefulness and sleep often results in vivid but ephemeral images. If people make a point of paying attention to the images, without becoming fully awake, they will continue to experience the images and be able to recall them later. *Sleepers, II* (1959) by George Tooker. Egg tempera on gesso panel, 16⅛ × 28 inches. Collection, The Museum of Modern Art, New York. Larry Aldrich Foundation Fund.

which he constantly kept hidden in his desk. We mentioned earlier that sensory stimuli often trigger memory images. By controlling their environment people can produce situations in which they are most likely to visualize.

In the first section we spoke of *hypnagogic imagery,* that is, visualizations that take place in the state between wakefulness and falling asleep. We noted that such imagery seems to be less under people's control than some of the other forms, such as daydreaming. The content of hypnagogic images is often fantastic and they have frequently been the acknowledged source of new ideas for artists and writers such as Edgar Allan Poe, Max Ernst, and Ray Bradbury.[3] It's not difficult for people to become aware of their own hypnagogic visualizations. Almost everyone experiences these images, although not everyone later recalls the experience. As with awake images it's helpful if

people are undisturbed, quite relaxed, and relatively free of purposeful thoughts. This is most likely to occur naturally if they are lying down and have nothing on their minds except resting. If people are exhausted when they lie down, they are likely to fall asleep immediately. People can produce heightened hypnagogic imagery by doing deep body relaxation when they first lie down (see page 108).

When people are in a hypnagogic state images come by themselves. All people need do is remain in a state of interested awareness. They may find that if they look too closely the images will disappear, or if they don't pay close enough attention to the images, they may fall asleep. Some people actually use specific techniques to keep themselves from falling asleep. For example, one such technique is for a person to bend his arm at the elbow, keeping his hand in the air; if he begins to go to sleep, his hand will drop and wake him. People have also ex-

137

perimented with talking into a tape recorder about what they see while in a hypnagogic state and with writing down their visualizations afterwards. While techniques like this are interesting, they are not usually necessary in order to become aware of and remember hypnagogic imagery.

Hypnopompic imagery, which occurs between sleep and waking, is similar to hypnagogic. It can occur when awaking in the middle of the night, after a nap, or in the morning—any time people are not required to fully awaken and immediately pursue concerns of ordinary consciousness. People who awaken spontaneously in the middle of the night frequently experience hypnopompic imagery if there is no pressing requirement being made of them. Likewise if people are able to awaken slowly after a nap or in the morning, they are more likely to experience such imagery. Most adults have a sense of having to awaken at a certain time in the morning in order to go about their work. For that reason, they are more likely to experience hypnopompic imagery when they have a day off and "sleep in" or when they are sick and know they won't have to be getting up. If people are interested in encouraging this kind of imagery, they can try waking a half hour or so before they actually have to get up. Then they can lie back and relax, peaceful in the knowledge they have nothing to do but let their minds wander, attentive to the images that will come.

A state of mind in which everyone experiences images is the *dream* state. People who bring their dreams to consciousness have a rich source of images to use in their life. Some people find it difficult to remember their dreams. The most common technique for bringing dreams to awareness is for people to tell themselves, as they are falling asleep, that they will remember their dreams when they awaken. When people wake, it is helpful if they can lie still and let the memories of their dreams come back. At first, even for the first few days, they may recall little. But as they continue this technique, day after day, they begin to recall more and more. At first people may recall a particular dream very fuzzily, then find that the longer they ponder it the more details they can recall. In fact, they may even find themselves remembering whole other dreams they did not, at first, recall. It's helpful if people remember dreams before waking thoughts attract their attention. Dream images do not necessarily follow the laws of ordinary consciousness and may therefore be especially difficult to grasp in the waking state. Some people find that they recall their dreams best in the hypnopompic state (that is, the state between sleep and waking), which seems somehow closer to the dream state than ordinary consciousness. What people are likely to recall of a dream at ten in the morning is a great deal less than they are likely to recall just as they awaken. Some people find it helpful to tell their dreams to another person or to write them down as soon as they awaken.

We've said before that visual imagery is closer to direct experience than verbal thought. Words are usually labels to describe an experience, whereas an image involves reliving the experience. This differentiation is particularly important in recalling dreams, because the images in dreams do not fit readily into the categories of verbal thought. Ehrenzweig, an American psychoanalyst, says, "In dreams, the impossible becomes possible. Often dream images appear to contain several totally different thing-forms, say a pram, a hearse, and a cannon at the same time, as though their shapes were superimposed upon one another. In our dreams we might see a thing which appears, while we are dreaming, quite ordinary and simple, but when we are awake and try to recall it we become aware of its 'too general content.' In trying to describe it we get into difficulties: 'I saw something approaching,' we might say, 'a pram perhaps or was it not a hearse . . . it could also have been a cannon . . ., etc.' What we are doing is again superimposing the several adult-things into the dream-thing; but the superimposition occurs only in the waking state after we have returned to the finer differentiation of the adult; the dream vision which appeared simple and clear in the dream, now appears vague and ambiguous or superimposed."[4]

Once people have learned to bring their dreams to awareness, the dream content can be of use in many parts of their personal life. Dreams have long been used by psychoanalysts

The dreamer enters a world rich with visualizations and boundless in its possibilities. Dream imagery is typically difficult to describe in words and full of superimposed, seemingly disparate forms and symbols. People can train themselves to remember their dreams and even participate in them. *Frog King Myth*. Photograph by Michael Samuels.

FIGURE A

Whether awake or asleep, a relaxed, restful state encourages visualizations. Once aware of this a person can increase his ability to visualize. Figure A, *A Maiden's Dream* by Lorenzo Lotto. National Gallery of Art, Washington, Samuel H. Kress Collection, 1939. Figure B, *Reverie* by Jean Honoré Fragonard. Copyright, The Frick Collection, New York.

as a door to the unconscious. Many artists and scientists have found working ideas in their dreams. Recently, people have become interested in influencing the contents of their dreams, that is, in putting thoughts from waking consciousness into them. Most people have experienced how events from everyday life may appear in their dreams. For example, a man may have a dream similar to a movie he has just seen. Or he may dream about an old friend after seeing her for the first time in years. Many people dream repeatedly about a very significant event in their life. Based on this knowledge, people can seek answers in their dreams, in the form of visualization images, to questions pondered in their waking state. Such a process often takes place naturally. It can also be encouraged. Before people go to sleep, they can concentrate on a question that concerns them and tell themselves that the answer will

140

FIGURE B

come in their dreams. When they awaken, they can recall the dreams in reference to the question which they were seeking to answer.

People can also affect the happenings in a dream. If they wish to have a particular kind of experience in a dream—such as a spiritual experience or a meeting with a particular person —they can focus on this before going to sleep. Another example of influencing dreams is given by the author Carlos Castaneda. He says

that his teacher, Don Juan, has told him that it's important to learn to consciously act in dreams as if they were taking place in the waking state.[5] In terms of this book, that means learning to achieve control over a form of visualization that people normally consider beyond their control.[6]

Up to now in this chapter we've discussed ways to encourage forms of visualization that everyone experiences. We will now briefly

141

mention some less common ways to encourage visualization. In the past twenty years there has been a great interest on the part of researchers and lay people in the use of *hallucinatory drugs,* including LSD, psilocybin, mescaline and peyote, hashish, marijuana, and amphetamines. All of these drugs have been known to produce visual images—often vivid, uncontrolled images—in people who have taken the drugs. These experiences have made many people aware of visualization phenomena for the first time. In terms of visual imagery, there is tremendous variability and variety in people's response to these drugs. Many people who have used drugs in the past to achieve visualization experiences have found that they can experience similar visualizations by other methods.

Sensory deprivation experiments have also been found to produce vivid visualizations in people. In a *sensory deprivation* experience a person is deprived of stimuli to one or more of the sensory modalities of touch, taste, sight, smell and hearing. This can occur naturally— for example to men working long hours in mines—or by experimental design. People who are in such situations are known to experience vivid, uncontrolled visualizations. In fact they might be called hallucinations.

Somewhat like sensory deprivation is a condition called *perceptual isolation,* which involves monotonous, unchanging sensory stimuation. Long distance truck drivers and pilots are particularly subject to such experiences. In such circumstances outside stimuli are at a minimum, yet the person is in a state of atten-

Driving down a straight, monotonous road can produce an almost trance-like state, in which a person's visualizations overlay and even overpower external reality. Photograph by Michael Samuels.

tion. It would seem in both sensory deprivation and perceptual isolation experiences that when the outside world recedes, the inner world surges forth, presenting itself in the form of visualizations.

Up to now, we've concentrated our attention on strengthening and holding images in the mind. It is also important that people believe in their images. It's been shown that an image is more stable and vivid if the person who is visualizing the image believes in it. For example, if a man is visualizing himself on the beach, he should be there, he should forget for a moment that he is lying on a couch and feel the sensations of warmth, sand and salt water. Although a person is convinced of the reality of his visualization, he need not confuse it with external reality. He can treat it with all the respect he would accord an external event, while knowing that it isn't one. He can have an attitude of full participation without attachment.

Secondly, it helps if people know that their visualizations affect their whole world. For example, the feeling of relaxation the man experienced during his beach visualization actually took place in his body. Although deep in his mind he knew he was visualizing, his body could not tell the difference between his visualization and the external experience.

Until people experience the effect of a visualization, they have to accept with faith the idea that mental images affect their outer world. That faith is based on intuition, as well as on knowledge about visualization gained from empirical reports. But everyone has felt the effects of his visualizations even though he hasn't necessarily created the images purposefully. For example, if a man visualizes a task as being difficult, he finds it difficult. If a number of people tell him the task is not hard, he will probably find it easier when he does that task again. As people experience the effects of visualization, their belief in the effectiveness of inner images deepens and in turn, as their belief deepens, the effectiveness of their visualizations increases. The knowledge that people gain is then based more firmly on their own direct experience.

Just as positivity and belief strengthen the effects of visualizations, so negativity and doubt can neutralize them. Insofar as they are able, it helps if people set aside worries, doubts and negative thoughts when they visualize. Here is a visualization exercise which is designed to consciously replace doubt with confidence. This exercise is like giving a positive program to one's bio-computer or like saying a prayer. Close your eyes. Breathe in and out deeply and slowly. Relax. When you feel deeply relaxed, say to yourself, "I am now deeply relaxed, in a calm, peaceful state of mind. My whole body feels healthy and strong . . . My mind feels clear and tranquil . . . I can now visualize vividly and easily. I can change what I see at will . . . My mind is open and receptive to images that will be helpful to me."

FOOTNOTES

1. Singer, J. *Daydreaming*, New York, Random House, 1966.
2. Horowitz, M. *Image Formation and Cognition*, New York, Appleton-Century-Crofts, 1970, p. 30.
3. McKim, R. *Experiences in Visual Thinking*; Belmont, Ca.; Wadsworth Publishing Co,. Inc.; 1972; p. 95.
4. Ehrenzweig, A. *Psychoanalysis of Artistic Vision and Hearing*, New York, Braziller, 1961, p. 31.
5. Castaneda, C. *Tales of Power*, New YOrk, Simon & Schuster, 1974.
6. Evans-Wentz, W. Y. *Tibetan Yoga and Secret Doctrines*, London, Oxford University Press, 1967, p. 221.

OTHER READING

1. Garfield, P. *Creative Dreaming*, New York, Simon & Schuster, 1975.
2. Lilly, J. *The Center of the Cyclone*, London, Paladin, 1973.
3. Ghiselin, B. *The Creative Process*, New York, New American Library, 1952.

Pure images from the inner center come in silence when the voice of the ego is stilled. Pure images are grounding when grounding is needed, soaring when it is time to soar. Wojciech Fangor, *Number 17*, 1963. Oil on burlap, 39½ × 39½ inches. Collection, The Museum of Modern Art, New York. Gift of Beatrice Perry, Inc.

Chapter 11

RECEIVING IMAGES

Whether or not a person realizes it, he pictures activities in his mind before doing them. His visualization may be simple and direct—for instance a person may picture in his mind, as he wakes up, something he will do that day. Or his visualization may be subtle and complex, such as his image of himself as being a friendly, outgoing person. People hold visualizations of the goals at which they are attempting to succeed and visualizations of themselves in relation to those goals. The goals may be both immediate and long-range, conscious and unconscious. They may be goals that people want to achieve or that they feel they ought to achieve. All of these goals are held in the mind in the form of visualizations.

This book tries to show how people can use visualization to improve the quality of their lives. Since the present quality of people's lives is the result of visualizations they already hold, consciously or unconsciously, if they wish to change some aspect of their life, they must first get in touch with their present visualizations. People make changes in order to try to improve their lives. The fact that they believe a change will enrich their lives shows that they are not presently fully satisfied with that area of their life. If they're not fully satisfied, then their present visualization of that area is, in a sense, negative. That is, they are measuring themselves or their lives against an inner standard which they do not meet. A correlate of this idea is that if they examine an area of their life with which they are satisfied, they will find they have a positive visualization of themselves with respect to that area. Such positive visualizations indicate areas in which people are following the course that is right for them. Negative visualizations are a sign that they are off their course. Through exploration of their negative visualizations people can gain information about the kinds of changes that can bring them back on course.

The science of *cybernetics* deals with the relationship between positive and negative messages and with reaching a particular goal. The word *cybernetics* was coined by the physicist Norbert Wiener from the Greek word *kubernetes,* or steersman.[1] People experience cybernetic feedback all the time. When a man reaches out to pick up a pencil off a table, the goal is the pencil. His hand moves toward the pencil, and his senses tell him where his hand is in relation to the pencil. The messages sent by his sense organs to his brain are perceived as "positive" when he is getting closer to the pencil, and "negative" if at any point he begins to move away from the pencil. Based on these messages his brain sends nerve impulses to the muscles of his hand and arm, causing them to expand and contract in such a way as to direct his hand to the pencil. What he may perceive as a smooth, steady, direct movement actually involves a series of "position-readings" and subsequent fine muscular changes as his hand literally zig-zags its way to the goal. When a person picks up a pencil, he feels as if his body is functioning automatically. He doesn't need to know the names of the muscles, or where the nerves are that innervate these muscles. He only needs to picture the goal; his body does the rest based on unconscious memories of other times he's successfully picked up a pencil. Babies, who lack the benefit of an adult's body experience, who are in fact just learning it for themselves, visibly and frequently alter the course of their hands when they first attempt to pick up an object such as a pencil.

In 1960, Dr. Maxwell Maltz, an American plastic surgeon extended the use of cybernetic theories to human behavior in his book *Psycho-Cybernetics.* Maltz writes, "The creative mechanism within you is impersonal. It will work automatically and impersonally to achieve goals of success and happiness, or unhappiness and failure, depending upon the goals which you yourself set for it. Present it with 'success goals' and it functions as a 'success mechanism.' Present it with negative goals, and it operates just as impersonally and just as faithfully as a 'failure mechanism.' Like any other servo-mechanism, it must have a clear-cut goal, objective, or 'problem' to work upon. The goals that our own creative mechanism seeks to achieve are MENTAL IMAGES, or mental pictures, which we create by the use of IMAGINATION."[2]

What Maltz calls the *creative mechanism* is not limited to muscular goals; it applies to any goal that a person may picture. As in the pencil example, for the servo-mechanism to work, there must be a goal that it is striving toward. Just as the man did not need to know the nervous innervation of the hand in order to pick up a pencil, people do not need to know the details or means of reaching other goals; they just have to be able to picture the goal. The mechanism works automatically. Maltz points out that mistakes or failures are not bad; in fact, they are essential. "All servo-mechanisms achieve a goal by negative feedback, or by going forward, making mistakes, and immediately correcting course . . . [After a goal has been achieved,] further learning, and continued success, is accomplished by *forgetting the past errors, and remembering the successful response,* so it can be imitated. You must learn to trust your creative mechanism to do its work and not 'jam it' by becoming too concerned or too anxious as to whether it will work or not, or by attempting to force it by too much conscious effort. You must 'let it' work, rather than 'make it' work. This trust is necessary because your creative mechanism operates below the level of consciousness."[3]

We said earlier that areas of a person's life with which they are not satisfied are accompanied by negative visualizations. A man may picture himself as being a failure, as being unable to reach a goal, as being uncreative or not intuitive, as unhealthy, or as having psychological problems. Like all visualizations, these negative visualizations become reality. In terms of cybernetics, the man has given his servo-mechanism a goal and it does whatever is necessary to reach that goal. For example, if a person has a visualization (unconscious or conscious) of failing at school, the failure will often occur. All of his actions will contribute toward it. He may study in a distracted way, wait until the last moment to begin a paper, and give up on an exam when he hits the first (and perhaps only) tough question.

If people find themselves dissatisfied with

People zig-zag toward goals using positive and negative feedback to guide them. Positive feedback tells people they are heading toward their goal, negative feedback tells them they are going off-course. People hold their goals in the form of visualizations. Allan d'Arcangelo. *Landscape.* 1968. Acrylic on canvas. 107¼ × 107 inches. Collection of the Whitney Museum of American Art. Gift of the Friends of the Whitney Museum of American Art.

one area of their life, in order to change it they have to remove the negative programs before they can replace them with positive ones. What they have to do to remove those negative programs is first to become aware of and stop them. These negative visualizations may be learned—that is authority figures may have told them to the person, or they may derive from a situation in which the person became aware of a "mistake" and from then on concentrated on the mistake rather than on the goal. Dissatisfaction can also be a message from a person's inner self telling him that changes are wanted in that area to better meet the needs of his inner self. The important thing with negative visualizations is to bring them to light; examine them in a detached, objective way; and then make a positive commitment to change them. Unrecognized negative visualizations counteract the effects of a positive visualization that people consciously hold in their mind. For that reason, it is important to deal with negative visualizations as well as to program positive ones.

We believe that it is an unconscious, primordial yearning of all people to feel good, that is, to feel satisfied with their life, to feel a sense of well-being, to feel at peace with themselves and in harmony with the universe. Most people have feelings of peace and satisfaction in certain areas of their life and feelings of dissatisfaction and yearning in other areas.

Many people believe that these feelings of satisfaction and dissatisfaction are guides that can help them to grow and fulfill themselves. Dr. Rammurti S. Mishra, a physician and yoga teacher in California, writing about Patanjali's Yoga Sutras, says, "It is common experience that when we do something good, a sentient rewarding feeling comes to the field of self-consciousness and, vice versa, when we do something evil a sentient unrewarding feeling full of guilt, anxiety, depression, etc., comes into the realm of individual consciousness."[4] The Principle which passes rewarding and punitive judgment on the individual soul and works within every soul as Absolute Judge is called Ishvara. Since Ishvara eternally guides consciousness it is called Teacher. No one is an exception to this guidance. "There [is] (in Ishvara) of utmost excellence the germ of om-

nipotence, omnipresence, and omniscience."[5] Mishra also says that to help hear the voice of Ishvara it is necessary to surrender the individual personality, which "is the seat of the ego, pride, lust, and desire."[6]

In a similar way, Dr. M. L. Von Franz, an Austrian psychoanalyst, in a discussion of Carl Jung's theories, speaks of the guide within people that is the source of inner images: "psychic growth cannot be brought about by a conscious effort of will power, but happens involuntarily and naturally . . . The organizing center from which the regulatory effect stems seems to be a sort of 'nuclear atom' in our psychic system. One could also call it the inventor, organizer, and source of dream images." Jung called this center 'the self' . . . Throughout the ages men have been intuitively aware of the existence of such a center. The Greeks called it man's inner *daimon*; in Egypt it was expressed by the concept of the *Ba-soul*; and the Romans worshipped it as the 'genius' native to each individual.

"In more primitive societies it was often thought of as a protective spirit embodied within an animal or a fetish . . . this creatively active aspect of the psychic nucleus can come into play only when the ego gets rid of all purposive and wishful aims and tries to get to a deeper, more basic form of existence. The ego must be able to listen attentively and to give itself, without any further design or purpose, to that inner urge toward growth."[7]

In a previous book, *Be Well*, which Mike Samuels wrote with Hal Bennett, the concept of the *Universal Self* is discussed. The Universal Self is "the personification of that part of a person which is always in harmony with universal law; a personification of the inborn healing abilities."[8]

The common thread of these ideas is that all people can have contact with the information necessary to direct their own growth and fulfillment. This information comes from a part of them deeper than their ego, a part *that works by itself*. It comes to them through feelings, intuitions, and strongly through spontaneous receptive visualizations. People can improve the quality of their life not only by concentrating on and continuing the positive visualizations that lie behind areas of satisfaction, but also by recognizing the negative visualizations behind areas of dissatisfaction, and by consciously inviting and holding positive visualizations related to those areas. Both of these methods bring people (in)to greater conscious awareness of their inner center. In terms of personal growth, it is the pure images from the inner center that are the most productive for concentration. These images are pure in that they relate directly to people's most fundamental needs.

At any moment, each person is aware of—consciously or unconsciously—those areas that are the most important in terms of growth, as well as those areas that are the most integrated and fulfilling. By getting in touch with images from his inner center, a person can become aware of both areas that yearn for change and resolution and areas that presently manifest harmony. Carl Jung has theorized that when a person feels weak, his inner center provides images of those areas in which he is strong. And again, when a person's ego becomes over-assertive, his inner center provides images of those areas that need work.[9] The inner center provides people with the images that are right

Feelings from the inner center can guide us. "When I shot this picture and printed it, I felt so good I knew it must be an important image for me." *Beach Rock I.* Photograph by Michael Samuels.

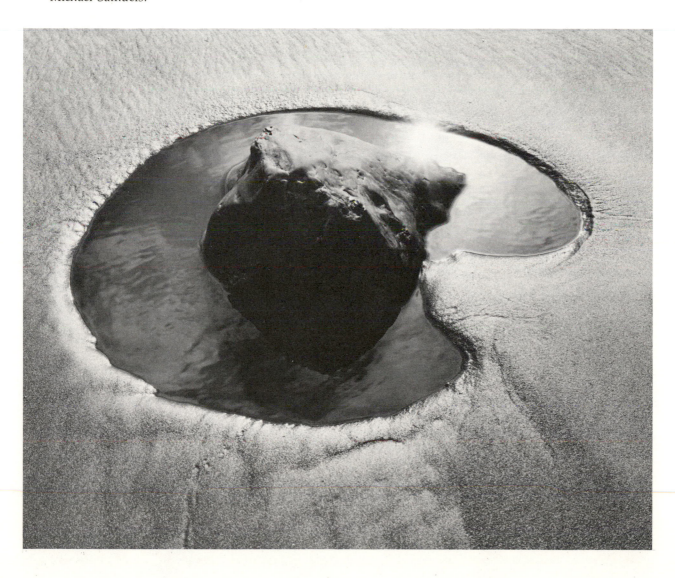

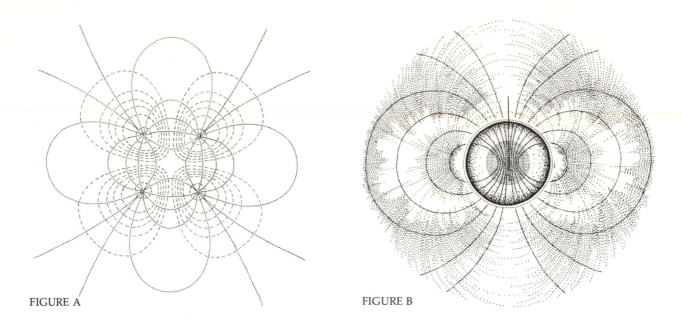

FIGURE A

FIGURE B

Many basic forms manifest themselves throughout the universe. For example, force fields around electrons resemble force fields around the earth. When a person looks at these forms and considers the relationship between the forms, he begins to feel his own kinship with the universe. He begins to sense the part of himself that is in harmony with the universe. Figure A, patterns of force around two positive and two negative charges. Figure B, electromagnetic force fields around the earth. Illustrations by Susan Ida Smith, from *Be Well*, by M. Samuels and H. Bennett.

for them at the moment, whereas the ego often provides images that are either over-inflated or overly negative. Overly-negative images can bring growth to a standstill and perpetuate unhappiness just as surely as over-inflated images. In the latter case, people assume a reckless, selfish attitude. With overly negative images people assume a hopeless, maudlin attitude of "It's not my fault—I am powerless to do anything." Images from the inner center avoid these snares of the ego.

People's egos, that is their conscious personalities, are always trying to find answers to life problems. These answers are generally forceful —that is they set out to solve problems, invent solutions, do a specific thing. The egos' answers are conditioned by people's habits and cultural biases. They are based on previous "losses and gains," on learned experience. Sometimes the decisions of the ego bring people fulfillment, sometimes quite the opposite. This is what makes ego visualizations different from pure images. Pure images are homeo-

static, that is they always foster harmony within people themselves and with the world around them. Pure images relate to long-term solutions, not just to immediate gain. Pure images contain the age-old knowledge of the species, even of the universe.

Images from the inner center have about them a universal quality. For thousands of years they have been the link between man and heaven. Richard Wilhelm has written, "Every event in the visible world is the effect of an 'image,' that is, of an idea in the unseen world. Accordingly, everything that happens on earth is only a reproduction, as it were, of an event in a world beyond our sense perception; as regards its occurrence in time, it is later than the supra-sensible event. The holy men and sages, who are in contact with those higher spheres, have access to these ideas through direct intuition and are therefore able to intervene decisively in events in the world. Thus man is linked with heaven, the supra-sensible world of ideas, and with earth, the material

150

Concentrating on pure images leads a person to discover his own harmony with the world around him. Circular, mandala-like figures have been envisioned by many people at crucial points in their inner development. Mandalas have always symbolized centering and the creation of the universe. Illustration by Susan Ida Smith.

world of visible things, to form with these a trinity of the primal powers."[10]

We've talked throughout the book of the effects of holding an image in the mind—effects on the visualizer and on the world around him. We've shown that people's bodies respond similarly to images whether they are of the inner or the outer world. Concentration on pure images brings about harmony. Whereas, concentration on ego visualizations has the same hit-or-miss effect as ego solutions have always had in people's lives.

Visualization, by its very nature, tends to get in touch with pure images. It does so because visualization involves participation and the loss of ego that accompanies giving oneself over to something. The ego tends to separate and elevate the "me-mine" from its surroundings, rather than to merge the self with its surroundings in a sharing experience. Images then are closer to the voice of the inner center, whereas words are closer to the voice of the ego. Psychologists have found that visual images tend to be most stable and vivid when we are relaxed, open, and positive.[11] This condition also tends to diminish the ego voice. When people are open and without fear they are least likely to resort to the learned security of verbal labels and most likely to apprehend pure images.

Several of the visualization techniques we have already discussed relate to receiving pure images. Body relaxation is the first and most basic (see page 106). Mind deepening techniques (see page 109) help people to go beyond ordinary consciousness into a place where the ego's voice is quieter still. This place is similar to that of hypnagogic and dream imagery. It is the place in people's inner world where it is easiest for them to receive pure images.

Receptive visualization provides us with the means for getting in touch with images from our inner center. The following exercise is a model for experiencing receptive visualizations. It includes an elevator image—long used as a mind-deepening technique by psychologists. It also introduces the use of a mental screen, a common visualization tool. Find a tranquil place where you will be undisturbed. Lie down with your legs uncrossed and your arms at your sides. Let your eyes close. Take a slow, deep breath, expanding your chest and abdomen. Pause a moment. Then exhale slowly, feeling your chest and abdomen relax. Breathe in this way until you begin to feel quite relaxed. As you become more relaxed, your breathing will become slow and even. You now feel calm and comfortable.

Feel your feet and legs. Imagine them becoming very heavy. Say to yourself, "My feet are relaxing; they are becoming more and more relaxed. My feet are deeply relaxed." Rest for a moment. In the same way relax your ankles, lower legs, thighs, pelvis, abdomen, back and chest. Rest again. Then relax your hands, forearms, upper arms and shoulders. Rest. Relax the muscles of your neck and jaw, allowing your jaw to drop. Relax your tongue, cheeks, eyes and forehead. Rest. Enjoy the feeling of total body relaxation.

You are now in a calm, relaxed state of being. To deepen this state imagine yourself in an elevator. Watch the doors close. Now look at the panel above the door which indicates the floor level. Imagine that number 10 is lit up. Feel the motion as the elevator begins to descend. As the elevator slowly passes each floor, you will become more and more relaxed, going to a deeper and deeper level of mind. Now see the number 9 light up. You are deeper and more relaxed. See number 8 light up. You are still deeper and more relaxed. Now 7. Deeper and more relaxed. 6. Still deeper. 5. Deeper still. 4. Deeper. 3. . . . 2. . . . 1.

You are now at a deep, open state of mind. See the elevator doors open. You are in a small, comfortable room that is dimly lit. On the wall in front of you is a large screen. Facing the screen is a soft, comfortable chair. Visualize yourself sitting in the chair facing the screen.

Say to yourself, "I am deeply relaxed. My mind feels clear and tranquil. I can visualize vividly and easily. My mind is open and receptive to images that will be helpful to me. I can look at the screen and see images come into view and disappear. If I wish to, I can hold the images on the screen or look closely at them. I can even influence what type of image will appear on the screen. If I have a question, I will see images that will help me find the answer. If I'm working on a problem, I will see images that will help me with its solution."

Contemplating the stars has given men a sense of universal order and filled them with awe as they watched the pantheon of constellations progress across the sky each night and change throughout the seasons. Albrecht Durer. Celestial Map—The Northern Hemisphere. German Woodcut, 1515. The Metropolitan Museum of Art. Harris Brisbane Dick Fund, 1951.

153

Moving through the heavens toward an area of white light is an image of particular expansiveness and receptivity. Globular star cluster—Messier-92 (NGC-6341). Photograph taken with a 120 inch reflector. Courtesy, Lick Observatory, University of California, Mount Hamilton and Santa Cruz.

Stay in this space as long as you wish. When you want to return to your everyday state of mind, simply enter the elevator and allow it to return to the tenth floor, watching the numbers light up as the elevator moves gently upward. At the tenth floor open your eyes. You will be at your everyday state of mind and feel rested, strong, and healthy.

Another method for achieving a relatively egoless state and receiving images is for a person to picture himself in space, moving to an area of white light. From time immemorial the concepts of space and light have produced feelings of expansiveness and receptivity. Contemplation of the heavens has always produced a sense of universal connectedness—from shepherds at the time of Christ to modernday astronauts.

Find a tranquil place where you will be undisturbed. Lie down with your legs uncrossed and your arms at your sides. Let your eyes close. Take a slow deep breath, expanding your chest and abdomen. Pause a moment. Then exhale slowly, feeling your chest and abdomen relax. Breathe in this way until you begin to feel quite relaxed. As you become more relaxed, your breathing will become slow and even. You now feel calm and comfortable.

Feel your feet and legs. Imagine them becoming very heavy. Say to yourself, ''My feet are relaxing; they are becoming more and more relaxed. My feet are deeply relaxed.'' Rest for a

The widely photographed space flights have provided stunning images of floating in space. This photograph shows Astronaut Edward H. White II floating in zero gravity outside the Gemini-4 spacecraft. Earth can be seen in the background. Courtesy of NASA.

FIGURE A

FIGURE B

Through *receptive visualization* (Figure A) a person spontaneously receives images. In *programmed visualization* (Figure B) a person holds a particular image in mind and concentrates on it. Illustrations by Susan Ida Smith.

moment. In the same way relax your ankles, lower legs, thighs, pelvis, abdomen, back and chest. Rest again. Then relax your hands, forearms, upper arms and shoulders. Rest. Relax the muscles of your neck and jaw, allowing your jaw to drop. Relax your tongue, cheeks, eyes and forehead. Rest. Enjoy the feeling of total body relaxation.

You are now in a calm, relaxed state of being. To deepen this state you can imagine yourself traveling into space. Visualize yourself drifting weightlessly and effortlessly through space. See the deep blue-black color of space all around you. Watch stars and planets slowly recede as you move past them further and further into space. As you see each star recede, you will become more and more relaxed, in a deeper and deeper state of mind. Now visualize an area of diffuse white light ahead of you. Picture yourself moving closer and closer to this area of light until you are bathed by its luminosity and can feel its energy. Travel into the light, toward its center. Visualize the center of the light as a space beyond light and darkness. In this space, you will feel open and clear. You will begin to see images before you. Look at them as long as they appear. These are pure images. They have

a life of their own, and they will appear and extinguish of their own accord. If any of the images evoke disturbing feelings in you, do not be afraid. Simply allow the images to pass.

Stay in this space as long as you wish. You can receive pure images whenever you go to it. To return to your everyday state of mind simply visualize yourself moving back through space to the place where you started. Count from 1 to 3. Then open your eyes.

Both of the exercises we've just given bring people to a place in their mind where they can receive visualizations. The next exercise is an example of a receptive visualization dealing with a specific area of a person's life. In the exercise a person goes to a receptive place in his mind and invites images of his inner vision of home life. Later in the exercise he works with the receptive visualization to make it clearer. Close your eyes. Breathe in and out slowly and deeply. Allow yourself to relax. Deepen this relaxation by whichever technique works best for you. Go to a level where you can visualize, where images flow freely and easily. Imagine a living space in which you feel completely comfortable. As an image forms, begin to look around you. Notice the walls. See what they're

156

made of. Notice any windows, pictures, cabinets, plants. Look at the floor. Notice what is is made of, whether it is covered with rugs. Look at the ceiling. Notice what it is made of. Notice lights, skylights, beams. Look around the room at the furniture. Notice chairs, tables, couches. Now walk around the house and look in any other rooms. In each room allow yourself time to look around. Notice the way each room feels. Notice the light in the room, the way the room smells. Walk around and touch the objects in the room, notice their texture.

Now move outside the house. Notice where the house is, whether it's in the country or the city. Notice whether it has a yard, a deck, a sidewalk. Notice what material the outside of the house is made of, the architectural style of the house. Notice what's immediately around the house—trees, plants, other buildings. Remain in this space and explore it as long as you wish.

You've now gotten in touch with your own vision of a comfortable living space. You can return to this space whenever you wish. On other visits you may find some differences or you may want to make some changes. All of this is possible in visualization. For example, recall a room in the home you visualized. Say that you visualized a window with potted plants on a wooden sill. Now change the window sill. Let it get wider, thicker. Imagine it's white. Imagine it's red. With each change, notice how you feel. Return to the visualization which feels best to you. By this method, you can change your inner visualization as your feelings change. And you can come closer to aspects of the visualization you were unaware of when you started the exercise.

Once you've gotten in touch with your inner vision, you can notice how it's similar to and different from the place you presently live. Then you can choose aspects of your inner vision which you wish to make real in your external world. You can choose small things or large things. For example, if the house in your visualization was filled with plants and your present house has few, you can easily begin by getting more plants. Or if your inner vision was of a small house with a yard and your present house is an apartment in the city, you could make plans for moving. Once you've decided on a change that you'd like to make, hold a visualization of the final state in your mind. Picture details in the scene. Be in the scene. Imagine how it feels, smells, sounds. Move around in the scene. See yourself living in the house you envision. Picture clearly the home you desire.

The last exercise is a model for using receptive visualization. It illustrates many of the principles we've discussed in this section. It involves relaxation, concentration, spontaneous visualization of memory and imagination images, moving within a visualization, changing objects in a visualization, using feelings to evaluate inner images, and holding an image in mind.

This exercise uses two basic types of visualization: *receptive visualization*, in which a visualizer spontaneously receives images, and *programmed visualization*, in which a visualizer either pictures specific images we have given in an exercise, or concentrates on and holds images he has spontaneously received. Both these visualization processes are involved in most visualizations, although one or the other may predominate in any exercise.

FOOTNOTES

1. Wiener, N. *The Human Use of Human Beings*; Garden City, N.Y.; Doubleday & Co., Inc.; 1956; p. 15.
2. Maltz, M. *Psycho-Cybernetics*, New York, Pocket Books, 1966, p. 12.
3. Maltz, M. p. 26.
4. Mishra, R. *Yoga Sutras*; Garden City, N.Y.; Anchor Books; 1973; p. 185.
5. Mishra, R. p. 184.
6. Mishra, R. p. 182.
7. Jung, C. G., Ed. *Man and His Symbols*; Garden City, N.Y.; Doubleday and Co., Inc.; 1968, pp. 161–163, from M.-L. von Franz, "The Process of Individuation."
8. Samuels, M. and Bennett, H. *Be Well*, New York, Random House/Bookworks, 1974, p. 156.

9. Jung, C. G. p. 50, from C. Jung, "Approaching the Unconscious."
10. Wilhelm, R., trans. *The I Ching*; Princeton, N.J.; Princeton University Press; 1967; p. lvii.
11. Richardson, A. *Mental Imagery*, New York, Springer Publishing Co., 1969, p. 88.

OTHER READING

1. Teilhard De Chardin, P. *The Phenomenon of Man*; New York; Harper & Row, Publishers; 1965.

SECTION III

VISIONS OF WHOLENESS

DAILY LIFE

PSYCHOLOGY

MEDICINE

PARAPSYCHOLOGY

CREATIVITY

SPIRITUAL LIFE

INTRODUCTION

In recent times, man has divided his life into areas of specialized function. Job, family and religion have all become somewhat independent activities. The advantage of this division is that people have been able to go into greater detail in a particular area of interest. In this sense social division functions as a device for concentration. A person may focus most of his energy in one work area, such as his job, in order to fulfill himself in that respect. But one of the prices a person pays for such division is the loss of a sense of wholeness. Because he concentrates on one aspect of life, other areas may remain unfulfilled.

We have structured this section of the book following the social divisions man has made in his life. We make a fundamental division in discussing the practical applications of visualization, separating them into internal and external realities. We've divided the first part of this section, the external world, into three areas: daily life, medicine and healing, and psychology. The chapter *Daily Life* involves those concerns that occupy people most frequently: family life, job, social relationships, and recreation. It concerns making decisions about and acquiring food, shelter, clothing. It involves working with objects that are perceived as real in time and three-dimensional space. The chapter *Medicine and Healing* deals with health, which concerns people's bodies—the link between their minds and the external world. Health underlies everything people do in daily life. Yet most people give little conscious thought to their health unless they are ill. The chapter *Psychology* concerns people's feelings and states of mind. It involves their emotions, their personal problems and their mental feelings of well-being. Most people consider their feelings to be responses to external events. At the same time people see their feelings less as objects and more as abstractions. And the abstract, ethereal nature of feelings ties them to the inner world.

The second fundamental aspect of man's life is his internal world. We've divided this section into three areas: creativity, parapsychology, and spiritual life. In *Creativity* we are concerned with inspiration, with imagination, with unique ideas that come from deep within a person. From such ideas artists create their work, scientists make their discoveries, and philosophers devise their theories. *Parapsychology* deals with mental abilities that are beyond the ordinary: extrasensory perception, telepathy, and psychokinesis. These abilities are involved with characteristics of the inner world that most people have not considered a part of their lives. The chapter *Spiritual Life* is concerned with man's conception of God, the life force, universal harmony, liberation and enlightenment.

The areas that we have chosen to delineate are arbitrary. They are so intertwined that each is inseparable from the whole. Obviously, for example, a person's psychological state affects his day-to-day life, his health, his ability to create. Likewise a person's day-to-day life affects his psychological state, as well as his health and creativity. Nevertheless, we feel that our arbitrary divisions play a real part in most people's lives. And they form a convenient way to tie visualization to the area of life in which a person is most interested. They provide a focus for visualization exploration. As a person works with visualization in these areas a process of unification and centering takes place. The person again feels whole.

Daily life is largely taken up with external realities. *Boulevard des Italiens, Morning, Sunlight.* Camille Pissarro, French, 1830-1903. National Gallery of Art, Washington, Chester Dale Collection.

Chapter 12

DAILY LIFE

Daily life forms the substratum of everyone's existence. It is the material setting, the background against which life unfolds. Daily life deals with food, clothing, social relationships and sex, the basic needs which everyone shares. The way in which people meet these needs varies with their personalities and with the environment into which they were born. For most people, meeting these needs takes up the major part of their waking hours and their creative energy.

Visualization almost seems an intruder into the events of everyday life. It is a quiet, subtle, inner experience, as opposed to the almost overwhelmingly material and outer-directed focus of daily activity. Moreover, everyone becomes habituated to viewing his daily existence as something he has little control over, or the control over which takes place on a causal plane. For example, a man is given a raise *because* he has worked a certain number of years for his company. From this point of view, visualization seems like an irrelevant act or an alien impossibility. For a man to picture a pay raise in his mind's eye, as he lies in bed in the morning, expecting it to occur in his everyday world, seems crazy or like a dream. There seems to be almost a magical quality to it. And indeed there is—the magic of joining inner and outer worlds.

The various aspects of a person's daily life come together to form a life style. In his inner center a person has a total vision of a life style that is right for him at that moment. He can get in touch with this vision through receptive visualization (see page 152).

Daily life, more than any other area, is subject to influences from outside the inner center. Each culture has characteristic values which are concretized in the form of specific styles of food, clothing, and shelter. Each culture values different material objects, different jobs, differ-

This soft, indistinct painting of the *House of Pere Lacroix*, by Paul Cezanne, evokes a person's images of an ideal home. The picture conveys warmth and security without dictating form. National Gallery of Art, Washington. The Chester Dale Collection.

ent kinds of leisure, different roles for family members. American culture is multi-faceted and extremely complex. In the United States, the blending of many diverse cultures was superimposed on a relatively young and rapidly developing industrial society. The result of this has been an historically unparalleled range of available choice in personal life style. In addition, we are now in a period of intense cultural evolution, in which the values that the culture upholds are undergoing rapid change, are often confused, and are sometimes in conflict. This situation forces every person to consult his inner center in making choices to create or evolve his lifestyle. There is no one lifestyle to follow, and he cannot copy a hundred. So he must create his own.

One of the most important elements in a person's lifestyle is the place in which he lives. While physical surroundings are more important to some people than to others, no one remains unaffected by his surroundings. Creating a home in touch with his inner vision gives a person the physical resting place that is most supportive of his growth and development. The following exercise is for visualizing such a home. It may be like other homes, or it may be quite different. It may be any size or shape. It may be made of any materials. Because this is a visualization, money is no object. What is important is how a person feels about his home.

Claude Bristol, author of the best seller *The Magic of Believing*, says, "You would like a new home and your imagination goes to work. At first you have only a hazy idea of the kind of house you would like. Then as you discuss it with other members of your family or ask questions of builders or look at illustrations of new houses, the picture becomes clearer and clearer, until you visualize the house in all of its particulars. After that the subconscious mind goes to work to provide you with that house. It may come into manifestation in any number of ways. You may build it with your own hands, or it may come to you through purchase or from the actions of outsiders. Its manner of coming is of no great consequence. The process is the same when you are after a better job or planning a vacation trip. You've got to see it in your mind's eye, see yourself as holding that job, or actually taking the trip."[1]

A person can extend his visualizations of a living space to include his vision of a community. For example, he might picture in his mind's eye how large the community is, what kind of people live there, what shops it has, and what kind of cultural life and resources the community provides.

Outside of their home, most people spend the largest part of their daily life at their job. Like a home, a job gives a person a focus, an identity. For most people, their job is a source of money and ego-gratification. Because job-money-success are so intertwined, and embody for the majority of people their basic life goals, most popular visualization books are largely devoted to this area. In this book, however, we see a person's job as an important part, but only one part, of his whole life.

Many people feel that they have less control over the job area of their life than they do over other areas. People's skills and cultural values, as well as economic necessity, influence the kind of jobs they hold. These aspects are not always in harmony, and this can lead to a person having ambiguous, even conflicting feelings about his work. Visualization can bring a person into contact with sources of satisfaction, as well as sources of tension, in his work. Visualizing a job is not limited by economics, skills, or education. A person can visualize himself working at any job.

The following work-success visualization is a personal model of Norman Vincent Peale's, given in his best-selling book of the early 1950's, *The Power of Positive Thinking*. "Begin to think prosperity, achievement, success. The process is to visualize; that is, to see Guideposts [an inspirational, self-help magazine that he was editing] in terms of successful achievement. Create a mental picture of Guideposts as a great magazine, sweeping the country. Visualize large numbers of subscribers, all eagerly reading this inspirational material and profiting thereby . . . Do not hold mental pictures of difficulties and failures, but lift your mind above them and visualize powers and achievements. 'How many subscribers do you need at the moment to keep going?' We thought

The American artist Joseph Pickett (1848-1918) has painted a warm, simple, timeless vision of a community. This picture, *Coryell's Ferry, 1776,* can serve as a model from which people can create a visualization of a community that matches their own inner vision. Oil on canvas, 37½ × 48¼ inches. Probably painted between 1914–18. Collection of the Whitney Museum of American Art, New York.

quickly and said 100,000. We had 40,000. Visualize 100,000 people being creatively helped by the magazine and you will have them. . . . As I write these words, Guideposts is nearing the half million mark."[2]

Many research studies done by psychologists in recent years have demonstrated the value of *mental practice,* that is, the value of visualizing an upcoming situation or "the symbolic rehearsal of a physical activity in the absence of any gross muscular movement."[3] The classic article on mental practice, reported in *Research Quarterly* by the Australian psychologist Alan Richardson, concerned the effects of visual-

ization on the free-throw scores of basketball players. The study involved three groups of students chosen at random, none of whom had ever practiced visualization. The first group practiced making free throws every day for twenty days. The second group made free throws on the first and twentieth days, with no practice in between. The third group also made free throws on the first and last days, but, in addition, they spent twenty minutes a day *imagining* sinking baskets. As in the external world, when these students (mentally) missed, they tried to correct their aim on the next shot. The first group who actually practiced,

A vibrant image of people working in harmony with the world around them. The people seem to be part of the landscape and the whole scene is full of energy. Visualizing a fulfilling work environment enriches a person's daily life. *The Olive Orchard,* by Vincent van Gogh, Dutch, 1853-1890. The National Gallery of Art, Washington. The Chester Dale Collection.

improved 24% between the first and last day. The second group, who had done no practice of any kind, did not improve at all. The third group, who visualized throwing the ball through the basket, improved 23%. Similar studies involving dart throwing and other athletic activities show the same kind of results.[4]

Richardson noted that vividness of imagery among the mental practicers is less important than their ability to control the image. In other words, for visualizers to benefit by mental practice, it is not necessary for their image to be as real as life, but it is important for them to be able to picture each part of the free-throw. For example, one of the students in Richardson's study who was not helped by mental practice found that he could visualize the court vividly, but he found that every time he mentally began to bounce the ball, the ball stuck to the floor and he was unable to proceed beyond that point.[5]

Richardson also concluded that mental practice is more effective if the visualizer "feels" as well as "sees" the activity he is symbolically practicing. For example, a person picturing free throws would have better results if he "felt" the ball in his hands and "heard" the ball bounce, as well as "saw" the ball drop through the basket.

As a result of studies like Richardson's and the experiences of people using visualization, the technique of mental practice has been widely applied in practical courses and psychology. Mental practice has been used in work, in athletics, and in relieving anxiety. In *Psycho-Cybernetics*, Maxwell Maltz, M.D. gives a number of examples of people using mental practice to improve their everyday lives. He describes how Conrad Hilton imagined himself owning a hotel years before he bought one, how Napoleon practiced being a soldier, in his imagination, many years before he actually went on a battlefield, and how salesmen increased their sales by imagining themselves in many sales situations, and mentally making a successful sale in each case. Salesmen can prepare for any sales situation ahead of time by imagining themselves and their prospect face to face. The salesmen picture themselves dealing competently with objections or problems that the prospective customer raises.[6]

Maltz talks about William Marston, a psychologist who developed a system of visualization called *rehearsal practice*. Marston tells a student who has an important interview coming up, such as a job interview, to plan for it in advance. He tells the student to go over in

Fatata Te Miti (By the Sea) was painted by the French artist Paul Gauguin in 1892, a few months after he arrived in Tahiti. It is a timeless image which stimulates all of the senses and makes a person feel the relaxation and warmth of a tropical beach. Holding such an image in mind, feeling the water and hearing the surf, can deeply relax a person even in a tension-filled situation in everyday life. The National Gallery of Art, Washington. Chester Dale Collection.

his mind the questions he is likely to be asked and rehearse the interview. Marston says that even if none of the rehearsed questions are asked, the rehearsal practice is still valuable because it builds confidence and helps a person ad lib and be spontaneous. Marston goes on to say that people always act out a role in life, so they may as well choose a successful role and practice rehearsing it.[7]

The following exercise is designed to enable a person to achieve a goal in an upcoming situation. It is particularly useful in a situation that a person is worried about or has had trouble with in the past. Everyone has experienced such situations at one time or another. For example, a person may be concerned about going to a job interview, taking an exam, having to make a speech, entertaining special company for dinner, or going to the dentist. This exercise is designed to supplant the negative visualization behind those worried feelings.

A Role Rehearsal Run: Sit or lie down. Make yourself comfortable. Close your eyes. Breathe in and out slowly and deeply. Allow yourself to relax. Deepen this relaxation by whichever technique works best for you. Go to a level where you can visualize, where images flow freely and easily. Allow an image to come to mind of a meeting room where you have been asked to give a talk. Picture yourself in the front of the room. Look across the room. Notice details—the color of walls, where the door is and what it's made of. Notice the windows and pictures on the walls. Now look at the chairs; notice how they are arranged and what they are made of. Look at the people. Notice the kinds of clothes they are wearing. See if you recognize any friends or colleagues in the group. Now imagine walking over to a table or lectern to begin your talk. Notice what the table is made of, put your hands on it and feel it. Take a few deep breaths until you feel calm, clear and relaxed. Listen as the people in the audience quiet down. Allow the quietness to enter you and make you calm. See the people looking at you in a friendly, interested way. Now hear yourself begin the lecture. Your voice is clear and loud enough for everyone to hear. Your speech is organized, interesting, and conveys exactly what you wish to say. As you're speak-

ing, you feel increasingly confident and comfortable. You can tell from the looks on their faces that the people in the audience have understood what you've said and are stimulated by it. As you end the lecture you hear excited talk begin among members of the audience. A number of people come up to you with stimulating questions and you answer them readily.

The goals of this exercise were to feel at ease while giving a speech and to have the audience enjoy it. This, like all specific visualizations described in this section, is a model. For example, people who do the role rehearsal run for giving a speech will each see details of a different room and a different audience, and hear themselves giving a different speech. The events in the example will further their own goals, whether they be feeling comfortable, convincing the audience, being liked by the audience, selling something to the audience, or teaching something to them. If, on the other hand, a person is concerned about another situation, such as a job interview, he can alter the details of this exercise to fit that situation. He can picture himself in *that* situation, in as much detail as possible, and see himself achieving his goals in that situation.

And it's important that a person "rehearse" the situation repeatedly. With repetition a person can make changes in his performance and perfect it. The more he repeats the visualization the more possible it seems and the more likely he is to have faith in it.

Another kind of exercise that can be useful is for a person to visualize the final state that he desires. For example, rather than visualizing the process of taking an exam, a student might visualize the returned exam with the grade on it that he desires. Here is an example of a final state visualization. Sit or lie down. Make yourself comfortable. Close your eyes. Breathe in and out slowly and deeply. Allow yourself to relax. Deepen the relaxation by whichever technique works best for you. Go to a level where you can visualize, where images flow freely and easily. Allow an image to come to mind of an exam paper or bluebook. See the size of the book, notice the color, feel the texture of the paper. See your name written on the top line and the name of the course written underneath.

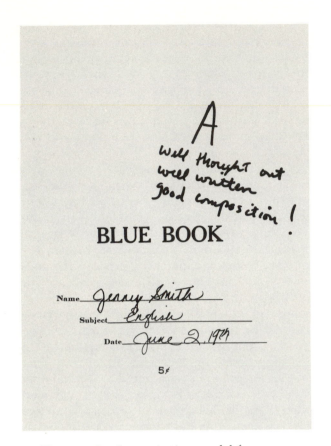

A

Well thought out well written good composition!

BLUE BOOK

Name *Jenny Smith*
Subject *English*
Date *June 2, 1974*

5¢

The exam book exercise is a model for final-state visualizations. A person pictures an image—in as much detail as possible—of a situation he wants to occur in his daily life.

Now open the exam book and see where the instructor has marked in red pencil the grade you hoped to get. Look at the letter, notice the way that it's drawn. For example, the legs of an A might be wide apart at the bottom, and the lines overlapping at the top. Fix the image in your mind. Read the instructor's comments below the grade—"Well thought out and well written . . ."—notice that they correspond with your goals in answering the exam questions.

Like a process visualization, this final-state visualization is a model. Final-state visualizations can be used in a number of situations. For example, a person might visualize the response to a report he has been asked to write at work. Or a person might visualize himself sitting at an executive's desk after he has been promoted. A person might even visualize his weekly paycheck with higher figures on it. The

point is to visualize an aspect of the final goal state, an image or a scene, in as much detail as possible.

Just as a person can visualize a paycheck with higher figures, he can visualize a specific material object that he desires. From ancient fertility rituals to modern occult literature, the visualization of material objects has been an important use of visual techniques. Visualization of desired material objects lends itself particularly to the final-state visualization method: objects have concrete images and are especially easy to visualize, whereas conditions of life do not usually have one specific visual referrent.

When people visualize a final state, with no thought or picture of how that state will come about, they often feel like it's magic when that state materializes. They feel they have expended no effort, no work, to gain the object, other than their visualization. And they feel there is no apparent connection between their holding an image in their mind and their acquiring the object. Every person who has had the extraordinary experience of having a visual-

The three ears of corn depicted on this American Indian pot are an ancient symbol of fertility and plenty. The Indians carved it on their pots in order to insure an abundant supply of food. It is a simple, beautiful image of material satisfaction. Pot by Grace Medicine Flower

170

ization become reality has their own theory of how visualization works. A psychologist might theorize that fixing an idea in the mind stimulates the subconscious to be continuously alert to situations that will further the goal and to signal the conscious mind to assertively act in those situations. A religious person might say that it is God hearing a person's prayer and answering it. An occult mystic might say that the energy surrounding the visualization directly influences objects and people in the world around it.

Each of the authors who has written about using visualization to acquire material objects has his own theories on how visualization works and his own hints on how to make it more effective. But all of them use the basic technique of visualizing a final state. The following is an example of a final state visualization from the book *Creative Visualization*, by Andrew Wiehl: "Say your objective is a car. First decide what make of car you want and what model. What color—black, blue, grey, green? Once you decide the make, type and color stay with it. Do not change your mind. . . .

"Place all your faith in your subconscious mind. Don't worry about the 'how' or the 'when.' . . . Go to your room where there is no disturbance. Relax and mentally visualize a screen . . . one inch by two inches . . . right between your eyes. It is better to have your eyes closed so that nothing in the room will attract your attention. As soon as the screen appears clear before your vision . . . inject into the screen the image of the exact kind of car you want. Speak in thought to your subconscious: 'I have it. I own it.' (naming the car's make). Feel yourself in possession of the car. See yourself driving it, going places. Notice particularly how well it handles, how smoothly it rides.

"Never set a time limit, or price limit. Just ask for whatever your heart desires, and have faith in yourself. Imagine yourself to be the owner of the car and leave everything else to the subconscious. It's amazing, the way it has of working out your problems and bringing about your desires! Once your objective is accomplished, set another immediately. You'll find the second easier of attainment, and each successive objective easier yet. When you gain

momentum, maintain it. As confidence increases, your power likewise will increase."[8]

Wiehl's hints include: whenever you visualize, visualize surroundings; have faith that your visualization will materialize; never change your objective once you've set it; keep your visualizations secret until they come about; always think in positive terms and give yourself positive mental suggestions; do not worry and do not stop visualizing.

In his book, *The Art & Practice of Getting Material Things Through Creative Visualization*, Ophiel, a Los Angeles author of occult books, suggests that a person only visualize things that he might reasonably expect to get, and that he limit his visualizations to one thing at a time. He also suggests that a person visualize things that he really wants and that the person feel himself in the visualization with the object he wants. Like Wiehl, Ophiel suggests that a person keep his desires private and, thus, free from other people's skepticism.[9]

Dr. Eikerenkoetter, a contemporary black evangelist better known as Rev. Ike, uses visualization in his United Church services. Rev. Ike's church seeks to bring peace, wealth and happiness to his parishioners. Rev. Ike includes in his meetings a visualization exercise which he calls *The Theater of the Mind*, an exercise in which parishioners are led into a "closing of the two outer eyes, the opening of the inner eye of faith." This process helps people to visualize, then attain, states of happiness and financial security they have always wanted. As Rev. Ike says, "I'm on that cruise to the islands, my bills are paid, I have money, I'm eating the steaks I enjoy. . . ."[10]

Most people working with the visualization of material objects suggest looking at and even hanging up pictures of a desired object so as to get a clearer image to visualize. Magazines, newspapers, and manufacturers' catalogues are rich sources of images. In this light, *The Whole Earth Catalogue*, for example, has functioned as a kind of dream book for selecting visualizations appropriate to produce an alternative life style. Advertisements and catalogues take advantage of a person's natural ability to visualize by providing images and suggesting his need for specific objects.

Because of the great emphasis placed on ma-

This image, *The Boating Party,* by Mary Cassatt (American, 1845-1926) provides a final-state visualization of a relaxed vacation with one's family. Visualizing such an image takes people away from the cares of everyday life. The National Gallery of Art, Washington. The Chester Dale Collection.

terial objects in our culture, and the persuasiveness of modern advertising, people may easily become confused about what things they really want or need. It is therefore important for a person to think carefully before visualizing a material object. Receptive visualization (see page 152) will give a person information about which objects are close to his inner vision. Receptive visualization also allows a person to experience what it would actually be like to possess an object. For example, a man visualized owning an expensive sports car and, somewhat to his surprise, found that it did not feel good to him. Much of his receptive visualization included worry over expensive servicing and repair bills, dents and scratches, and poor gas mileage.

One of the basic aspects of daily life involves relationships with other people. This may mean getting along with family members, friends, co-workers or classmates, or it may involve dealing with strangers, authority figures, or employees. Visualization provides a person with a method for getting in touch with his inner images of personal relationships and gives him a method for making them manifest. Through visualization he can mentally try on different roles to see how they feel and also practice the particular roles that feel good to him.

A classic, serene family image by Carl Anthony Tollefson called *The Fisherman's Family*. A pure image such as this, in harmony with a person's inner vision, can help to crystallize his or her family life. n.d. Oil on canvas. 12 × 11 inches. Collection of the Whitney Museum of American Art, New York.

Swirl Nude. Photograph by Michael Samuels.

The receptive visualization exercise on page 152 gives a person a model that he can apply to personal relationships to discover his inner visions. Allow an image to come to mind of a situation involving the person in whom you are interested. See details in the scene you have visualized. Notice particularly yourself and the people in the scene and how they are relating to each other. For example, a woman visualizing about her family might see herself sitting in the grass having a picnic with them. She might notice that the day is warm and sunny, the people's movements slow and languorous. She might see herself hugging her spouse and her children, feeling warm and loving toward them. She could then hold this visualization in order to bring about similar situations in her external life.

Visualization also plays a role in sex, which is simply a part of a special kind of social relationship. Men and women have dual arousal systems—that is, they can become aroused by sensory stimuli or by mental images. Mental images may originate in the external world, as for example a picture of a person provocatively dressed, or they may originate in a person's mind, as an erotic fantasy. Mental arousal can then lead to physical arousal in both men and women. Robert Chartham, a British researcher and author on sexual activity, has said that sexual imagination is one of the most important sexual attributes a person can have. From his research he has concluded that "the great majority of people make love more frequently in response to the promptings of their 'voluntary' sex-drive than to their 'involuntary' sex-drive. That is to say, they deliberately turned on to, or allowed themselves to be turned on by psychological stimuli more often than they were turned on by physiological stimuli. They put their sexual imaginations to work in order to have a sexual experience rather than wait for the chemicals in their bodies to regulate their sexual activity."[11] Just as a person might visualize a particular family scene in order to bring about a similar situation in everyday life, so a person might visualize a particular sexual situation in order to arouse himself or herself and bring that situation about.

Visualization has always been important in athletics. For example, many golfers visualize a perfect swing, visualize the path of the ball from the tee to the cup, or visualize the ball rolling up to the cup and dropping in.

Another area of daily life to which visualization has frequently been applied is sports. Many professional athletes, in thinking over the reasons for their success, have realized the importance of holding images in the mind's eye. A number of athletes have written books about, and developed whole teaching systems based on, visualization. From a scientific point of view, the role played by visualization in athletics is much easier to understand than the role played by visualization in obtaining material objects. Not only does positive visualization increase a player's confidence, it also directly affects his muscles. In his experiments the physiologist Edmund Jacobson showed that a person's muscles demonstrated small (not visible), but detectable amounts of the electrical activity associated with movement when that person imagined a specific activity.[12] A person develops *muscle memory* of an activity by imagining that activity, as well as by actually engaging in it. The value of mental practice in relation to physical action was further demonstrated by Richardson's study that found increased basketball free throw scores among the students who used visualization.

In *Psycho-Cybernetics* Maxwell Maltz gives the following examples of how visualization can be used to improve golf scores. He talks about Alex Morrison, a professional golfer who has written a book called *Better Golf Without Practice*. Morrison says a person must have a clear mental image of the correct thing before he can do it successfully.[13] Morrison has a person sit in a comfortable chair, relax, and visualize a correct swing. Ben Hogan has described mentally rehearsing each shot, "feeling" the clubhead strike the ball, and "feeling" himself follow through in the correct manner. Johnny Bulla, another professional golfer, believed in picturing the end result. He instructed people to mentally see their ball dropping in the cup, to know that it would happen.

In *The Inner Game of Tennis*, W. Timothy Gallwey, a tennis professional from California, instructs people to picture hitting the ball where they want it to go and then to let it happen: ". . . stand on the base line, breathe deeply a few times and relax. Look at the can [a tennis ball container placed in the backhand corner of one of the service courts]. Then visualize the path of the ball from your racket to the can. See the ball hitting the can right on the label. If you like, shut your eyes and imagine yourself serving and the ball hitting the can. Do this several times. If in your imagination the ball misses the can, that's all right; repeat the image a few times until the ball hits the target. Now, take no thought of how you should hit the ball. Don't *try* to hit the target. *Ask* your body . . . to do whatever is necessary to hit the can, then let it do it. Exercise no control; correct for no imagined bad habits. Having programmed yourself with the desired flight of the ball, simply trust your body to do it. When you toss the ball up, focus your attention on its seams, then let the serve serve itself."[14]

Because of visualization's powerful effect on the body it has been used in a number of fields relating to body image. One of these fields is weight control. When a person visualizes himself as thin, and visualizes himself as eating less, he automatically begins to lose weight. A. T. W. Simeons, M.D., an Italian physician specializing in weight control, uses visualization as one part of his treatment program. First a patient is instructed to visualize himself looking thin and healthy at a beach. Next he is told to visualize himself eating a cold sour dill pickle. This pronounced taste-tactile sensation demonstrates to the patient that he has control over the ability to visualize food sensations. Then the patient is presented with an exercise that Simeon calls "visualizing yourself at the dining room table." The patient is told to "see yourself eating less at meal times. You are taking smaller bits of food and are chewing very slowly . . . See yourself eating and enjoying only the foods that are good for you, such as fish, meat, fruits, milk and fresh vegetables. See yourself refusing dessert and having coffee. Smell the coffee . . . Feel relaxed and soothed . . . Visualize yourself leaving the table with a comfortable feeling. Visualize yourself standing tall and feeling responsible and successful in your own ability to properly handle your food intake."[15] This type of visualization exercise has also been used successfully by psychologists and hypnotherapists for other types of habitual actions such as smoking.

Visualization has also been used as the basis for several systems for increasing memory. This is not surprising since the whole process of remembering is tied up with images. One widely-used system involves picturing a simple figure like a cat in association with whatever is to be remembered. In the most popular formulation of this method, a person memorizes ten key words which stand for easily visualizable objects: for example, one is a bun, two is a shoe, and so on. The person then attaches an image of the first thing to be remembered to the bun.[16] For example, if the first word a person was trying to remember was "boy," he might use an image of a boy standing on top of a bun.

Another method involves converting each object to be remembered into a graphic visual image. For example, to remember the word green, a person might use an image of a green tiger. Often bizarre images are constructed because they are easier to remember. A

More than any other perception, the way a person sees himself is a visualization. *Girl Before A Mirror*, 1932, Pablo Picasso. Oil on canvas, 64 × 51¼ inches. Collection, The Museum of Modern Art, New York. Gift of Mrs. Simon Guggenheim.

A well-known mnemonic device involves visualizing a list of objects to be remembered along a well-known street or path. Each object—the rug, the comb, the winged candle, the cat, and the egg—is visualized next to a familiar landmark. To recall the objects the person mentally walks down the street and notes the objects as he sees them. Illustration by Susan Ida Smith.

modification of this method which is used for memorization of long lists involves a mental walk. The person distributes the constructed images along a street that is visualized, generally a familiar street such as one between home and work. For example, a green tiger might be placed in the first doorway. To recall the list of memorized objects, the person has only to mentally walk down the street and see the objects as he distributed them.[17]

Visualization is a tool people can use to create a day-to-day life in harmony with their inner visions. It allows people to gain an element of control over their world and to shape their daily life into something more beautiful and enjoyable.

FOOTNOTES

1. Bristol, C. *The Magic of Believing.* Englewood Cliffs, N.J.: Prentice-Hall, Inc., 1948, p. 82.

2. Peale, N.V. *The Power Of Positive Thinking.* Englewood Cliffs, N.J.: Prentice-Hall, Inc., 1952, p. 208.

3. Richardson, A. *Mental Imagery.* New York: Springer Publishing Co., 1969, p. 56.

4. Richardson, A. p. 56.

5. Richardson, A. p. 57.

6. Maltz, M. *Psycho-Cybernetics.* New York, Pocket Books, 1966, pp. 33–36.

7. Maltz, M. p. 34.

8. Wiehl, A. *Creative Visualization.* New York, Greenwich Book Publishers, 1958, pp. 67–68.

9. Ophiel, *The Art and Practice of Getting Material Things Through Creative Visualization.* Los Angeles, Peach Publishing Company, 1972.

10. Eikerenkoetter, F. from a speech.

11. Chartham, R. *What Turns Women On.* New York: Ballantine Books, 1974, p. 199.

12. Jacobson, E. *How To Relax and Have Your Baby.* New York: McGraw-Hill Book Co., 1965, p. 110.

13. Maltz, M. p. 35.

14. Gallwey, W.T. *The Inner Game of Tennis,* New York, Random House, 1974, p. 59.

15. Simeons, A. T. W. *Pounds and Inches.* Los Angeles: Medical Weight Control, 1966, p. 159.

16. Pavio, A. *Imagery and Verbal Processes.* New York: Holt and Rineheart, 1971.

17. Pavio, A.

This line drawing by Pablo Picasso, "Nessus and Dejanira" (1920), depicts the Greek myth in which a centaur tries to ravish Hercules' wife, Dejanira. It is a striking imagination image of a person having intercourse with a mythological creature. Images of the inner world obey their own laws. Courtesy of The Art Institute of Chicago.

Chapter 13

PSYCHOLOGY

In daily life we are concerned with the material background or setting of a person's life, the outer world against which his life is played out. In psychology we are concerned with a person's thoughts and ideas about his life, his feelings and moods, the inner world which observes, reacts to and motivates the actions of the outer drama. Whereas visualization seems at first to be an intruder in the material outer world, it seems completely natural in the inner world. In fact, philosophers and psychologists consider images to be a basic element of thought. The previous chapter was based on the concept that an image held in the mind becomes manifest in the outer world. An image held in the mind, whether or not it is manifest in the outer world, is a direct experience in the inner world. In terms of the inner world, that is, any image is real not in the sense that it can't be differentiated from the external world, but in the sense of being an inner experience. In terms of the inner world, if a person is involved in a fantasy of sexual intercourse his experience is real; the image *is* experience in the inner world. While a person is daydreaming, the outer world may recede and disappear. The person's body, which is the link between inner and outer worlds, can become aroused and respond physiologically to the inner image just as strongly as if intercourse were actually taking place.

In the outer world, we are limited by the laws of matter in what we can experience. In the inner world, there is no limit to what we can experience. For example, a person can experience an image of having intercourse with a person they've never met, with a person who lived in the 18th century, or even with a giant mythological creature. The images a person experiences directly affect that person's mood, feelings, thoughts, and ideas. Their images can make a person sad or happy, anxious or at ease, afraid or confident, in turmoil or at peace.

With the discovery of the function of the unconscious at the turn of the century, man realized that he could get in touch with images within himself of which he had previously been unaware. Both memory and imagination images come from the unconscious. Freud found that a patient who was deeply relaxed or hypnotized could recall images of childhood events they had long forgotten. Jung found that when relaxed he experienced images of caves, wise men, and serpents that he had never seen. Both Freud and Jung found that bringing certain emotionally-charged images to awareness relieved neurotic symptoms and made a person's inner world more whole. It was as if simply experiencing certain basic images allowed a person to feel better and to grow emotionally.

Releasing an image from the unconscious and bringing it to awareness seems to be a basic growth process in the inner world. The person who experiences such an image is somehow changed by that experience. The person is completed, made whole—it's as if a piece necessary for that person's growth has been found. Once found, the piece fits itself automatically into the unfolding puzzle of a person's mind. Using another metaphor, we may liken each person's inner life to a painting. Successive images, flowing from the unconscious into awareness, fill in one area of the picture after another. Finally a complete painting appears. As this natural inner process takes place, the person develops and comes to feel whole. Becoming aware of these images from the unconscious and having one's life improved by them can be called the *automatic function of images*.

The first use of images in psychology involved what we have called *receptive visualizations*. The images that early psychiatrists were interested in were those memory and imagination ones that were tied to traumatic emotional experiences. Freud referred to these visualizations as "intensely emotional fancyimages."[1]

The first doctor to use the elicitation of images for treating a patient was Dr. Joseph Breuer, whom Freud credited with creating psychoanalysis. Breuer was a practicing

Viennese physician, already known for his physiological and pharmacological discoveries. In 1881 (when Freud was still a student), Breuer was treating a patient named Anna O. Anna was a girl of twenty-one with hysterical paralysis of both extremities, severe alteration of her personality, and a number of other physicalpsychiatric symptoms. In the course of his observation, Dr. Breuer noticed that during Anna's period of psychic "alteration" or "absence" she mumbled to herself. Dr. Breuer put her in a sort of hypnosis and suggested to her that she talk about her mumblings. She related to him "fancies, deeply sad, often poetically beautiful, day dreams, we might call them, which commonly took as their starting point the situation of a girl beside the sickbed of her father. Whenever she had related a number of such fancies, she was, as it were, freed and restored to her normal mental life. . . . Symptoms of the disease would disappear when in hypnosis the patient could be made to remember the situation and the associative connections under which they first appeared, provided free vent was given to the emotions which they aroused."[2]

Later, when Freud began to use Breuer's techniques in his own work, he achieved the same kind of results. Both Freud and Breuer felt that a patient, in describing such images and giving vent to the emotions they aroused, experienced a catharsis. At first they used the cathartic technique only when their patients were hypnotized. But when Freud found he was unable to hypnotize certain patients, he tried to achieve the same kind of catharsis without the use of hypnosis. At first he would "assure them that they did know [the memory], that they must just tell it out, and I would venture the assertion that the memory which would emerge at the moment that I laid my hand on the patient's forehead would be the right one."[3]

Freud later abandoned the technique of placing his hand on the patient's forehead in lieu of free association and analysis of dreams and symptomatic acts. Freud concluded from this type of work that the memory images thus aroused were not lost to the person, but were locked away in their unconscious.

In Freud's later work he concluded that

images were more primitive than verbal thought, primitive in that they developed earlier in childhood. In fact, Freud linked images to "primary process thought." Primary process thought, which is characteristic of

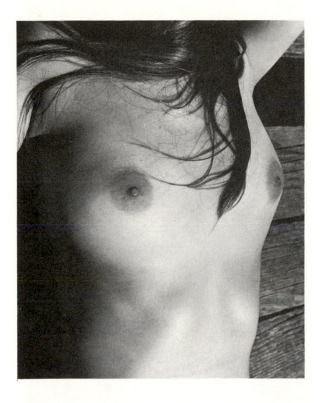

infancy and early childhood, is direct, immediate, fantastic, wish-oriented and magical. One example of primary process thought given by Freud is that of an infant hallucinating a breast to temporarily gratify himself while his mother is absent. Freud felt that verbal thought developed later, and was more realistic, that is, it gave more credence to the laws of matter. Freud thought that images were close to actual perceptions, to actual experiences, and could therefore come closer to gratifying a person. He believed that images were formed rapidly and spontaneously, unrestrained by logic. These characteristics of images permit "novel combinations of divergent ideas . . . condensation and symbolization."[4]

Freud wrote, ". . . it is possible for thought processes to become conscious through a reversion to visual residues. . . . Thinking in pictures . . . approximates more closely to unconscious processes than does thinking in words, and is unquestionably older than the latter both ontogenetically and phylogenetically."[5]

Carl Jung, a psychiatrist contemporary with Freud, gave images great importance in his theories. In his confrontation with his own unconscious, Jung endeavored to "translate the

The mother's breast is a primary visualization of mankind. It is the first object to be associated with nourishment, warmth, and love, and may be the first image a baby visualizes. Photographs by Michael Samuels.

''I let myself drop . . . I plunged down into dark depths . . . Before me was the entrance to a dark cave, in which stood a dwarf with a leathery skin . . .'' From C. G. Jung, *Memories, Dreams, Reflections*. In order to get in touch with his fantasies Jung often envisioned precipitous descents. Like most people Jung was fascinated by, but also feared, his unconscious images. Illustration by Susan Ida Smith.

emotions into images, that is to say, to find the images which were concealed in the emotions."[6] He felt that the more images he was able to bring to consciousness, the more he was "inwardly calmed and reassured."[7] He felt that emotionally-laden images left in the unconscious could tear a person to pieces or produce neuroses; but for a long time he was afraid to look directly at these images in himself.

One day in December 1913, Carl Jung experienced a decisive visualization: "I was sitting at my desk once more, thinking over my fears [of plummeting down into his fantasy images]. Then I let myself drop. Suddenly it was as though the ground literally gave way beneath my feet, and I plunged down into dark depths. I could not fend off a feeling of panic. But then, abruptly, at not too great a depth, I landed on my feet in a soft, sticky mass. I felt great relief, although I was apparently in complete darkness. After a while, my eyes grew accustomed to the gloom, which was rather like a deep twilight. Before me was the entrance to a dark cave, in which stood a dwarf with leathery skin, as if he were mummified."[8] This visualization, quoted from Jung's autobiography, *Memories, Dreams, and Reflections,* goes on in vivid detail.

Jung continued to describe visualization after visualization as he explored his own unconscious. He later wrote that, "the years when I was pursuing my inner images were the most important in my life."[9] To explore his images, Jung used a number of techniques. To get to "a level where he could visualize freely and easily," Jung would imagine steep descents, making several attempts to get to the bottom. He would imagine himself on the edge of cosmic abysses, imagine himself voyaging to the moon, or descending into empty space. He would visualize figures, and visualize himself talking to them as if they were real people. He would even visualize and converse with animals.[10]

Jung often recorded his images in written form. In an attempt to further explore his images he would draw or paint them on canvas. Many of Jung's inner images appeared as mandalas. At one point in his life, Jung sketched a mandala in his notebook every morning. The mandalas changed daily and through them he observed inner changes within himself. He felt that the mandalas were "cryptograms" which portrayed the state of the self and reflected its constant changes. He believed that the mandala is a symbol for centering and that following one's images inevitably leads one to his own center.

Jung felt that his images were autonomous: "There are things in the psyche which I do not produce, but which produce themselves and have their own life. . . . Their autonomy is a most uncomfortable thing to reconcile oneself to, and yet the very fact that the unconscious presents itself in that way gives us the best means of handling it."[11] Jung felt that while he was visualizing it was important to ground himself in the world. He did so by embedding himself in his family and in his professional work. He felt that otherwise his visualizations could drive him mad. The knowledge that, "I have a medical diploma from a Swiss university, I must help my patients, I have a wife and five children, I live at 228 Sees Strasse in Kusnacht . . . proved to me again and again that I really existed, that I was not a blank page whirling about in the winds of the spirit like Nietzsche. Nietzsche had lost the ground under his feet because he possessed nothing more than the inner world of his thoughts—which incidentally possessed him more than he it."[12]

This quote by Jung expresses the age-old fear of the voyage into the unknown, the unconscious, through visualization. Jung believed that the images experienced during visualization must be understood by a person and incorporated into his day-to-day life.

In order to help his patients benefit from his experiences, Jung developed a technique called *active imagination.* In active imagination, a patient is instructed to meditate, remaining free of any goal or program. The person then invites images to appear and watches them without interference. If the person wishes, he or she can interact with the images by talking to them or asking questions. Subsequently the patient discusses the visualizations with the therapist. The technique of active imagination differs from Freud's early analytic techniques in that it is more likely to bring forth imagination rather than memory images. Jung believed that images experienced during active imagination

In this painting, *Oedipus and the Sphinx*, Gustave Moreau (1826-1898), the French Symbolist, illustrates the Greek myth in which Oedipus guessed the riddle posed by the Sphinx and became king of Thebes. This incident illustrates the hero overcoming obstacles and succeeding in his quest. The Metropolitan Museum of Art, Bequest of William H. Herriman, 1921.

were archetypal. That is, the patient often saw images of figures similar to those described in myth. Jung considered them to be primordial images that are part of man's mind and that manifest themselves in fantasy as symbols. Examples of archetypal situations are the hero journey, the initiation ritual, the earth mother, and beauty and the beast. Archetypal images, which are full of emotion, express symbolically situations that are important to a person's growth. When the archetype is brought to awareness and corresponding emotions are experienced the person grows and feels fulfilled. Jung believed that archetypal images are primitive in that they were first experienced by ancient man. Modern man, experiencing the archetypes anew through visualization, can reflect on them and, for the first time, understand them.

Like Freud, Jung used receptive visualization to get in touch with inner images. Techniques that we have described for receptive visualization (see p. 152 and p. 156) can be used in a way similar to Freud's free association and Jung's active imagination. The techniques we've described for breathing, relaxing and going to a deepened level correspond to Freud's "sort of hypnosis" and Jung's meditation in preparation for active imagination. Both Freud and Jung subtly suggested to their patients topics for visualization. Freud told patients to relate images about problem areas; Jung told patients to invite any images from their inner center. Because both Freud and Jung were psychotherapists, it was implicit in the situation that the patient would visualize images pertinent to their analysis. For the reader to visualize following the paths of Freud or Jung, he or she can go to a receptive visualization level and make autosuggestions similar to the ones above. Because no therapist will be present, the process will be different from psychoanalysis. We have gone into detail in describing Jung's personal techniques for visualization in order that readers can make use of them in the same way as they might use one of our exercises. The same will be true for the techniques of other schools of therapy we will discuss in this chapter.

In his painting *Saint George and the Dragon* Raphael (Umbrian, 1483–1520) illustrates a common mythical incident in which the hero does battle with a fearsome monster in order to rescue a helpless maiden. The National Gallery of Art, Washington. Andrew Mellon Connection.

This photograph conveys the feelings of a dream or fantasy image from the past. The whole scene is reflected in a large mirror which heightens the dream-like quality. The two shadowy figures are barely perceptible. Images such as this, visualized in reverie states, can evoke memories of childhood events. Re-experiencing emotionally laden childhood events can help a person with present problems. Photograph by Michael Samuels.

As psychotherapeutic techniques developed, the use of visualization expanded and also became more specific. Several techniques, developed after Freud and Jung, were also based on receptive visualization, but made use of it in a more directed way. In 1943, Kubie, an American neurologist and Freudian analyst, described a technique for using induced reveries to enhance image formation. Kubie worked with the hypnagogic state, which he referred to as a *dream without distortion*. He found that "guilt and anxiety seem to play a less active role than in dreams with the result that the reveries can come through with less disguise."[13] He induced a hypnagogic state by several means, including amplifying a patient's breath sounds, then playing them back through earphones; playing a monotonous sound repeatedly; and using Jacobson's progressive relaxation techniques. Kubie felt that the reverie state frequently produced visual memory images which had "all of the attendant sensations and affects"[14] of the original experience. Kubie used *induced hypnagogic reverie* when he wanted to speed up analysis and when he found that free association and conventional dream analysis were not producing satisfactory results.

Sacerdote, an American psychotherapist who used hypnosis, developed a technique which he called *induced dreams*. Sacerdote hypnotized patients and suggested to them that they "begin to have an interesting, possibly strange dream, with a pleasant conclusion, that will help you further with your past and present problems."[15] He would use free association techniques to interpret the dream. Then he would hypnotize the patient again and suggest that the patient dream a dream related to the previous one. In this way he would draw out a succession of related dreams. Sacerdote felt that this technique circumvented resistances in the patient.

Recently, a University of Pennsylvania psychiatrist named A. Beck described techniques he teaches to his patients to control spontaneous visualization. These were patients who complained of anxiety over recurring, uncontrollable fantasies. One patient again and again visualized himself driving a car which crashed over a wall. When the patient ex-perienced the visualization, he would become as anxious as if the event were really happening. Beck found that if he clapped his hands loudly while the patient was envisioning the scene, the patient's visualization would disappear, as would the anxiety. Beck then instructed the patient to clap his own hands whenever the visualization recurred. After the patient had stopped the anxiety-producing visualization, he was instructed to visualize a pleasant scene that made him feel good.

Beck also used a technique which involved encouraging the patient to repeat at will his unpleasant visualization. He found that with repetition the patient came to feel he had control over the visualization and could cut off as well as induce it. Beck believes that a person's fantasies play an important part in his state of mind. "If the dominant theme of the fantasy is negative, then his mood . . . is unpleasant."[16] Beck felt that the effect of fantasies on mood was based on the fact that "A person visualizing an episode may react as though the episode were actually occurring."[17]

Another technique used by Beck and other therapists involves *forward time projection*. The patient is asked to visualize himself in a situation in the present, and then to visualize himself in the situation as it will be in three months, six months, a year, even five years. An example might be a woman who feels anxious about a hernia operation her child is to have. The patient is asked to visualize herself before the operation, and she sees herself as tense and worried. She is then asked to visualize herself directly after the operation, and she sees herself feeling relieved that the operation has gone well, but still somewhat anxious. Finally she is asked to envision the situation six months after the operation, and she sees her child as completely healed and sees herself as relaxed and happy. This technique enables the patient to see beyond their moment of anxiety to a time when the source of anxiety is past and the situation has worked out well. Such forward time projection helps to put the patient's anxiety into perspective and relieves tension over the impending event.

The use of visualization to lessen anxiety leads us into the techniques of the behavior therapists. In the 1960's American psychiatrist

Joseph Wolpe, a prominent behavioral therapist, developed a technique called *systematic desensitization*. In this technique, Wolpe has patients relax, then visualize a series of situations related to the source of their anxiety or phobia. Wolpe and the patients arrange the situations in a hierarchy ranging from situations that make them mildly anxious to ones that make them extremely anxious. The following is an example of a Wolpe-type hierarchy concerning fear of cats:

- the person in front of his or her house on a sunny day talking with a friend who mentions the word "cat,"
- the person coming across a picture of a cat in a magazine,
- a good friend sitting with a cat 2 blocks away,
- a cat in the next room,
- a cat in an airline's travel cage in the same room,
- a cat sleeping in a chair across the room,
- a cat sitting on the patient's lap.

In systematic desensitization Wolpe begins by teaching patients to relax deeply through Jacobson's progressive relaxation (see page 106) or through autosuggestion (see page 108). The patients are then told to visualize the least frightening scene in the hierarchy. If they experience the least anxiety, they are told to stop the visualization and relax themselves more deeply. Then they are asked to visualize the scene again. When patients are able to visualize a particular scene without anxiety, they are instructed to visualize the next scene in the hierarchy. In this manner, stopping to relax further whenever they experience any anxiety, patients are gradually led to picture one scene after another until they are able to visualize without discomfort what has been the most anxiety-producing image in their hierarchy. Through these visualization exercises patients lose their fear of cats. They are trained or conditioned to replace their feelings of anxiety with the pleasant sensations of relaxation.

Similar conditioning techniques have been used with negative or unpleasant stimuli in order to stop a patient from doing something. Psychiatrists call this technique *aversive training*. This technique has been applied to smoking, compulsive eating, alcoholism, drug addiction, homosexuality, transvestism, and fetishism. In one technique, patients are told to visualize clearly the acts they wish to stop. For example, if the patient is a man who wants to stop smoking, he is told to visualize clearly lighting a cigarette, putting it in his mouth, and inhaling. When the patient begins to feel the pleasure of this act, he is instructed to immediately visualize an experience that is intensely unpleasant to him, such as falling or becoming sick. The repeated association of the unpleasant image with the patient's habit is believed to diminish the patient's desire for and pleasure in the habit.

More extreme versions of aversive therapy involve the use of electroshock, and drugs which produce nausea or terror. Patients are asked to visualize their habit, and when they begin to experience pleasurable sensations, they are administered shock or a drug. Therapists using this technique often bypass the use of visualization and introduce concrete stimuli such as food or alcohol. These therapies, which are described in Wolfe's book, *The Practice of Behavior Therapy*,[18] and are in actual use, are similar to techniques portrayed in the Stanley Kubrick movie *A Clockwork Orange*. In that film a sadistic criminal was shown violent and sexually-arousing movies and, at the same time, given a nausea-producing drug. Many people, including the authors of this book, question the moral right of therapists to use treatments of this kind.

Another form of treatment based on principles of conditioning is *implosive therapy*, a technique which was developed by the American therapist T. G. Stampfl in the 1960's.[19] He begins with the common psychiatric assumption that repressed memory of a traumatic experience causes anxiety. Stampfl believes that making a person vividly aware of such traumatic events, while the person remains unharmed, causes the anxious response to diminish. Stampfl suggests that patients visualize the most anxiety-producing situations that they can. For example, a woman with a rat phobia might imagine a rat actually biting her and devouring her organs. Stampfl says the patient will find the imagined experience less anxiety-producing than she had feared, and will realize that she can control her thoughts.

Examples of images Stampfl uses are aggression, punishment, cannibalism, rejection, bodily injury, loss of control, and guilt. Stampfl believes that experiencing these basic fears and negative images in fantasy allows the patient to pass through his or her anxiety.

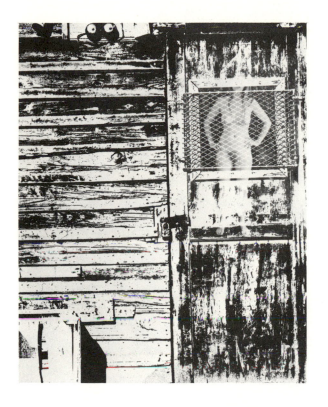

Hypnosis is one of the oldest techniques in psychology to use visualization. As we mentioned earlier, it was through hypnosis that Breuer and Freud first discovered memory images in the unconscious. Many of the hypnotic techniques in use today were originated by old-time mesmerists in the early 1800's. Despite the fact that the techniques have proven useful and are over 100 years old, little is known scientifically about how they work. And there is probably more misconception than knowledge about hypnosis and its relation to sleep, meditation, and altered states of consciousness. Leslie LeChron, a clinical psychologist in Los Angeles and leading authority on hypnosis, says in his book, *Techniques of Hypnotherapy* (1961), that "the most common misconception is that there will be a loss of consciousness when one is hypnotized. . . . Actually, unconsciousness never occurs even in the deepest stages of

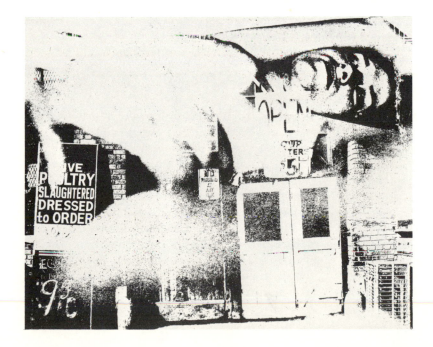

Certain images call up basic fears that are shared by everyone. The image of a woman behind a grate evokes the fear of imprisonment and loss of liberty. The image of a sleeping woman superimposed on the image of a slaughter house calls up deep-seated fears of physical injury. Confronting and learning to control negative imagery can relieve a person's anxiety. Photographs by Michael Samuels.

191

The Surrealist painters used a technique similar to automatic writing to produce images for their art. They allowed their hands to move without conscious direction. The Surrealists believed that art produced in this manner was as valid as consciously-directed art. Jean Arp. *Automatic Drawing,* 1916. Collection, The Museum of Modern Art, New York.

hypnosis. There is always complete awareness.''[20] LeChron goes on to say that ''daydreaming, concentration on a book, a television program, or a motion picture, or any similar focusing of attention may produce spontaneous hypnosis.''[21] Techniques for inducing hypnosis are similar to the exercise for inducing receptive visualization, page 152. There are many specific techniques used in hypnosis for bringing forth images. Freud used hypnosis to uncover memory images; Sacerdote used hypnosis to induce dreams. Hypnotists have also used *automatic writing* to uncover images.

A person is hypnotized, given pencil and paper, and told that the inner mind will take muscular control of the hands and fingers and write. Doodling is a form of automatic writing which we have all experienced. In one visualization technique that hypnotists use to release inner images ''the subject may be instructed to imagine a blackboard in front of him. He is told to see words come on the imaginary blackboard, as though a hand were writing with white chalk. Whole sentences may appear, or just a word which will offer a clue [to a traumatic memory].''[22]

192

Another interesting technique used by hypnotists is *age regression*. The hypnotized subject is asked to "re-experience what had happened with all five of his senses."[23] In this way, a person can re-experience an event from any time in his past. Many hypnotists even claim they can take a subject back to the time of his birth or to previous lifetimes. Hypnotists use several different visualizations to promote age-regression experiences. "It can be suggested that the subject is floating on a magic carpet. Looking down below him he will see a broad river, which is the river of time. The past is upstream and the carpet is directed to move upstream. There is a milepost below on which is a number—the present date. The carpet moves on back and another milepost is seen—the previous year. Speeding up, one milepost after another is passed and the carpet is then directed to stop at the desired time.

"Another technique . . . is to suggest visualization of a large book, open at the middle pages. This is the book of life. The subject is instructed to see pictures on the pages and to turn back rapidly page by page until he reaches the page representing the desired date.

"Still another method is to suggest the illusion of a large grandfather's clock, the hands seen as moving counterclockwise, in reverse. Below the face of the clock the subject is told to see a dial showing the month, date, and year. As the hands turn backwards they go faster and faster, and the dates on the dial change. This may be continued until the desired time is reached."[24]

The complimentary technique to age regression is *age progression*. Using similar visualizations the subject is asked to move forward in time. Another hypnotic technique is called *time distortion*. In time distortion a person experiences in a few minutes a mental activity that would normally require hours. People working with hypnosis have discovered that many subjects are capable of giving themselves the suggestions used to induce hypnosis, a process known as *autohypnosis*. All of the exercises in this book which involve the reader's repeating to himself verbal suggestions are techniques similar to autohypnosis.

Thus far, the psychotherapeutic techniques that we've discussed are primarily based on re-

ceptive visualization. People open themselves up to their memory and imagination images. The memory images may be of meaningful situations in childhood, of traumatic events from the past that have caused anxiety, or of situations that have brought pleasure. The imagination images may be images from their inner center, archetypal or mythological images, images of forthcoming events that make a person feel pleasure or anxiety, or images that exist purely in fantasy that a person does not expect to happen. Receptive visualization techniques stimulate a person to receive images. Modern psychological theory holds that these images come from the "unconscious" and, when brought to awareness, can improve a person's state of mind and result in personal growth.

The next group of therapies that we will discuss involve more programmed uses of visualization. In these techniques, the therapist provides suggestions for the content of visualizations, as well as suggestions for their manipulation and control. The therapies in this section all have similarities to one another, all share common techniques, and are all broadly related in their historical development. Because the therapies often overlap, we will not discuss each one in detail; we will discuss selected therapies, citing some of the techniques that they employ.

Wolfgang Kretschmer, a German psychiatrist, has called many of these techniques "meditative." By meditative he means that the patient strives toward "self-realization, psychic freedom and harmony, and a lively creativity. At best, one achieves a Nirvana-like phenomena of joy and release."[25] Kretschmer summarizes meditative techniques as follows: "After a general bodily relaxation has been achieved, symbolic fantasies are skillfully induced. Then colors and objects are visualized. One endeavors to experience a symbolic representation of ideas . . . in a way which allows the psyche to make unconscious tendencies symbolically visible."[26]

Dr. Carl Happich, a German internist with knowledge of both Oriental meditation techniques and Western psychotherapy, developed a technique in the 1920's and 1930's which is now used by a number of therapists in Europe and the United States. Happich theorized that there is a level of consciousness called *symbolic consciousness,* which lies between consciousness and unconsciousness. At this level, the "collective unconscious" expresses itself with symbols. Happich first instructed his patients to relax deeply. He then directed them to imagine leaving the room, going across fields to a meadow. When patients had visualized the meadow, they were asked to describe in detail what they experienced there. This visualization exercise was called the *meadow meditation.* In

The meadow is a basic symbol which represents the primordial, creative basis of a person's life and is a natural departure point for visualizing other symbolic images such as a forest or a stream. Illustration by Susan Ida Smith.

The mountain symbolizes spiritual elevation. In ascending the mountain a person must
work to overcome obstacles. The mountain can also symbolize a person's ambition,
career, and worldly goals. When a person visualizes climbing the mountain inward
transformation takes place. *Mountain Number 21,* by Marsden Hartley, 1929–30. Oil on
canvas. 34 × 30 inches. Collection of the Whitney Museum of American Art, New York.
Gift of Mr. and Mrs. Herman Schneider.

later sessions Happich used the *mountain meditation*, in which patients visualized themselves climbing a mountain and describing the view; the *chapel meditation*, in which patients entered into a chapel and remained there; and finally, a meditation in which people visualized themselves sitting on a bench by an old fountain, listening to the water. Happich believed that at a meditative level of mind the meadow, mountain and chapel images go beyond everyday life and become archetypal, primordial symbols. The meadow symbolizes "youthful Mother Nature in her serene and beneficent aspect,"[27] the positive, creative side of a person's life. The ascent of a mountain represents man achieving the goal of psychic freedom. A forest, experienced in reaching the meadow or in climbing a mountain, represents the dark and fearful side of a person's nature and often is the home of demons. The chapel represents a room within the person's inner self, wherein the person confronts the central problems of his or her life.

After patients had spent time visualizing these scenes, Happich directed them to the *design meditation*. The patient was instructed to visualize a mandala, to "psychically identify himself with the symbol and integrate the meaning of the symbol with his psychic life."[28] It is interesting to note that while Jung found archetypal symbols and mandalas are often perceived spontaneously during receptive visualization or free association, Happich directly presented such symbols to his patients for their exploration.

Hans Carl Leuner, a prominent German psychiatrist from the University of Goettingen, developed a therapy called *Guided Affective Imagery* (GAI) in the 1950's and 1960's. In GAI therapy the patient lies on a couch in a quiet, partially darkened room. The patient is given verbal suggestions to relax. Leuner says, "It is essential to understand that when the patient is in this state of induced relaxation, the mind is functioning differently than in situations of alert consciousness. During GAI, the patient's state of consciousness is similar to that which occurs in meditative states. It is often surprising to hear him excitedly describe vivid colors and detailed forms which are experienced as parts of a totally new world. The patient paradoxically seems to be living in this fantasy world while he simultaneously knows that he is doing this with his therapist for purposes of treatment."[29] When thoroughly relaxed, the patient is asked by Leuner "to imagine a meadow, any meadow that comes to mind."[30] Leuner allows the patient to develop his own visual fantasy around the word

Cathedrals and chapels are symbols of the religious function in man. They represent the deep place in man's psyche where he relates to psychic transformation and faces the basic questions of existence. Claude Monet (1840-1926), the French Impressionist painter, in his *Rouen Cathedral, West Facade,* has portrayed the shimmering peace of a cathedral in a way that makes it easy for a person to visualize going inside and meditating. The National Gallery of Art, Washington. Chester Dale Collection.

This primordial-looking forest by Rodolphe Bresdin, a 19th century French Symbolist, seems to draw the viewer into its depths. The image of a forest serves to stimulate the emergence of deeply-repressed symbolic figures. The darkness and earthiness of a forest symbolize the perils of the unknown, the home of demons and dark creatures. In the center of this print Bresdin has drawn a clearing, which not only draws the viewer in, it provides a safe escape. The viewer can either watch creatures in the clearing or confront them there. *Clearing in a Forest*, courtesy of The Art Institute of Chicago.

"meadow." The meadow is the first of "ten standard imaginary situations" that the patient is asked to visualize. According to Leuner, the meadow may represent a fresh start, the patient's present mood, the Garden of Eden, or a patient's mother-child relationship.

In the second situation the patient is directed to find a path in the meadow that leads through a forest to a mountain. Then the patient is asked to climb the mountain and describe the view. Leuner says that the symbolism of the mountain pertains to the patient's career and achievements.

In the third situation, the patient is directed to look around the meadow, find a brook, and follow it, either downstream to the ocean, or upstream to the source. The brook symbolizes the flow of psychic energy and potential for emotional development. The brook or spring can also represent magic healing fluid. Some people visualize themselves bathing in the liquid, rubbing it on their bodies or drinking it.

In the next situation, the fourth, the patient is directed to visualize a house and to explore the rooms. The house is a symbol of the pa-

In this painting, *The Nymph of the Spring*, Lucas Cranach, the Elder (German, 1470-1553), depicts a young woman resting next to a beautiful rock pool fed by a spring. The Latin inscription in the upper left hand corner identifies the spring as sacred. Springs are age-old symbols of refreshment and healing. In psychoanalytical terms the waters of a spring can be identified with the womb. A person visualizing himself next to a sacred spring feels relieved and refreshed by the magic fluids. The National Gallery of Art, Washington. Gift of Clarence Y. Palitz.

tient's personality, onto which he can project all his fears and wishes.

In the fifth situation, the patient is asked to return to the meadow and then to visualize a close relative. The patient's description represents his emotional relationships. In the sixth situation, the patient is asked to visualize sexual situations. In the seventh situation, Leuner asks the patient to visualize a lion in a cage, jungle or desert. The patient's visualization of the lion is seen to represent his aggressive tendencies. In the eighth situation, the patients are asked to visualize a person of their own sex. Typically, patients visualize someone who they would like to be, helping them to work out their own identity.

In the ninth situation, the patient is asked to visualize himself or herself at a safe distance from the forest or cave.[31] The patient is directed to watch for a creature to emerge. This visualization helps to stimulate the emergence of deeply repressed symbolic figures—witches, giants and monsters. In the tenth and final situation, the patient is asked to visualize a swamp in the corner of the meadow and describe a figure emerging from it. Leuner feels this figure is symbolic of deeply repressed, archaic sexual material.

Leuner says that the patient may be intensely frightened by the images experienced in the last two situations. He uses two techniques to deal with the deep fears that may arise. In the

Looking into the dark opening of a cave often evokes fearsome creatures that represent repressed material. The images may be of an archaic, instinctual nature. The cave, seen in this way, represents the unconscious. *Cave at Pendynne,* photograph by Michael Samuels.

The star is a symmetrical form which radiates from a central point. A five or six-pointed white star has always been a symbol of light as opposed to darkness. The shape itself is believed to have transforming power when it is visualized. Illustration by Susan Ida Smith.

first technique, *confrontation,* the patient is directed to stare into the eyes of the frightening creature. Leuner believes that this confrontation helps the patient to discover what the creature means and eventually serves to banish the creature or transform it into a known person or into a more benign form. During this process, the patient is supported and encouraged by the therapist. The second, milder, technique Leuner uses to deal with these apparitions involves *feeding.* The patient is directed to feed the creature, in fact to overfeed the creature, until it is satiated and goes to sleep. Leuner also uses two supplementary techniques for dealing with the creature— *reconciliation,* in which the patient attempts to make friends with the creature, and, a dangerous last resort in which the patient exhausts and kills the monster.

Leuner says, "I often give control of the therapeutic process to the patient's psyche. There appears to be a spontaneous inner pacemaker whose influence over the treatment process can be invoked by the GAI method. This is accomplished by asking the patient to let himself be guided by one of his own benign symbolic figures."[32] Leuner uses GAI to help people stimulate their imagination, to help psychotherapists diagnose a patient's illness (using the ten standard situations like a Rohrschach test), as a basis for free association in therapy, and as a therapy in itself.

Psychosynthesis, a series of techniques described by the Italian psychiatrist Roberto Assagioli, aims toward "harmonious integration"[33] of human nature. Among its techniques is *symbolic visualization.* In this technique patients sit in a comfortable chair, close their eyes, and relax. Patients are then directed to visualize various symbols in their mind's eye. In discussing the uses of symbolic visualization, Robert Gerard, a Los Angeles psychologist, notes that at first patients are often troubled by intrusive thoughts and images and that they must learn to control their imaginative processes in order to focus on specific images. Gerard believes that as patients learn to focus on an image they increase their control over their inner and outer lives. Gerard uses four types of symbols in therapy. He has the patient visualize, then hold the image of these symbols. The first group of symbols is of synthesis, integration and balance. Examples of such symbols are sunflowers, a white dot at the center of a white circle, a cross, a five- or six-pointed white star, and various mandalas. The second group of symbols relates to "harmonious human relations."[34] An example of this group is two hands clasping one another. The third group concerns symbols of masculinity and femininity: for example, a shining sword (masculine) or a gold cup (feminine). The fourth group is symbols of affective states. Gerard uses color visualization to bring about affective states. For instance, patients may picture themselves in a globe of light of a particular color, or they may visualize an object of a particular color. Gerard also directs patients to change images. For example, a seed might be changed to a tree, a worm to a butterfly.

Gerard has the patient picture sequences of images in scenes symbolic of the patient's problem. For example, a man rebuilding his personality might visualize rebuilding a house. If such images do not come spontaneously to the patient Gerard will suggest an image. Gerard uses several techniques of receptive visualization to promote symbolic imagery. If patients have any bodily feelings of tension, they are asked to visualize associated images. To visualize affective states, patients are directed to imagine a door with the name of an affective state, such as love, written on the door. Patients are then asked to open the door and describe what they see. Similarly, patients may be asked to visualize a large heart, bigger than themselves, with a door which they can walk through. Gerard also asks patients to hold a word or thought in their minds, such as justice or altruism, and to watch for an associated visual image to appear. All of these techniques are designed to help the patient find a visual image that corresponds to verbal thought. These images can then be held in the mind in order to achieve personal goals.

R. Desoille, a French psychologist, has developed a therapy which he calls *Rêve Evéillé* or *Directed Daydreams.* Desoille instructs his patients to "psychically wander"—visualizing and experiencing what they see. Desoille is especially interested in patients' visualizations of ascent or descent. In their psychic

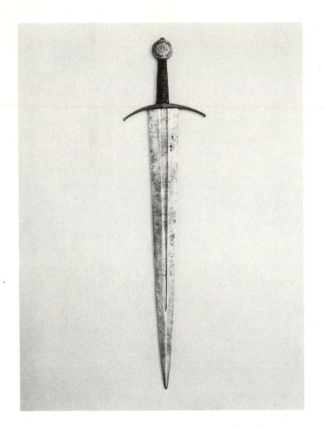

The image of a sword is associated with traditional masculine qualities—power, strength, liberty and aggression. Visualization of a sword and restoration of it if it is in disrepair can strengthen the masculine side of a person's personality. *15th century Italian sword,* The Metropolitan Museum of Art. The collection of Giovanni P. Morosini, presented by his daughter Giulia, 1932.

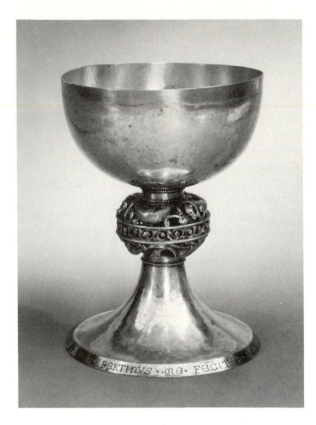

The chalice or cup symbolizes the feminine qualities of receptivity and containment. Visualization and cleaning or polishing of the cup strengthen feminine aspects of a person's personality. *Bertinus Chalice,* 1222. The Metropolitan Museum of Art, The Cloisters Collection, Purchase, 1947.

wanderings, patients encounter obstacles, as well as helpful and malevolent figures, all of which they recount to Desoille. As the therapist is told about the visualization, he "suggests to the patient a symbolic means of changing his (the patient's) situation by climbing or descending. The therapist does not suggest the whole fantasy; rather, he gives only a direction and maintains control of the fantasy by offering helpful symbols which can serve as points of crystallization for the fantasy."[35] The visualized *ascent* symbolizes "creative sublimation," that is, transformation of the psyche and development toward psychic freedom. Visualized *descent* symbolizes man's instinctual motivations. Learning to visualize such symbolic ascents and descents helps patients to control their archetypal images, and thus lose their fear of them. As patients ascend, they encounter images of spiritual figures and situations; as they descend, they encounter symbolic situations related to basic drives.

Another form of visualization therapy was developed by Walter Frederking, a German psychotherapist of the 1940's. He referred to his technique as *deep relaxation and symbolism.*[36] In this technique patients are led through a deep relaxation run and then told to describe their visualizations. Frederking encourages patients to visualize *symbolic strip thought,* like scenes

Allegory, by Lorenzo Lotto, the 16th century Venetian painter, represents the ascent of a spirit who has chosen virtue over vice. The naked child playing in the sunlight represents Renaissance virtue and culture; the drunken satyr portrayed in gloom and darkness on the right represents vice. Virtue's victory is portrayed by the tiny spirit climbing the path in the left-hand background. This Renaissance visualization negatively depicts descent, or instinctual drives, symbolized by the ship in the storm. The National Gallery of Art, Washington. Andrew Mellon Collection.

A striking image of ascent.
Photograph by Dr. I. Samuels.

from a movie. Patients are further encouraged to interact with the figures in the scenes they visualize. Other therapists have expanded this technique to have patients become identified with elements from their fantasies. For example, a woman may be asked to imagine that she is a figure or an object in her visualization and then be asked to reenact the visualization from that point of view. Present day Gestalt therapists on the West Coast such as Fritz Perls ask their patients to imagine that they are each of the figures in a scene in succession. For example, if a man visualizes a person hitting a dog with a stick, he is directed to visualize himself as the person, then as the dog, then as the stick, reporting the incident from each point of view.

Yet another visualization therapy was developed by the German psychotherapist Friederich Mauz in the 1940's. His therapy is a

An extraordinary image of falling and descent by the 16th century Netherlandish artist Hendrik Goltzius. This print depicts Phaeton, the son of Helios, the Greek god of the sun. Phaeton was struck down by Zeus when he drove the chariot of the sun too close to earth and almost set it on fire. The Metropolitan Museum of Art, Harris Brisbane Dick Fund, 1953.

Sunday Afternoon on The Island of La Grande Jatte, by George Seurat, is a painting of remarkable serenity. The viewer can feel the warmth of the later afternoon sun and sense the people's delight at being outdoors. The dreamlike stillness heightens these sensations of relaxation and pleasure and conveys a profound sense of psychological harmony that is shared by all of the figures in the painting. Such an image of security and pleasure has creative power when it is experienced firsthand or in visualization. When a person visualizes an image that is personal and impersonal at the same time—as in this painting—he is led into the realm of meditative reality. Courtesy of The Art Institute of Chicago.

narrower and more directed form of visualization. Mauz developed this therapy in his work with psychotics because he thought that less structured techniques might be dangerous for such patients. Mauz directs his patients to visualize scenes full of positive symbols. Mauz asks patients to recall very pleasant memories from their childhood such as Christmas Eve, family celebrations, parades, a river at sunrise, or a page from a children's book. Mauz talks to the patients about these scenes using their own words and images and directs them to visualize the scene. He also has patients visualize Happich's "meadow," but he suggests a number of positive images the patient will encounter. Mauz feels that visualization of these highly positive scenes unlocks suppressed emotions and stimulates a natural healing in the patient.

In this chapter we have given an overview of many of the contemporary therapies that use visualization techniques. We have described in detail a number of those techniques. We have not included actual visualization exercises. However, these techniques as a whole are very graphic and bear strong similarities to visualization exercises elsewhere in this book. The techniques described in this chapter lend themselves to use both as receptive and programmed visualizations. We hope that readers will be stimulated to adapt some of these techniques for use in exploring their own inner world.

Psychology, that is the area of study dealing with a person's state of mind, broadly overlaps the other areas in this section of the book. The reader will find other techniques applicable to, and used in, psychology throughout the rest of the chapters and in *Daily Life*. The technique of role playing or role rehearsal is discussed in another chapter (page 169). The technique of autogenic training will be discussed in detail in the chapter on healing (page 223–226).

FOOTNOTES

1. Freud, S. *The Origin and Development of Psychoanalysis.* Chicago, Henry Regnery Co., 1955, p. 6.
2. Freud, S. p. 6.
3. Freud, S. p. 20.
4. Freud, S. *The Ego and the Id.* New York: W. W. Norton & Co., 1960, p. 19.
5. Freud, S. *The Ego and the Id.* p. 19.
6. Jung, C. G. *Memories, Dreams, Reflections.* New York: Vintage Books, 1963, p. 177.
7. Jung, C. G. p. 177.
8. Jung, C. G. p. 179.
9. Jung, C. G. p. 199.
10. Jung, C. G. pp. 181–188.
11. Jung, C. G. pp. 183, 187.
12. Jung, C. G. p. 189.
13. Kubie, L. "The Use of Induced Hypnagogic Reveries in the Recovery of Repressed Amnesiac Data," *Menninger Clinic Bulletin,* 7:172–182, 1943.
14. Kubie, L. pp. 172–182.
15. Sacerdote, P. "Induced Dreams," *American Journal of Clinical Hypnosis.* 10:167–173, 1968.
16. Beck, A. T. "Role of Fantasies in Psychotherapy and Psychopathology," *Journal of Nervous and Mental Diseases.* 150:3–17, 1970.
17. Beck, A. T. pp. 3–17.
18. Wolpe, J. *The Practice of Behavior Therapy.* New York: Pergamon Press, 1969.
19. Stampfl, T. G. and Lewis, D. J. "Essentials of Implosive Therapy," *Journal of Abnormal Psychology.* 72:496–503, 1967.
20. Lecron, L. *Techniques of Hypnotherapy.* New York, The Julien Press, 1961, p. 3.
21. Lecron, L. p. 4.
22. Lecron, L. p. 26.
23. Lecron, L. p. 46.
24. Lecron, L. p. 50.
25. Tart, C., ed. *Altered States of Consciousness.* Garden City, N.Y.: Doubleday & Co., Inc., 1969, p. 225, from Kretschmer, W., "Meditative Techniques in Psychotherapy, pp. 224–233.
26. Tart, C. p. 224.
27. Tart, C. p. 226.
28. Tart, C. p. 228.
29. Leuner, H. "Guided Affective Imagery (GAI)," *American Journal of Psychotherapy.* 23:6, 1969.
30. Leuner, H. p. 5.
31. Leuner, H. p. 11.
32. Leuner, H. p. 16.
33. Assagioli, R. *Psychosynthesis.* New York: Hobbs, Dorman & Co., 1965.
34. Gerard, R. "Symbolic Visualization—A Method of Psychosynthesis," *Topical Problems in Psychotherapy.* 4:70–80, 1963.
35. Tart, C. p. 229.
36. Tart, C. p. 230.

The modern physician's authority rests on his knowledge of scientific methods, drugs, and surgery. The shaman of ancient and contemporary times bases his authority on his ability to visualize the cause of disease and the cure. Among Northwest American Indians the shaman was sometimes portrayed as a doll-like image with small figures at his side who possibly represented his assistants. *Shaman Group,* Haida, 19th century. M. H. de Young Memorial Museum, San Francisco. Lent by H. Del Richards.

Chapter 14

MEDICINE AND HEALING

The use of visualization techniques for physical healing dates back well before the rise of experimental science. In fact, visualization may be the most ancient healing technique used by primitive man. The earliest records of such techniques are found on cuneiform slabs from Babylonia and Summaria. We can assume that there were antecedents for these techniques among ancient primitive tribes. Even today, Indian tribes such as the Canadian Eskimo and the Navahos of the American Southwest use forms of healing based on visualization. These tribes have in common a world view that includes a belief in spirits, gods, sorcerers, and magical figures, of whom the malevolent ones are thought to be the cause of disease. The practice of the healing art in these tribes centers around their *shamans*, special members of the tribe who are believed to have the power to heal disease. Shamans are in contact with tribal spirits through dreams, visions, and mystical experiences, that is, through visualization. Shamans heal through ceremonies or rituals in which disease-causing, malevolent spirits are confronted by positive forces, and the power of the spirits is dissipated. Such confrontation often involves the shaman traveling mentally to the land of the spirits. On the physical level, the shaman may even suck a foreign object out of the body of the sick person and show it to that person.[1]

Among the Canadian Eskimos, the shaman goes into a trance and visualizes himself journeying to the bottom of the sea where he visits Sedna, the sea goddess, to find the cause of the illness (or to ask for more animals to hunt or to seek help in calming a storm).[2] The Eskimo shaman also performs complicated rituals in which he, while in a trance, invokes a spirit helper to aid in discovering the cause of an illness. The shaman's role encompasses a number of facets—he acts as physician,

In order to discover the cause of illness the Eskimo shaman would visualize animal spirits. This mask is the concrete form of a shaman's visualization of the seal (right) and its spirit or *inua* (left). Wearing the mask helped the shaman to contact the seal spirit. Photograph courtesy of the Museum of the American Indian, Heye Foundation. Driftwood mask, Good News Bay, Alaska, 1875-1900.

psychiatrist, seer, and religious leader—curing physical and mental disease, foretelling the future, mediating between the spirits and the tribe, and seeking solutions to the daily problems of food and shelter. His ability to function in all these spheres rests on his power of visualization.

Some shamanistic ceremonies are accompanied by monotonous chanting or drumming which induces a trance-like state in all the participants and serves to heighten the group visualization. The Navaho shaman instructs helpers in the making of highly complicated, traditional sand paintings which are symbolic of the gods of the Navaho universe and the patient's relation to them. Among the Navahos the roles of healer and diagnostician are separated. A *hand trembler* is called in to ascertain what is wrong with the patient. The trembler goes into a trance and in a ritual ceremony visualizes the cause of the patient's illness. He then advises the patient to call in the *singer* or shaman who can perform the appropriate "sing" or ceremony (and sand painting) to effect a cure. The Navaho and many other tribes also have herb healers who are called in for minor illnesses. The herb healer, in a trance or dream state, visualizes and locates the correct mixture of herbs to relieve the patient's symptoms. Among the Cheyenne, this mixture was called the medicine bundle.

The Northwest Coast shaman wore beautifully-carved ivory or bone charms around his neck while he was communicating with the spirits during a healing. These charms depicted the particular spirit which the shaman wished to contact.
M. H. de Young Memorial Museum, San Francisco.

210

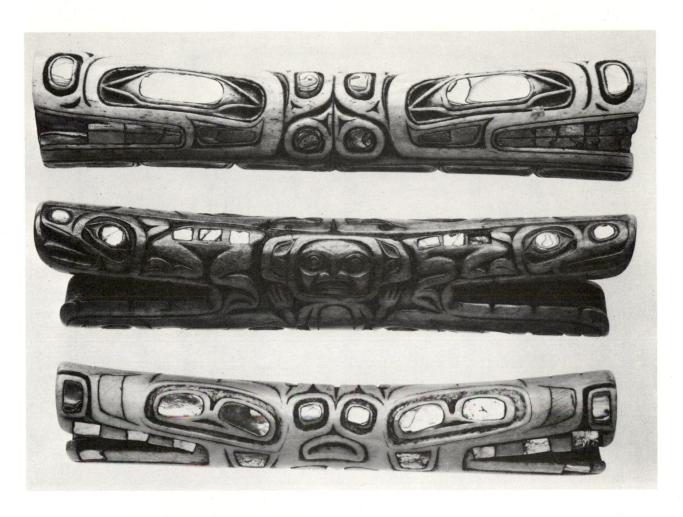

The shaman's charms on this page help the shaman to contact spirits when he is visualizing. The three charms at the top of the page are carved bone "soul catchers." The top two, Kitksan, British Columbia; the third, Niska, Lower Nass River, British Columbia. The bottom two objects are bone charms made by the Tlingit of Alaska. The bottom charm represents a spirit canoe made in the shape of a sea lion and an octopus. It contains seven spirits. Photographs courtesy of The Museum of the American Indian, Heye Foundation.

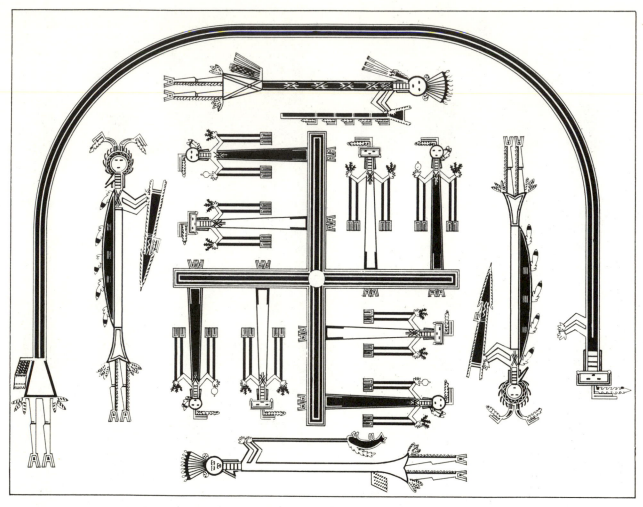

Navaho sandpaintings are holy altars, made on the ground, on which a patient sits during a healing ritual. The sandpainting illustrates episodes in the specific ceremony being performed. In this sandpainting the cross-bars represent pine logs, the central circle represents water. The figures are gods and goddesses. Above all the figures the rainbow goddess stretches. Illustration from *American Indian Design and Decoration*, L. Appleton, Dover Publications, Inc.; New York.

Ancient civilizations used visualization in similar ways. In Babylonia and Assyria people believed illness was caused by evil spirits. Treatment constituted an appeal to the deities to exorcise a demon from the patient. Special priests acted as diagnosticians and interpreted signs and omens from the sun and storm gods. They referred to the position of the sun, moon and planets, and to markings on the livers of sacrifical animals (using them like a DaVinci screen—see page 116). Most importantly, the priests referred to their own dreams. The pa-tient himself might also receive a healing dream by sleeping in the temple. This temple sleep or "incubation" was used both for medical emergencies, and for the cure of chronic diseases. Here is a Babylonian visualization exercise designed to invite a healing dream:

"Reveal thyself unto me and let me see a favorable
  dream,
May the dream that I dream be favorable,
May the dream that I dream be true,
May Mamu the goddess of dreams stand at my
  head."[3]

This ancient Near Eastern plaque 750-720 B.C., depicts a bearded man grasping a tree. Above him is a winged female thought to represent the sun goddess. Assyrian priest-healers consulted the sun gods in their diagnosis. The Metropolitan Museum of Art, Rogers Fund, 1959.

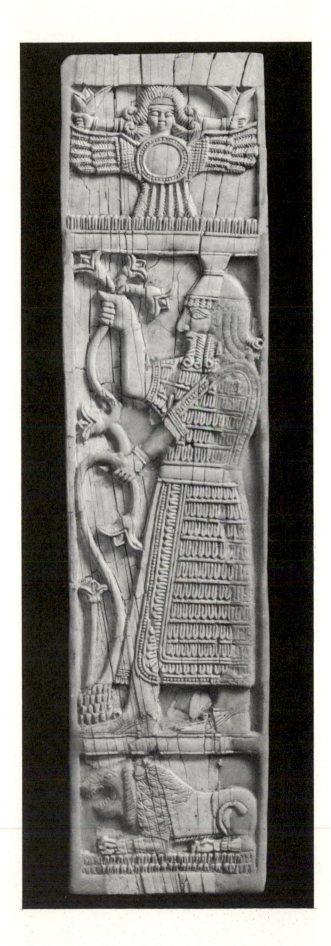

Another Babylonian visualization technique used by the physician-priests involved the use of fire, which was considered a healing element. An image of the demon to be exorcised from the patient was made of wax. The gods of fire were thus invoked to consume it:

"Nusku [Fire God], great offspring of Anu,
I raise the torch to illuminate thee, yea, thee.
(Sorcerers, sorceresses, charmers, witches who
    had bewitched the sick man),
Those who have made images of me, reproducing
    my features,
Who have taken away my breath, torn my hairs,
May the fire god, the strong one, break their
    charm.
I raise the torch, their images I burn,
Of the utukku, the shedu, the rabisu, the
    skimmu,
And every evil that seizes hold of men.
Tremble, melt away, and disappear!
May your smoke rise to heaven,
May the fire god,
The great magician restrain your strength(?)."⁴

Egyptian, Greek and ancient Indian and Oriental civilizations used visualization techniques for healing similar to the Babylonian ones we have described. Like the Babylonians, the ancient Egyptians believed that supernatural beings and demons caused disease. Healing consisted of magical and religious rites. The Egyptians had a well-developed system of magic, which it was said could control the weather, bring people back to life, and divine the future. In a healing ceremony, the magician-priest would perform incantations and prayers, and also use herbs and devices invested with magic. In extreme cases, dream divination was used. The priests' incantations were both prayers and visualizations.

This Egyptian sculpture of the Ptolemaic Period, 332-30 B.C., depicts three gods: Osiris, the god of the underworld and judge of the dead; Isis, the goddess of motherhood and fertility; and Horus, the god of the day. All three gods were invoked in healing rituals. The Metropolitan Museum of Art, Rogers Fund, 1942.

The Greeks also ascribed disease to superhuman agents. And they likewise invoked the power of the gods for healing. The Greeks healed both by direct means—through the laying on of hands or the application of herbs to the patient—and, more commonly, by indirect means—that is through dreams and visions. A dream might be responsible for effecting an immediate healing, so that the patient awoke healed, or the dream might contain regimens or remedies for the patient to use in

effecting a cure. The Greeks were famous for their healing temples, which contained shrines for the healing gods, dormitories where patients stayed, gymnasiums, libraries, stadiums, theaters and beautiful surrounding grounds.

Patients came to a temple, often from great distances. Their first step in seeking a cure was to take a purifying bath. Then they were put on a special diet or a fast. Later they were taken to visit one of the shrines, where they made an offering of food and touched the affected part of

214

An Egyptian faience made of glass and bronze which was used in magic rituals. 18th dynasty. The Metropolitan Museum of Art, Museum Excavations, 1911-12.

their bodies to the image of a healing god. In the evening they were dressed in white and went to a special room to sleep. During the night, priests dressed in the costumes of gods entered the room, touched patients' diseased parts and sometimes talked to the patients. Patients, being asleep or in a hypnogogic state, experienced divine dreams. The next morning, patients were either healed or began to carry out the instructions given to them in their dreams.[6]

In the healing systems we've mentioned thus far, disease, visualized in the image of a demon, was exorcized by a figure of authority, a physician-priest. And that figure derived his authority from his ability to visualize an infinitely higher authority, a spirit or god. Therefore the god was believed to heal through the priests.

Evolving alongside this shamanistic mode of healing was a more subjective mystical philosophy based on people experiencing visualizations themselves. This mystical tradition permeated the thought of Hermetic philosophers in Egypt, Platonic philosophers in Greece, Sufis in Persia, and Buddhists and Hindus in India and the Orient. In the Middle Ages in Europe it expressed itself in the mysticism of Christian Gnostics, Jewish Kabbalists, and secret occult societies like the Rosicrucians.

This Greek relief shows a sick man in incubation sleep. The healing god Asklepios is seen to come in a dream and cure the patient. In the relief a snake, a symbol of Asklepios, is shown biting the sick man's shoulder. Asklepios himself is seen on the far left healing the patient. Courtesy of The National Museum, Athens.

215

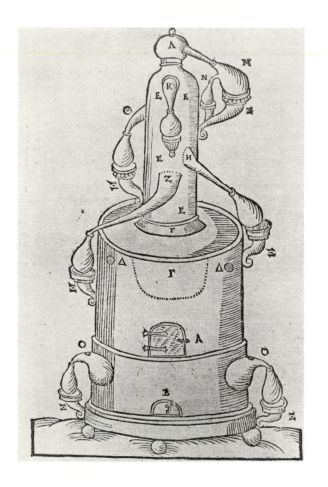

The philosophies of these groups had in common a belief in a spiritual center which formed the universe. This center could be reached by an individual through meditative techniques and visualization. These philosophies believed in the primacy of spirit over matter, of mind over body; they believed that matter is a manifestation of spirit. They believed that visualizations manifest themselves as health or disease in the physical body.

Philippus Aurelus Theophractus Bombastus Paracelsus von Hohenhein, known as Paracelsus, was a Renaissance physician whose medicine embodied the link between occult mysticism and science. He worked in the early 1500's in Switzerland. He is considered the father of modern drug therapy and scientific medicine. Nevertheless Paracelsus opposed the idea of separating the spirit from the healing process. Among his medical theories, Paracelsus held that imagination and faith were the cause of magic phenomena, that imagination was the creative power of man. "Man has a visible and an invisible workshop. The visible one is his body, the invisible one is imagination (mind) . . . The imagination is sun in the soul of man. . . . It calls the forms of the soul into existence. . . . Man's physical body is formed from his invisible soul."[7]

Paracelsus also said that, "The spirit is the master, imagination the tool, and the body the plastic material. . . . The power of the imag-

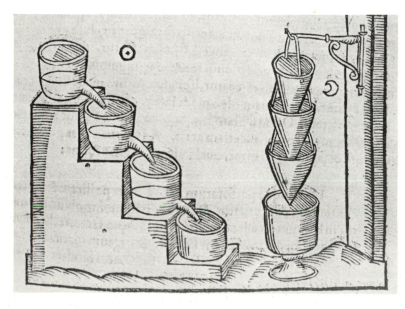

Medieval alchemists believed that the impure human body must be purified. Purification involves separation of the different elements in a person's consciousness. Alchemists used the chemical metaphor to represent mental transmutation. The image of a substance becoming purer and purer is an ancient healing image. Andrae, *Alchymia*, 1633.

216

Paracelsus is considered the father of modern medicine because of his work with chemicals used as drugs. Paracelsus also stands out in the history of visualization healing because of his belief in the relationship between man's imagination and his body. This etching of Paracelsus by Balthazar Jenichen was a broadsheet used after Paracelsus' death. Paracelsus holds in his hands a flask with the word "azoth" on it, which means mercury—a symbol of transformation and healing. Reproduced from *Medicine and the Artist (Ars Medica)* by permission of the Philadelphia Museum of Art. C. Zigrosser; Dover Publications, Inc.; New York.

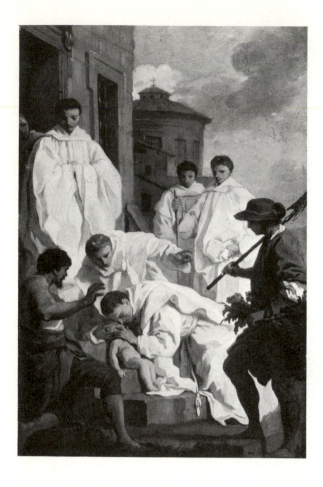

There have been many miraculous healings associated with Christianity, from Christ's time to the present. This theme is expressed in the painting, *The Miracle of St. Benedict,* by the 18th century French painter Pierre Subleyras. M. H. de Young Memorial Museum, San Francisco. Gift of Dr. and Mrs. Walter Heil.

ination is a great factor in medicine. It may produce diseases in man and in animals, and it may cure them. . . . Ills of the body may be cured by physical remedies or by the power of the spirit acting through the soul."[8] Paracelsus believed that evil spirits and witches could cause disease. And he believed that a physician could heal by tapping the power of God. He also believed that dreams gave man clairvoyance (the ability to see a man or an event a long distance away) and the ability to diagnose that person's illness. Paracelsus' methods differed from earlier shamanistic ones in that he believed people could be healed by their own thoughts, as well as by gods and spirits.

Since Paracelsus' time "religious" and "practical scientific" methods of healing have split into two distinct systems. Scientific healing, in the form of drug therapy and surgery, has grown to become the dominant Western treatment modality. Nevertheless, the tradition of religious healing has remained alive. Faith healers, Christian Scientists and shrines such as the one at Lourdes have maintained the tradition of religious healing in our time.

Since 1900 medical scientists have begun to explore the role the mind plays in healing. Doctors have traditionally acknowledged the limits of scientific medicine. In critical situations they have been known to say, "We've done all we can do. It's in God's hands now," or "It depends upon the patient's will to live." And every physician has witnessed recoveries inexplicable to scientific understanding. "Spontaneous remission" of terminal cancer is one of the most well-known contemporary examples. Physicians have also long recognized the efficacy of placebos, which are substances with no known pharmacological action. Placebos have been found to work in both physical and mental illnesses. In one study of placebos, "patients hospitalized with bleeding peptic ulcer showed 70 percent 'excellent results lasting over a period of one year' when the doctor gave them an injection of distilled water and assured them that it was a new medicine that would cure them."[9]

In another study, painting warts with a brightly-colored inert dye, described to patients as a powerful medicine, was found to be as effective as surgical excision of the warts. "Apparently the emotional reaction to a placebo can change the physiology of the skin so that the virus which causes warts can no longer thrive. . . . In this connection it may be worthwhile to recall that until the last few decades most medications prescribed by physicians were pharmacologically inert. That is, physicians were prescribing placebos without knowing it, so that, in a sense, the 'history of medical treatment until relatively recently is the history of the placebo effect.' "[10]

A striking phenomenon found with placebos was the part the patient's expectations played in the effects of the drug. In one study a patient was given ipecac, a drug which normally causes nausea and vomiting. But the patient was told that the drug would stop the symptoms of nausea and vomiting they were (already) experiencing and it did![11]

Dr. Jerome Frank, a psychiatrist at Johns Hopkins Medical School who has written a book about the relationship between persuasion and healing, postulates that a placebo is a symbol of healing. It is as if the symbol (the placebo) triggers in the patient a healing visualization. The fact that a drug has been administered to the patient by a doctor lends authority to the patient's visualization of the drug's effectiveness.

An extreme example of the relationship between the mind and physical illness is taboo death. This phenomenon is common among the Murngin, a North Australian tribe. If a Murngin is told that his soul has been stolen, and it becomes general knowledge, he will die within several days. In such cases, scientists have found no illness present in the corpse. On the other hand, a Murngin hovering near death frequently recovers if he is told that the curse or spell has been broken.[12] Similar phenomena have been reported about laboratory animals placed in stressful situations. Dr. Frank hypothesizes that taboo death may be caused by prolonged over-stimulation of the adrenal glands as a result of fear-induced over-activity of the vagus nerve which innervates the heart.[13]

Dr. Frank believes that a person's "conviction that his predicament is hopeless may cause or hasten his disintegration and death."[14] He cites increased death rates in elderly people after admission to mental hospitals. In these cases too, there is commonly no adequate cause of death found upon autopsy. Increased death rates have also been noted among people who have recently retired and among prisoners of war who have given up hope. Dr. David Cheek, a San Francisco gynecologist and hypnotist, mentions a number of cases in which patients reacted poorly after surgery for no apparent medical reason. When hypnotized, the patients recounted ominous-sounding remarks made by their surgeons during the operations. When the remarks were explained to the patients' satisfaction, the patients improved. Through his experience with many such cases, Dr. Cheek has come to believe that patients hear, record in their subconscious, and are affected by what is said while they are anesthetized.[15]

All of us have experienced less dramatic examples of the relationship between body and mind in our daily lives. When we are frightened, our body responds with an increased rate of heartbeat, more rapid breathing, butterflies in our stomach, and excess sweating. W. B. Cannon, a famous American physiologist who did pioneering research on the sympathetic nervous system and homeostasis in the 1920's, named these reactions the "fight and flight" response. This response to emergency situations readies the body for action by stimulating the sympathetic part of the autonomic nervous system and by stimulating the adrenal glands to release epinephrine. Such stimulation causes a shift in blood flow from the digestive organs to the muscles, lungs and brain. Blood pressure rises, oxygen consumption increases, and stored glucose is released into the bloodstream. Our body is in fact ready to fight or run. Blushing and sexual arousal are other common examples of our bodies responding to a situation perceived by the mind. Our bodies react regardless of whether the situation has

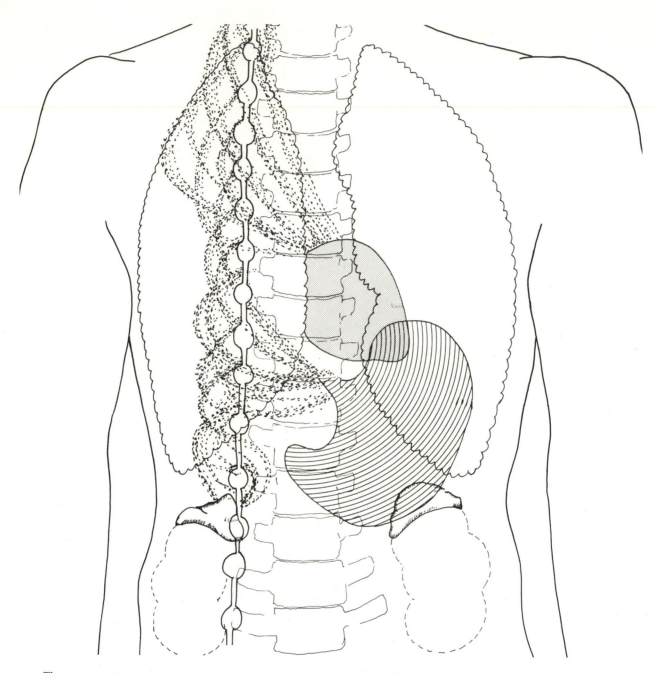

The autonomic nervous system connects the mind with every cell in the body. Through the autonomic nervous system a thought held in the mind affects hormonal balance, blood flow, and metabolism. Thus thoughts—visualizations—can produce a state in which disease or health occurs. Illustration by Susan Ida Smith.

occurred in the external world or is an image held in the mind.

Scientists have long known the anatomy of the neural connections between the brain and the body. "All parts of the body are connected directly or indirectly with a central governing system and function under the control of the central organ. The voluntary muscles as well as the vegetative organs, the latter via the autonomic nervous system, are influenced by the highest centers of the nervous system."[16] Scientists also know that the endocrine glands, which regulate basic bodily processes such as metabolism, are in turn regulated by the central nervous system. "All emotions are accompanied by physiological changes: fear, by palpitation of the heart; anger, by increased heart activity, elevation of blood pressure, and changes in carbohydrate metabolism; despair, by a deep inspiration and expiration called sighing. All these physiological phenomena are the results of complex muscular interactions under the influence of nervous impulses, carried to the expressive muscles of the face and to the diaphragm in laughter, to lacrimal glands in weeping, to the heart in fear, and to the adrenal glands and to the vascular system in rage."[17]

Just as we have all experienced fear and other forms of excitation, we have all experienced the feelings associated with relaxation. These more subtle feelings include a slowing of heartbeat and breathing, and lack of tension in the skeletal muscles. Until recently, little attention was paid to studies made by physiologists such as Jacobson on the effects of body relaxation. Since the late 1960's, Dr. Herbert Benson of Harvard Medical School has been studying the body's physiological response to relaxation. In one study he taught people to relax by concentrating on a constant stimulus such as an object, a sound, or a phrase that was repeated again and again. The subjects rested in a quiet, dimly lit room and closed their eyes. They were told to disregard distracting thoughts and not to worry about how well they were doing. Dr. Benson found that after twelve minutes of relaxation the subjects' oxygen consumption decreased by an average of 13% (from their control value), their carbon dioxide production decreased by 12%, and their respirations decreased from sixteen to eleven breaths per minute. Dr. Benson has named these physiological changes *the relaxation response*.

In other studies, Dr. Benson found that the relaxation response was accompanied by decreased blood lactate (a waste product of metabolism), relatively low blood pressures, slightly increased forearm blood flow, decreased heart rates, and intensification of Al-

Physiologic DATA from J. Beary and H. Benson M.D., adapted from *Psychosomatic Medicine* 36:2 (March-April 1974).

	Control Mean Sitting Quietly.	During Relaxation Technique Period.	% Decrease	Just Closing Eyes.
Oxygen Consumption ml/minute	258.9	225.4	13%	251.4
CO_2 Production ml/minute	242.4	214.1	12%	237.9
Respiratory Rate breaths/minute	15.7	11.1	4.6%	14.8

pha brain waves. Based on these studies, Benson has hypothesized that the relaxation response is the opposite of the fight and flight response. Benson calls the relaxation response a hypometabolic state (that is, one of lowered metabolic processes) resulting from decreased sympathetic nervous system activity. Benson goes on to say, "There are many religious and secular techniques which elicit the physiological changes characteristic of the relaxation response. Some of these are autogenic training, [Jacobson] progressive relaxation, sentic cycles, cotension, yoga and zen, and transcendental meditation."[18]

One of the implications of Benson's work is the understanding that a person is able to control, in a general way, their body physiology. That is, people can do things—through meditation, yoga, relaxation—that result in a lowered output of the sympathetic nervous system, which is a division of the autonomic or so-called "involuntary" nervous system. The lowered output of the sympathetic nervous system is an "integrated response," that is, the body exhibits a group of general changes every time relaxation takes place. Dr. Benson postulates that learning to relax voluntarily may have a role in treating diseases, such as hypertension, that are caused by prolonged excitation of the sympathetic nervous system.[19]

For years medical scientists have heard remarkable stories of the ability of yogis to control specific bodily functions such as heartbeat and metabolic rate. These reports have not been given much credence and scientists have continued to believe that the autonomic nervous system is beyond conscious control. Recent studies, however, have shown that control over the autonomic nervous system can be learned. In the late 1960's, Drs. Miller and Dicara, physiologists at Rockefeller Institute, in a pioneering study of visceral learning in rats, found that rats could learn to alter their blood flow, blood pressure, stomach acidity, and brain wave patterns in response to reward. The rats' control was specific in that the animals could precisely increase and decrease blood flow to a single area of their bodies.[20] The human outgrowth of, and correlate to, experiments like this has been the birth of *biofeedback*, which, as Dr. Barbara Brown, au-

thor of *New Mind, New Body*, says, is "simply the feedback of biological information to the person whose biology it is." For example, a person is attached to an apparatus which graphically and continuously shows their blood pressure. It has been found that a person can lower his or her blood pressure by simply concentrating on the dial dropping.[21]

Their minds opened by research like Miller's and Dicara's, scientists have now vertified in the laboratory the ability of yogis to control specific body processes. In 1970 Elmer Green, a bio-feedback researcher at the Menninger Foundation, conducted a number of studies on Swami Rama. Green described the results of one study: "He [Swami Rama] caused two areas a couple inches apart on the palm of his right hand to gradually change temperature in opposite directions (at a maximum rate of about 4°F. per minute) until they showed a temperature difference of 10°F. The left side of his palm, after this performance (which was totally motionless), looked as if it had been slapped with a ruler, it was rosy red. The right side of his hand had turned ashen gray."[22]

Using an electrocardiograph machine, Green demonstrated that Swami Rama could raise his heartrate at will from 70 beats per minute to 300 beats per minute. 300 beats per minute represents a state which doctors call "atrial flutter." The Swami could also control his brain waves, and produce, while he was awake, waves previously seen only in people in deep sleep.[23]

Specific self-regulation of the autonomic nervous system, such as that demonstrated by Swami Rama, has indicated to researchers a potential area of medicine largely unexplored and untapped. Spectacular demonstrations of specific bodily controls are described in great detail by W. Y. Evans-Wentz, an Oxford University scholar who visited Tibet in the early 1900's. He tells of yogis who were able to sit naked in the snow for hours at a time, actually melting the snow in a circle around them. These yogis generated tremendous bodily heat with the aid of visualization: "Visualize in the tri-junction of the three chief psychic-nerves (below the navel nerve center, in the perineum, at the base of the organ of generation), a sun."[24]

Research into the effects of visualization on the control of specific bodily processes was done in the Soviet Union in the 1930's as part of a group of studies on S., a famous stage mnenonist (a person who can demonstrate amazing feats of memory). The studies were conducted by Dr. A. R. Luria, a research psychologist, and his colleagues at the All-Union Institute of Experimental Medicine. Dr. Luria described the studies in a fascinating and highly readable small book called *The Mind of A Mnenonist.* In the book, which is a classic on visualization, Dr. Luria describes how the subject S. was able to call forth at will images (eidetic) he had recorded years earlier. S. was also able to control his heart rate and body temperature. He demonstrated to Dr. Luria that he could alter his pulse from his normal rate of 70 beats per minute to 100 beats, and then back to 70. S. told Dr. Luria, "What do you find so strange about it? I simply see myself running after a train that has just begun to pull out. I have to catch up with the last car if I'm to make it. Is it any wonder then that my heart beat increases? After that, I saw myself lying in bed, perfectly still, trying to fall asleep. . . . I could see myself beginning to drop off . . . My breathing became regular, my heart started to beat more slowly and evenly."[25]

In another experiment Dr. Luria measured the skin temperature of S.'s hands. In one minute S. raised the temperature of his right hand 2° and dropped the temperature of his left hand 1½°. In describing how he did it, S. said: "No, there's nothing to be amazed at. I saw myself put my right hand on a hot stove. . . . Oi, was it hot! So naturally, the temperature of my hand increased. But I was holding a piece of ice in my left hand. I could see it there and begin to squeeze it. And, of course, my hand got colder."[26]

Luria and his colleagues also documented that S. could alter the time it took the pupils of his eyes to adapt to the dark by visualizing various degrees of light, and could depress the alpha waves of his brain by visualizing a light flashing in his eyes. S.'s visualizations could also produce an involuntary reflex action— when he *imagined* hearing a sudden sound, his pupil size changed (the cochlea-pupil reflex).[27] The implications of all this data for the field of medicine are extraordinary. Through visualization a person can learn to control and use the body's own mechanisms for self-healing.

Visualization techniques have been used for healing, both by affecting body physiology in a general way (that is, via the relaxation response) and in a specific way (that is, by increasing blood flow to one area of the body). *Autogenic therapy*, a psychophysiologic technique developed in the 1930's in Germany by Dr. J. H. Schultz, a psychiatrist and neurologist, has worked successfully with both general and specific visualization effects. Autogenic therapy uses a series of standard visualization exercises to "facilitate autogenic (brain-directed, self-generating, self-regulatory) processes of a self-normalizing nature . . . which normally participate in homeostatic, recuperative . . . processes."[28] The exercises are done with patients sitting or lying in a relaxed state, with their eyes closed. Patients are advised to adopt an attitude of "passive concentration," that is they are told that (1) they should imagine that they are in "mental contact" with the part of their body they are concentrating on; (2) they should keep repeating a given formula, either visually or verbally; and (3) they should have a casual attitude toward the results of the exercise and toward their body.

There are six standard, 60-second autogenic exercises directly oriented to body physiology. In the first exercise, the patient concentrates on a feeling of heaviness in his arms and legs. Right-handed persons repeat to themselves, "My right arm is heavy." At the same time, the person can repeat a background image, "I am at peace," or visualize an image of a peaceful scene. Such background images are considered to enhance the effect of all the exercises. The feeling of heaviness in the arm characteristically spreads to the other extremities and is reinforced by verbal suggestions such as, "My leg feels heavy." Dr. Schultz states that the heaviness exercise produces relaxation and other physiological changes associated with self-healing.

The second standard exercise is similar to the first, but concentrates on feelings of warmth in the extremities. This exercise increases peripheral blood flow, relaxes blood vessels, and, again, promotes self-healing physiological changes.

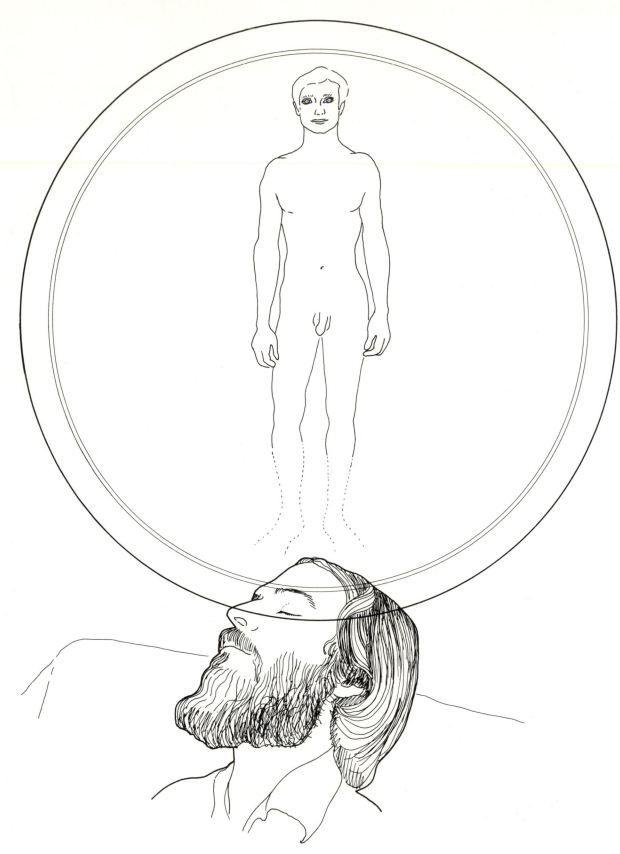

The Renaissance physician Paracelsus said man's physical body is formed by imagination from his invisible soul. Through visualization man creates health or disease. Illustration by Susan Ida Smith.

In the third exercise the patient repeats, "Heartbeat calm and regular." Dr. Schultz states that this exercise strengthens the self-regulatory processes of the heart. Dr. Schultz has found that "mental contact" with the heart is increased if the patient is instructed to become aware of his heart beating before he or she does this exercise.

In the fourth exercise patients are told to repeat to themselves, "It breathes me," or "Breathing calm and regular." This exercise promotes slow, deep, regular breathing.

In the fifth exercise the patient mentally repeats, "My solar plexus is warm." The patient can support this formula with the phrase, "Heat rays are warming the depth of my abdomen." Dr. Schultz says that this exercise calms the central nervous system, improves muscle relaxation, helps sleep, and increases blood flow to the abdomen.

The last exercise consists of the patient saying, "My foreheat is cool." Some patients use images such as, "The wind is blowing over my forehead." This exercise is found to be generally calming.

After a patient has learned the six standard exercises and can evoke those feelings quickly, he may go on to a series of meditative exercises. These exercises direct the patient to (1) spontaneously visualize colors, (2) visualize colors at will, (3) visualize objects at will, (4) visualize concepts such as happiness, (5) visualize feelings and people, and (6) ask questions of his unconscious, inner self. Dr. Schultz observes that all the positive effects of the standard exercises are reinforced by this meditative training.

Autogenic therapy is widely used in Europe and has been extensively researched. A seven-volume work on autogenic therapy by Schultz and Luthe cites 2400 studies.[29] Researchers examining the effects of the standard autogenic exercises have demonstrated a decrease in muscle potentials and a decrease in knee-jerk reflex (heaviness exercise), an increase in skin temperature (warmth exercise); and changes in blood sugar, white blood cell counts, blood pressure, heart and breathing rates, thyroid secretion, and brain wave patterns. Researchers have found that Autogenic Training profoundly affects body physiology in general and specific ways. The standard exercises affect the body in a general way by causing the hypothalmus to moderate the autonomic nervous system, producing homeostatic, normalizing and healing physiological changes. A particular exercise may affect a specific organ or physiological process.

Autogenic Training has been used in coordination with standard drug and surgical procedures in Europe to treat a broad range of diseases, including ulcers, gastritis, gall bladder attacks, irritative colon, hemorrhoids, constipation, obesity, heart attacks, angina, high blood pressure, headaches, asthma, diabetes, thyroid disease, arthritis, and low back pain. It has also been used in obstetrics and gynecology, dermatology, ophtamology, surgery, psychiatry and dentistry. Extensive research has been done which demonstrates the efficacy of Autogenic Training in the treatment of a number of chronic diseases. For example, in the treatment of asthma the standard exercises are used, postponing the breathing exercise till last and adding the formulas, "My throat is cool," and "My chest is warm." Four studies showed between 50 per cent and 100 per cent of the patients becoming symptom free after doing the exercises regularly[30] Patients with high blood pressure are given the standard exercises, with the heart exercise postponed until last. The heart exercise is changed to "Heartbeat calm and easy;" the forehead exercise is changed to "Forehead is agreeably cool. My head is clear and light." In the studies on high blood pressure some patients have shown excellent response.[31]

Patients with gastritis are given the standard exercises with the exception that patients with acute gastritis omit the formula "My solar plexus is warm" because it increases gastric blood flow and motility, which is contraindicated. One study of gastritis showed 70% of the patients were improved.[32] In another study Dr. Schultz had a patient with excessive gastric secretion gaze at the texture and dryness of blotting paper and imagine "absorbent dryness." Tests showed that the patient's excessive secretions normalized within 10 days of using these visualizations.[33]

Examples of specific formulae that Autogenic therapists use include the following:

Angina: "Heartbeat calm and easy."
Hemorrhoids: "My anus is heavy," "My pelvis is warm," "My anus is cool."
Itching or Pain: "Coolness."
Gynecological disorders: "My pelvis is warm."
Low-back pain: "My spine is heavy."

Autogenic Training has been designed to be used under the supervision of a therapist. Precautions, such as not using "My solar plexus is warm" in certain abdominal conditions, are included in Schultz's writings. Dr. Schultz also discusses other symptoms which arise and disappear during the therapy, discharges which he feels are caused by the patient's brain releasing tensions.

We have gone into detail discussing Autogenic Training because it is the most thoroughly researched and widely applied of all the systems of visualization used in healing. Autogenic training has many characteristics in common with hypnotherapy (especially autosuggestion), certain psychic healing techniques, relaxation healing techniques (such as Jacobson), ancient yogic techniques, and the more recent healing techniques taught in mind control courses.

Since 1965 Dr. Carl Simonton of Fort Worth, Texas, a radiologist specializing in the treatment of cancer, has been using visualization in the treatment of cancer with some success. While treating cancer patients, Simonton was struck by the fact that some of the patients who were classified as terminal recovered against all

odds. Doctors have long known of this phenomenon, which they call "spontaneous remission." (In 1958, one researcher compiled a list of 90 documented cases of spontaneous remission which could not be attributed to the patient's medical therapy.)[34] Simonton noticed that patients of his who improved against overwhelming odds had a consistently positive attitude toward life and toward the possibility of recovery. He also noticed that many terminal cancer patients lived to see an event which they had been looking forward to. Simonton believes that "everyone has cancer many times during his lifetime."[35] Normally a person destroys the "bad cells" with his immunological system. And Simonton knew that the mind can influence a person's immunological responses. Based on this information, he developed techniques designed to affect a patient's attitude toward living, and toward curing the cancer. Simonton's technique begins with teaching the patient how to go into a state of relaxation. The patient is then instructed to visualize a peaceful, natural scene. Next the patient is told to see his cancer in his mind's eye and to " 'picture his immune mechanism working the way it's supposed to work, picking up the dead and dying cells.' Patients are asked to visualize the army of white blood cells coming in, swarming over the cancer, and carrying off the malignant cells which have been weakened or killed by the barrage of high energy particles of radiation therapy. . . .

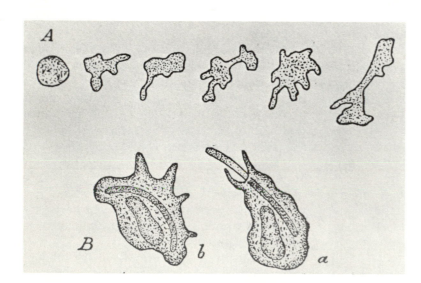

This drawing shows a white blood cell engulfing a disease bacteria. This process is one of the basic ways the body heals itself. Visualizing this sequence helps a person's body cure infection. This drawing is from *The Modern Physician*, by Andrew Wilson, 1882.

These white cells then break down the malignant cells which are then flushed out of the body. Finally, just before the end of the meditation, the patient visualizes himself well."[36]

Bob Gilley, a 40-year-old executive with cancer worked with Dr. Simonton using visualization. Before seeing Dr. Simonton Gilley's survival was estimated at 30%. Of his work with visualization Gilley has said, " 'I'd begin to visualize my cancer—as I saw it in my mind's eye. I'd make a game of it. The cancer would be a snake, a wolverine or some vicious animal. The cure, white husky dogs by the millions. It would be a confrontation of good and evil. I'd envision the dogs grabbing the cancer and shaking it, ripping it to shreds. The forces of good would win. The cancer would shrink— from a big snake to a little snake—and then disappear. Then the white army of dogs would lick up the residue and clean my abdominal cavity until it was spotless.' Gilley did this three times a day for 10 to 15 minute intervals. After six weeks of meditation, an examination revealed his tumor had shrunk by 75%. After two months Gilley had a cancer scan. There was no trace of the disease left in his body."[37]

Simonton's patients are educated about the functioning of their immune mechanism and are shown their own x-rays, as well as pictures of tumors healing. This procedure gives them specific images to visualize. Simonton also uses psychotherapy groups oriented toward the patient's discovering and confronting his or her deep negative attitudes and replacing them with more positive ones.

Simonton has found that patients who "follow instructions implicitly and are enthusiastic about getting better [show] marked relief of symptoms and dramatic improvement of condition"[38] (9 out of 9 patients). The implications of a study such as Simonton's are that a person's visualizations play a fundamental role in the cause of disease and its cure.

We have said that visualization can affect a person's blood flow, heart rate, and immune response—his total physiology. Moreover, visualization affects the creation of the body, the creation of all of its cells. Harold Burr, an anatomist from Yale Medical School, has said that all the protein in the body is renewed every six months or more frequently: "When we meet a friend we have not seen for six months there is not one molecule in his face which was there when we last saw him."[39] Burr says that electro-dynamic fields cause the molecules in cells to arrange themselves in particular patterns (for example, as a friend's face, or as healthy or diseased tissue).

There is evidence accumulating now that

PATIENT (CANCER) RESPONSE			Uncooperative doesn't follow instructions	Uncooperative rarely follows instructions	Usually follows instructions	Follows instructions and shows some initiative	Full cooperation. Follows instructions implicitly and is enthusiastic about getting better	
			− −	−	+ −	+	+ +	
Marked relief of symptoms and dramatic improvement of condition.	Excellent		0	0	0	11	9	20
Relief of symptoms, general condition improved	Good		0	2	34	31	0	67
Mild relief of symptoms	Fair		0	14	29	0	0	43
No relief of symptoms	Poor		2	17	3	0	0	22
	Totals		2	33	66	42	9	152

PATIENT ATTITUDE

Two-Year Study of 152 Patients Treated by Carl Simonton, M.D.

visualization affects the electric fields of the body. Scientists have shown that visualization drops skin resistance over acupuncture points as effectively as acupuncture therapy.[40] Scientists have postulated that acupuncture points and lines correspond to a flow of energy, possibly bio-plasmic energy (see the chapter on parapsychology).[41]

Researchers working with Kirlian photography have demonstrated that the energy field or colored, light area around a person's fingers varies with that person's visualizations or state of mind.[42] This line of research indicates that visualization affects the body in ways unknown to classical physiology, ways that are just beginning to be studied. These changes in the body's electric fields, or bio-plasmic energy fields, have long been thought to be related to health and disease. This energy concept has been called "chi" by the Chinese, "prana" and "kundalini" by the Indians, "baraka" by the Sufis. People have studied and experienced this energy through specific visualization exercises. They believe the exercises are related to healing, as well as to spiritual growth.

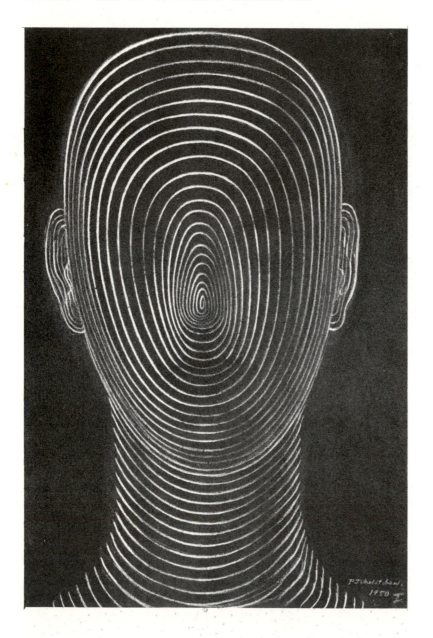

An artist's expression of an inner image which conveys the feeling of force fields. Pavel Tchelitchew. *Head*, 1950. Collection of The Museum of Modern Art, New York.

Healing energy can be moved through physical and mental exercises. This drawing of Marilyn Monroe illustrates the freeing of the body's energy. Illustration by Susan Ida Smith.

The visualizations we've been discussing in this chapter, like others in this book, may be either receptive or programmed. They may deal with a process (such as visualizing cancer cells being carried off by white blood cells) or with a final state (such as visualizing oneself recovered and healthy). Receptive visualizations in healing may concern (1) becoming aware of feelings concerning an illness, (2) determining the cause of an illness, (3) diagnosing an illness, and even (4) determining things that will help in its treatment. To work on their own healing, people can do a receptive visualization run, page 152. When they are at a receptive level, they can open themselves to images and feelings that surround their illness. For example, a person can open himself up to areas of dissatisfaction involved with his job, his homelife, his family and friends, his lifestyle. He may find sources of tension or dissatisfaction that are negative visualizations which are affecting his body's physiology. The book *Be Well*, by Mike Samuels, M.D. and Hal Bennett, contains a system of receptive visualization designed to help in determining the cause of an illness.[43] We will discuss the use of receptive visualization for diagnosis and treatment in the chapter on parapsychology.

Another way to use visualization in healing is to do a programmed visualization of the healing process. Examples of the healing process, given in *Be Well,* are, "erasing [or killing] bacteria or viruses, building new cells to replace damaged ones, making rough areas smooth, making hot areas cool, making sore areas comfortable, making tense areas relax, draining swollen areas, releasing pressure from tight areas, bringing blood to areas that need nutriment or cleansing, making dry areas moist (or moist areas dry), bringing energy to areas that seem tired."[44] People can invent their own programmed visualization using these processes as the basis. Images of healing may come from medical books, biology and science textbooks, and x-rays or lab values (see bibliography).

People can even create a fantasy image that symbolizes for them the healing process that they want to take place. "If you have a virus infection you might imagine the virus as tiny dots on a blackboard and then imagine yourself

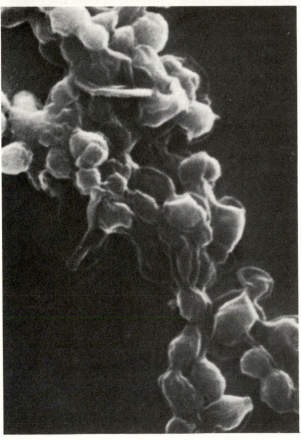

This photographic sequence shows *Candida albicans,* the organism that causes vaginal yeast infections, under a scan electron micrograph, magnified 5,000 times. The top picture shows flourishing Candida, the bottom picture shows Candida dying. The two images form a graphic example of healing in process. Visualizing images of disease organisms dying reinforces the body's natural healing mechanisms. Courtesy Ortho Pharmaceutical, New Jersey.

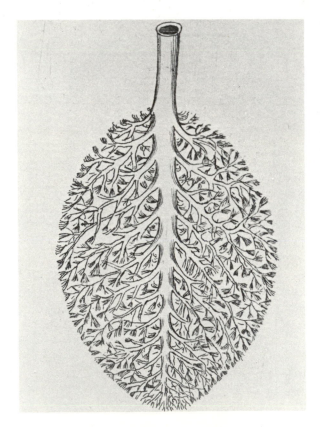

A drawing of the blood vessel structure of the lung from a 17th century medical text, *Dr. Collin's Anatomy.* The resemblance of the vessel structure to a tree is striking. A person visualizing this structure pulsing with blood will increase blood flow to their lungs.

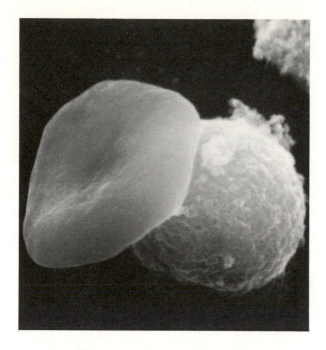 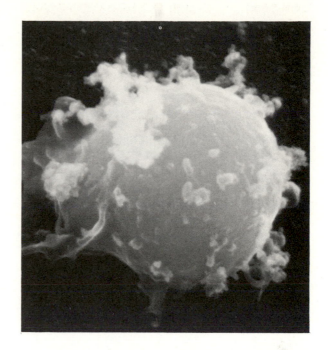

The lefthand photograph shows a red blood cell to the left and a white blood cell to the right. The right hand photograph also shows a white blood cell. Both are from the spleen of a mouse. Scan electron micrograph, magnification about 14,000 x. Images such as these help people to visualize healing processes within the body. Photographs courtesy of Ralph Camiccia.

erasing those dots."[45] If you have a cut or a broken brone, you might imagine new cells filling in the gap like stones being laid up by a mason. If you have chronic sinus problems, picture "The tubes leading from your sinuses to your nose. Imagine the tubes opening and the fluid draining out from the sinuses"[46] like a sink unclogging. If you have a headache, "imagine you have a hole in your head near the area of your headache. As you exhale your breath imagine that the pain is going out through that hole and is colored a murky muddy color."[47] A woman with a Fallopian tube infection can "Concentrate on relaxing the area around your Fallopian tubes. Imagine that the area is warm and pulsing with energy. Think about an area of your body that feels perfectly healthy to you; now imagine that feeling is spreading down to the area of the infection. Picture the Fallopian tubes themselves; imagine that they are open and draining and lined with pink, healthy mucosa."[48]

This last description not only involves the visualization of a healing process, it ends with an image of the healed or final state. Examples of healed states, which are provided by people's own bodies when they feel good, are "smoothness, comfort, gentle warmth, suppleness, moistness (not too wet, not too dry), resiliency, strength, ease and harmony."[49] For instance, if your throat is sore, you can "Imagine the mucous membrane in the back of your throat becoming pink, slightly moist, and feeling very comfortable, just as it feels in its most well state."[50] If you have a skin rash, "picture the skin being smooth, supple, vibrant, and soft"[51] and your normal skin color.

Another example of a final-state, healing visualization is provided by the Rosicrucians, a brotherhood of mystic masters in existence since the Renaissance: "1. Sit erect and relaxed with feet touching and hands clasped in your lap. 2. Visualize the sun, a great white flaming orb of prodigious energy. 3. Mentally lift your

231

consciousness from your body and go 'in spirit' to the sun. Enter into its flaming aura and proceed to the body of the sun itself. 4. Have no fear. You are a son of the sun and this is your rightful home. Let the sun's tremendous energy flow through your entire being invigorating and strengthening every particle. 5. After one minute return to your body, rise and go on with your daily tasks."[52]

The Rosicrucians use this visualization especially to increase energy[53] in the body to promote healing. The term *energy* as it is used here and in many other exercises is itself a visualization. It has no specific scientific correlate, but it may perhaps correspond with glucose, with bloodflow, with bioplasmic energy, with chi or with prana. In any case, throughout the ages, the image of energy flowing has been a part of the basic symbolism of healing.

Another Rosicrucian healing visualization deals with "white light." Like energy flow, "white light" is an ancient healing symbol used in visualizations by many mystical groups. A person is instructed to visualize himself surrounded by a cloud, a very brilliant white light like sunshine on fresh fallen snow. Then he is told to see that light becoming more and more concentrated in the area that is ill.[54] The Rosicrucians also direct that the white light be visualized along the spine near the injured area. This exercise is similar to a number of yogic techniques; visualizing white light along the spine corresponds to visualizing kundalini energy located in spinal energy centers or

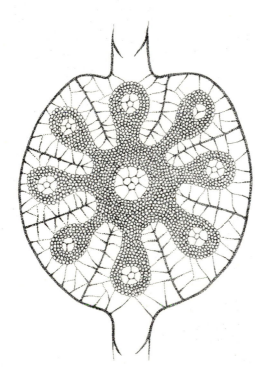

This diagrammatic cross-section of a lymph node helps people to visualize an important self-healing system in their body. The lymph node is a filter; it traps bacteria and viruses that have been ingested by the white blood cells and breaks them down. The cross-section of the lymph node, like many natural structures, is a mandala. Illustration by Susan Ida Smith, from *Be Well*.

Visualizing the sun or white light is a powerful final-state visualization for healing. The sun is the source of all life and energy on earth and is a symbol of rebirth. When a person visualizes himself surrounded by the sun he brings healing energy into his body and frees his body's own homeostatic mechanisms. Illustration by Susan Ida Smith.

chakras.[55] In *Psychic Healing*, by Yogi Ramacharaka, this exercise is given: "Form a mental picture of the inrushing Prana [vital force] coming in through the lungs and being taken up at once by the solar plexus, and then with the exhaling effort being sent to all parts of the system, down to the fingertips and down to the toes."[56]

In some circumstances the general nature of final-state visualizations allows the healing process to take place more naturally than more directed, process visualizations. An example of this is the contra-indication, in Autogenic Therapy, of having a patient with an ulcer visualize their solar plexus as warm, which would serve to increase blood flow to the area and increase acidity, possibly making the patient's condition worse.[57] Final-state visualizations like visualizing the stomach as healed and healthy avoid these kinds of problems.

Visualizing a healed state can involve simply seeing oneself as radiantly healthy. "See yourself in your mind's eye as you wish to be. . . . See yourself as healed, with your parts, organs and cells functioning normally."[58]

Visualizing oneself as healthy, rather than visualizing one's disease, is a basic technique in Christian Science healing. Christian Scientists teach a person not to be afraid that disease is an image of externalized thought. To cure disease a person is taught to break the dream of his senses, to argue mentally that he has no disease, that harmony is a fact and sickness is a dream.[59]

Most of the visualization exercises we've discussed in this chapter are general enough in nature that they can be used in any illness. In fact, their physiological mode of action involves a total body response.

Visualization has been used in interesting ways in specific medical areas. We will mention a few of the numerous examples available. In the early part of this century, William Bates, an American opthamologist, developed a natural system for vision-building.[60] One of his basic theories, and its accompanying techniques, is based on visualization. Bates' theories are based on the fact that seeing involves both a sense impression from the eye and the interpretation of that impression by the brain (see page 57). According to Bates, "When you can remember or imagine a thing as well with your eyes open as you can with your eyes closed your vision will improve promptly."[61] When a person visualizes a scene sharply and clearly, his eye actually relaxes, attains its normal shape, and send impressions which the brain recognizes as sharper. "Perfect memory of any object increases mental relaxation which results in a relaxation of the eyes and both together result in better vision."[62] "Mental picture work —true visualization"[63]—brings about relaxation. Bates used several visualization techniques in his work. He had his patients visualize things that they loved—peaceful scenes from nature, winning card hands, balloons drifting across the sky, breakers coming in on beaches—in order to relax their eyes.

Bates also devised a technique that involved swinging a visualized black dot. This technique, called "Shuttling the 'O'," relieved pain, increased blood circulation to the eye, and cleared the eye of debris. "1. In your mind's eye, that is, with eyes closed and in memory, draw a big black round 'O'. . . . 2. On the left black curve put a black dot; on the right curve put another black dot. . . . 3. Point your nose and attention from one dot to the other, from one black side of the 'O' to the other, from side to side until the 'O' seems to shuttle out of your way as you travel from one dot to the other."[64]

This exercise, one of ten similar Bates exercises, brings about relaxation and causes a person to concentrate (and hence forget about pain). In another exercise, Bates has his patients visualize jet blackness. He says that when a patient is able to do this, his eyes and mind will be completely relaxed.

Visualization has also played an important part in modern obstetrics and natural childbirth. Grantly Dick-Read, a world-famous British obstetrician, thought the effects of visualization were so significant that he devoted the second chapter of his book, *Childbirth Without Fear, The Original Approach to Natural Childbirth*, to mental imagery. Dr. Dick-Read says that "the memory, or even the visualization of an incident may surround a natural and physiological function with an aura of pain or pleasure so vivid that normal reflexes are dis-

Moving attention from one dot to the other and back until the circle seems to shift causes the eyes to relax and improves vision. This exercise was developed by the opthalmologist William Bates. Illustration by Susan Ida Smith.

turbed. . . . Fear of childbirth, then, becomes the great disturber of the neuromuscular harmony of labor."[65] Read goes on to say that young women are exposed to negative imagery through legends of suffering, from personal sources, even through religious history. In other words, the culture a woman is raised in is often the source of fear-producing images of childbirth. "When through association or indoctrination there is fear of childbirth, resistant actions and reactions are brought to the mechanism of the organs of reproduction. This discord disturbs the harmony or polarity of muscle action, causing *tension,* which in turn gives rise to nervous impulses interpreted in the brain as *pain.* . . . The fear of pain actually produces true pain through the medium of pathological tension. This is known as the 'fear-tension-pain syndrome' . . ."[66] Read says that fear affects blood flow to the uterus, allows waste products to build up in the tissues, and causes stimulation of the sympathetic nervous system. Read believes that an important part of natural childbirth involves educating the mother toward a positive image of childbirth,

thereby preventing the "fear-tension-pain syndrome."

This discussion of natural childbirth leads us into a discussion of the more general use of visualization in preventing and alleviating pain. It's now known that the perception of pain depends upon a person's visualization. Dr. L. S. Wolfe, an anesthesiologist who works with hypnosis, says pain is a learned sensation.[67] Let us give an example by way of illustration. All of us have had the experience of cutting ourselves when we were not aware, and only feeling pain when we later noticed the cut. The fact that pain is a sensation like touch, which is mediated in the mind, makes it particularly susceptible in the effects of visualization.

Glove-anesthesia is a visualization technique that has been used for years by hypnotists. For example, to induce glove anesthesia in a woman, a therapist tells the subject to imagine that her hand is relaxing, falling asleep, or immersed in cold water. When she feels tingling and numbness, she is told to concentrate on that sensation and deepen it. Within a short time, most subjects will not feel pain from a pin-prick. They will feel pressure, but no pain. A subject can then move the feeling of anesthesia to other parts of her body by placing her anesthetized hand on an area and allowing the feeling of anesthesia to flow from her hand to that area.

Another visualization to relieve pain involves picturing pain flowing out of the body. In Luria's book, *Mind of a Mnemonist,* the subject S. describes two visualizations he has used to control pain. "Let's say I'm going to the dentist. You know how pleasant it is to sit there and let him drill your teeth. I used to be afraid to go. But now it's all so simple. I sit there and when the pain starts I feel it . . . it's a tiny, orange-red thread . . . I'm upset because I know that if this keeps up, the thread will widen until it turns into a dense mass. . . . So I cut the thread, make it smaller and smaller, until it's just a tiny point. And the pain disappears.

"Later I tried a different method. I'd sit in the chair but imagine it wasn't really me but someone else. I, S., would merely stand by and observe "him" getting his teeth drilled. Let him

"Let your ideas of all disease symptoms become bubbles in your consciousness. Now imagine that these bubbles are being blown out of your mind . . . Watch them disappear over the horizon." This visualization is both healing and liberating. It helps a person to let go of images of disease and worry. It is especially useful when a person is learning about disease or is afraid of becoming ill. Illustration by Susan Ida Smith.

feel the pain. . . . It doesn't hurt me, you understand, but "him." I just don't feel any pain."[68]

We've seen in this chapter that visualization affects a person's health, both in underlying his assumptions and in specific disease processes. Following is a visualization which deals with people's attitudes about whether or not they will get sick and how they will heal.

Close your eyes. Breathe in and out slowly and deeply. Relax your whole body by whatever method works best for you. "Then let your ideas of all disease symptoms . . . become bubbles in your consciousness. Now imagine

that these bubbles are being blown out of your mind, out of your body, out of your consciousness by a breeze which draws them away from you, far into the distance, until you no longer see them or feel them. Watch them disappear over the horizon.

"Now imagine that you are in a place that you love. It may be the beach, in the mountains, on the desert, or wherever else you feel fully alive, comfortable, and healthy. Imagine the area around you is filled with bright, clear light. Allow the light to flow into your body, making you brighter, and filling you with the energy of health. Enjoy basking in this light. . . ."[69]

FOOTNOTES

1. Service, E. R. *A Profile of Primitive Culture*. New York: Harper & Brothers, Publishers, 1958, p. 24.
2. Service, E. R. p. 81.
3. Jayne, W. *The Healing Gods of Ancient Civilizations*. New Haven, Conn.: Yale University Press, 1925, p. 102.
4. Jayne, W. p. 111.
5. Jayne, W. p. 46.
6. Jayne, W. p. 46.
7. Hartmann, F. *Paracelsus: Life and Prophecies*. Blauvelt, N.Y.: Rudolf Steiner Publications, 1973, p. 111.
8. Hartmann, F. p. 112.
9. Frank, J. *Persuasion and Healing*. Baltimore, Md.: Johns Hopkins Press, 1961, p. 68.
10. Frank, J. p. 66.
11. Frank, J.
12. Frank, J.
13. Frank, J.
14. Frank, J. p. 42.
15. Cheek, D. personal communication.
16. Alexander, F. *Psychosomatic Medicine*. New York: W. W. Norton Co., 1950, p. 36.
17. Alexander, F. p. 38.
18. Beary, J. and H. Benson, "A Simple Psychophysiologic Technique Which Elicits The Hypometabolic Changes of the Relaxation Response," *Psychosomatic Medicine*. 36:119, 1974.
19. Beary, J. and Benson, H.
20. Miller, N. "Learning of Visceral and Glandular Responses," *Science*. 163:434–445, 1969.
21. Brown, B. *New Mind, New Body*. New York: Harper & Row, 1974, p. 4.
22. Green, E. From a speech at De Anza College, Cupertino, Cal.: Oct. 30, 1971.
23. Green, E.
24. Evans-Wentz, W. Y. *Tibetan Yoga and Secret Doctrines*. London, Oxford University Press, 1967, p. 203.
25. Lauria, A. *The Mind of A Mnemonist*. New York: Basic Books, Inc., 1968, p. 140.
26. Luria, A. p. 141.
27. Luria, A. p. 143.
28. Luthe, W. *Autogenic Therapy, Vol. I*. New York: Grune & Stratton, 1969, p. 1.
29. Luthe, W.
30. Luthe, W. *Autogenic Therapy, Vol. II*. p. 96.
31. Luthe, W. p. 72, Vol. II.
32. Luthe, W. p. 14, Vol. II.
33. Luthe, W. p. 16, Vol. II.
34. Everson, T. C. "Spontaneous Regression of Cancer," *Connecticut Medical Journal*, 22:637–643.
35. Bolen, J. "Meditation & Psychotherapy in the Treatment of Cancer." *Psychic*. July, 1973, p. 20.
36. Bolen, J. p. 20.
37. ____. *New Age Journal*. April 1974.
38. Bolen, J. p. 21.
39. Burr, H. S. *The Fields of Life*. New York: Ballantine Books.
40. Krippner, S. *Galaxies of Life*. New York: Interface, 1973.
41. Krippner, S.
42. Krippner, S.
43. Samuels, M. and Bennett, H. *Be Well*. New York: Random House-Bookworks, 1974.
44. Samuels, M. and Bennett, H. p. 144.
45. Samuels, M. and Bennett, H. p. 142.
46. Samuels, M. and Bennett, H. *The Well Body Book*. New York: Random House-Bookworks, 1973, p. 227.
47. Samuels, M. and Bennett, H. *The Well Body Book*. p. 219.
48. Samuels, M. and Bennett, H. *The Well Body Book*. p. 270.
49. Samuels, M. and Bennett, H. *Be Well*. p. 145.
50. Samuels, M. and Bennett, H. *Be Well*. p. 144.
51. Samuels, M. and Bennett, H. *Be Well*. p. 144.
52. Weed, J. *Wisdom of the Mystic Masters*. West Nyack, N.Y.: Parker Publishing Co., Inc., 1968, p. 79.
53. Weed, J. p. 78.
54. Weed, J. p. 80.
55. Evans-Wentz, N.Y.: p. 247.
56. Ramacharaka, Y. *The Science of Psychic Healing*. London: L. N. Fowler & Col. Ltd., 1960, p. 87.
57. Luthe, W. *Autogenic Therapy, Vol. II*.
58. Ramacharaka, Y. p. 87.
59. Eddy, M. B. *Science and Health*. Boston, Mass.: First Church of Christ, Scientist, 1934, p. 410–418.
60. Bates, W. *Better Eyesight Without Glasses*. New York: Henry Holt & Co., Inc., 1918.
61. Corbett, M. D. *Help Yourself to Better Sight*. No. Hollywood, Cal.: Wilshire Book Co., 1974, p. 221.
62. Bates. W.
63. Corbett, M. D. p. 44.
64. Corbett, M. D. p. 50.
65. Dick-Read, G. *Childbirth Without Fear*. New York: Harper & Row, 1953, p. 14.
66. Dick-Read, G.
67. Lecron, L. *Techniques of Hypnotherapy*. New York: The Julien Press, 1961.
68. Luria, A. *The Mind of A Mnemonist*. p. 141.
69. Samuels, M. and Bennett, H. *The Well Body Book*. p. 284.

Poets, artists, and creative people receive ideas through visualization. During visualization the artist is in a state of relaxed attention and often feels as if ideas come to him. Some artists feel their images come from their unconscious, others feel the images or ideas come from outside themselves. The Greeks visualized the source of ideas as a goddess, a Muse. In this painting Henri Rousseau has depicted *La Muse du Poete Guillaume Apollinaire.* Courtesy of Phoenix Art Museum.

Chapter 15

CREATIVITY

Elmer Green, a prominent biofeedback researcher at the Menninger Foundation in Topeka, Kansas, said in a speech given in 1971, "It seems increasingly certain that healing and creativity are different pieces of a single picture. . . . The entrance, or key, to all these inner processes we are beginning to believe, is a particular state of consciousness . . . [called] 'reverie'."[1] Visualization is a reliable means for getting access to the reverie state.

Dr. G. Wallis, a psychologist, theorizes that the creative process consists of four stages, a theory that is widely accepted by researchers in the field of creativity.[2] The four stages Wallis describes are based on the accounts of famous people's creative experiences. He calls the first stage *preparation*. In this stage, people consciously collect data and methodically file away potential images. They get together the tools and raw materials that seem applicable to the problems they are working on. During this preparatory stage a person's mood is often that of excitement and perplexity.

The second stage is called *incubation*. In this stage, people often release their conscious hold on the problem. They may rest, relax, or turn their attention in another direction. It is theorized that during this stage images in the unconscious shift and realign themselves. Most current researchers feel that this is the critical stage in creativity. Because this stage involves a non-ordinary state of consciousness and deals in images, we will discuss it at length in this chapter. In the incubation stage a person may get sudden glimpses of parts of the solution they seek.

The third stage Wallis calls *illumination*. It is the stage during which the solution or inspiration spontaneously occurs, often at an unexpected moment, usually accompanied by feelings of certainty and joy. This is the moment of discovery, when an artist sees the outlines of a new painting or a poet records the central lines of a new poem.

The fourth and final stage is called *verification* or *revision*. In this stage people work out details and make their ideas manifest in a form or structure. For a scientist this last stage involves organizing the data and conducting the experiments which will prove his theory. For a sculptor this stage involves solving the technical problems of pouring the bronze and polishing the finished product. This is a stage of effort and skill. Verification, like preparation, the first stage, is largely a conscious process.

The word imagination contains within it the word image, image meaning a mental picture. Most current theories of creative imagination hold that images exist and are stored in the unconscious mind, and that the conscious mind can become aware of them. It is believed that within the unconscious images can become associated to form streams of images, that they can juxtapose to form combination images, or coalesce and recombine to form entirely new images. All of this activity takes place without a person's awareness, but sometimes the results of these processes surface in conscious thought and catch his or her attention.

New images come to awareness as novel ideas, illuminations or flashes in ordinary consciousness. They seem to come most readily in a state of reverie. The reverie state includes dreams, daydreams, fantasies, visions, hallucinations, hypnagogic and hypnopompic imagery. All of these forms of the reverie state are closer to unconscious thought than to ordinary consciousness, and they provide access to consciousness for images from the unconscious. Receptive visualization likewise provides access to unconscious images. It gives people a more controlled means of getting in touch with the spontaneous new images that form the basis of their creativity.

Doing a receptive visualization, like experiencing other reverie states, allows new images to surface free of censorship from the ego. Ego censorship often inhibits the formation of new images and/or tends to make potential images combine in known, stereotyped ways.

Another characteristic of receptive visual-

ization is that it puts a person in an attitude of relaxed awareness. This state of relaxed awareness is also achieved by Eastern meditation techniques which have been used throughout history by artists in India, Tibet and Japan to stimulate their creative efforts.

Because creative images come from the unconscious part of the mind, which is not under the control of the ego, many people feel that such images come automatically—from outside themselves. For this reason some artists have felt that they must surrender to the creative impulse or even become possessed by it.

Psychiatrists have noted that images from the unconscious are often symbolic in nature. Creative people likewise frequently receive solutions to their problems in the form of symbolic images. The chemist Kekulé's apocryphal dream of a snake holding its tail in its mouth is one common example. Kekulé translated this symbol into workable scientific language with his conception of the benzene ring.

Once an idea comes to awareness a person works to complete his vision and give it form. Programmed visualization provides a means of trying out alterations in, and elaborations on, the original idea. Creative people have written about the importance of intuition and esthetic feeling in guiding them to choose which images to pursue. They have often found that the "correct" solution to a problem was the simplest solution and the one that felt good to them. In the Appendix we discuss ways that people can use their feelings to judge how closely an image or idea corresponds to an image from their inner center. This method works equally well for the creative person who is refining and fleshing out an idea.

E. W. Sinnott, an American biologist and philosopher, has postulated that creativity is a natural manifestation of life. Sinnott looks at imagination as a person's ability to picture in his mind's eye something he had not seen, something never experienced.[3] Like other creativity researchers, Sinnott believes the creative process takes place in the unconscious. "In dreams and half-dreaming states the mind is filled with a throng of images and fantasies . . . here the natural tendencies and predilections of living stuff come to expression. More

240

1930. B.6.   Gruppe W

In the mind unconscious images join, rejoin, become interlocked, and form entirely new images. This concept is beautifully expressed in this whimsical drawing by Paul Klee, *Group W, B.6* (1930). The mind seeks to find images that fit a particular set of data or solve a specific problem. In an attempt to make sense of the drawing most people find in the shapes a variety of figures. The Solomon R. Guggenheim Museum, New York.

than all, I think, here the organizing power of life fashions into orderly patterns the floating fantasies of the unconscious mind. . . . Among the throng of random images and ideas, the unconscious mind rejects certain combinations as unimportant or incompatible but sees the significance of others. By its means, order—intellectual, esthetic, perhaps spiritual order—is here distinguished from randomness. . . . One must recognize the operation in the unconscious of such an organizing factor, for chance alone is not creative. Just as the organism pulls together random, formless stuff into the patterned system of structure and function in the body, so the unconscious mind seems to select and arrange and correlate these ideas and images into a pattern. The resemblances between the two processes is close. The concept is worth considering that the organizing power of life, manifest in mind as well as in body—for the two are hardly separable—is the truly creative element. Creativity thus becomes an attribute of life."[4]

We can learn more about the biological basis of creativity from R. W. Gerard, a neurophysiologist from the University of Michigan. Gerard agrees with the four stages of creativity we discussed in the beginning of this chapter and with the idea that imagination involves the formation of new images in the unconscious. Gerard has considered the physiology of perception (see The Nature of the Image) in relation to imagination in detail. He states that three areas of the cerebral cortex act successively in the interpretation of visual stimuli. Research has shown that "direct stimulation of area 17 in a conscious patient produces an awareness of lights; when the next area, 18, is stimulated, the lights move about; and, if the next brain region is excited, complete pictures flash into consciousness—as of a man somersaulting toward the observer."[5] Thus awareness of sensation, awareness of an organized precept, and awareness of a formed image can be related to nervous impulses in specific areas of the brain. Gerard goes on to say that "in

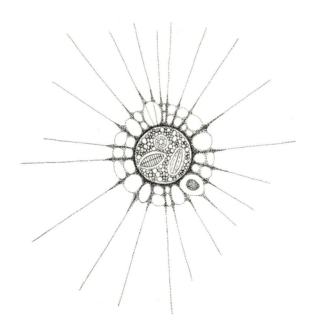
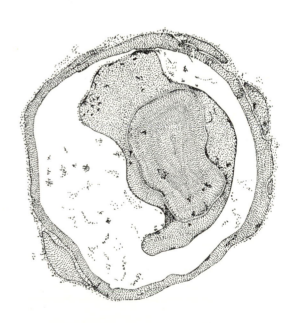

All life exhibits remarkable physical organization—from the simplest to the most complex organisms. Creativity involves finding patterns and ordering random, disparate elements. Thus life itself is creative. The drawing on the left illustrates a one-celled animal, Actino-sphaerium, magnified about 500 times. The drawing on the right illustrates a red blood cell in a capillary, from the muscle of a lizard, magnified 20,000 times. Illustrations by Susan Ida Smith, from Be Well, by M. Samuels and H. Bennett.

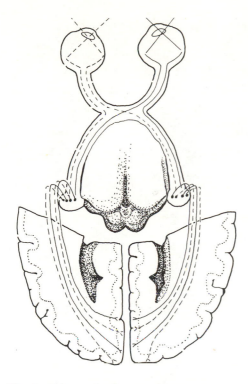

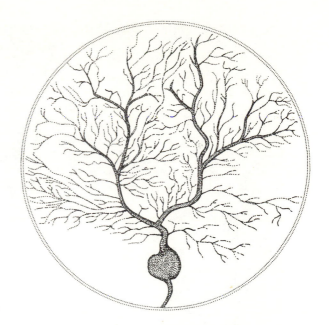

The brain's cerebral cortex interprets visual stimuli. Electrical impulses from the eye are read by a person as visual images. Illustration by Susan Ida Smith.

Each nerve cell in the brain is connected to many other cells in the brain and is affected by them. Thus nerve cells can fire one after another in loops. The whole brain can hum with activity, loops starting, summing, influencing each other. Each loop can be thought of as an image or idea. Illustration by Susan Ida Smith from *Be Well*.

supplying the substratum for thought, vision in man is surely of overwhelming importance. . . . Modern man is eye-minded."[6]

The eye sends impulses along the optic nerve to the brain. And each nerve cell in the brain is connected to many other areas by nerve fibers —"like an egg packed in sticky excelsior"[7]— and influenced by electric currents in neighboring cells. The nerve cells in the brain are also influenced by adjacent blood vessels, by oxygen, by the levels of blood sugar and salts, by temperature. As a result of these many influences, a particular nerve cell may or may not fire. An example of this is found in the fact that epinephrine (a hormone produced in the adrenal glands which is responsible for triggering the fight and flight response) lowers the threshold of electric current necessary for a nerve cell to fire. In the brain, nerve cells are continuously active and fire in circuits or loops "with excitation going round and round like a pinwheel . . . throwing off regular sparks of activity on each cycle."[8] Because the firing of a

nerve cell is dependent on many influences, including the firing of many cells around it, the whole brain is like a loom with loops of activity affecting each other.

Each loop can be looked upon as a "closure." "Closure is a basic property of mind. It is . . . the ability to separate a figure from its ground, to formulate a gestault, or form, to identify an entity."[9] Closure, then, can be thought to represent an idea, a new image put together from separate images—each caused by the firing of a group of neurons—the new image put together by the formation of a neuronal loop. "By such various mechanisms, then, great masses of nerve cells—the brain acting as a great unity— act together; and not merely do two or a billion units sum their separate contributions, but each is part of a dynamic fluctuating activity pattern of the whole. This is the orchestra which plays thoughts of truth and beauty, which creates creative imagination."[10]

The mechanism by which an idea remains in the brain is unclear. If a loop is fired again and

The ability to discern figures, to recognize meaningful patterns, is a basic attribute of the brain. This ability has been called *closure* since it is thought to be the result of the closure of a loop of firing neurons in the brain. Georges Seurat's work in particular evokes a feeling of closure because of his use of dots which, when observed from a distance, are interpreted by the viewer as shapes and figures. *Child in White (Study for ''A Summer Sunday on the Grande-Jatte'')*, 1884, The Solomon R. Guggenheim Museum, New York.

again, it becomes stable and may be more easily fired again. Some researchers have speculated that the nerve cells themselves change and/or that new proteins are synthesized.

In the early 1960's, Harold Rugg, an educator at Columbia University, proposed a theory of creativity which embraced the theories of Sinnott and Gerard and added to them. Rugg wrote that "the brain-mind works continually as a modeling computer, averaging through feedback the organism's learned (stored) assumptions . . ."[11] To Rugg this meant that the impulses sent from the eye to the brain had to be interpreted by the mind: for example, if you hold a smoking pipe in front of you and turn it around, the impulses registered by the eyes provide the brain with entirely different data at each moment. The interpretation of this data as a discrete object, rotating upon its own axis, involves the equivalent of highly complicated projective geometry. (To experience this yourself, see our visualization example with the tea kettle, page 126). In its interpretation, the mind's computations serve to average or pool the data until it fits in with a learned concept, in this case, "pipe." Rugg said that "the brain-mind's alpha rhythm [one of a number of brain wave patterns] is the mechanism that scans for best fit."[12] Each visual concept, such as "pipe," that the mind holds is, in a real sense, a symbol, in that it suggests a meaning for a seemingly random set of visual impulses.

In cybernetic terms, man is looked at as a goal-seeking animal, one who reacts to a particular situation "by seeking the simplest possible act in response to what the situation demands."[13] In terms of visual stimuli, the brain responds to a particular set of visual data by seeking the simplest possible visual concept that fits that data. In its creative expression, Rugg said, the mind is seeking a solution to a problem, is striving to create a metaphorical image—be it visual, poetic, etc.—that interprets disparate sensations, feelings and/or data.

Rugg postulated that all this work goes on or takes place in the *transliminal mind*, a "dynamic ante-chamber" between the conscious and unconscious mind. He felt that the threshold between the conscious and unconscious is the only part of the mind that is free from censorship. Rugg believed that the transliminal

mind, the operating ground of creativity, is the area identified with Eastern meditation states, with light auto-hypnotic trances, with intuition, and with hypnagogic states. The transliminal mind is characterized by a state of relaxed readiness or relaxed concentration. In this state, a suggestion to create is accepted and the creative ideas are viewed by the person as real. To solve a problem, then, the transliminal mind freely, without censorship, scans its images to come up with the simplest meaningful symbol-image that answers the problem confronting it. When such a symbol-image is found, an idea is born. This is the creative flash. This moment, this flash, is what makes possible a new work of art or an experimental breakthrough.

Rugg felt that the creative flash is inseparable from, and necessary to, physical manifestation of a creative idea. He believed that the creative moment naturally results in action—like an ideo-motor action in which an imagined activity is accompanied by minute but measurable amounts of muscular activity (as demonstrated in Jacobson's experiments). Neuromotor enhancement studies have shown that these minute muscle movements resulting from a mental image are vastly intensified as the sensory system relays back to the mind impulses which confirm that the body is responding to the image. This is the first step toward the physical manifestation of a mental image.

Sinnott, Gerard and Rugg would likely agree that stored images in the mind, which are the basis of new, creative ideas, are derived from a person's past perceptions. The most graphic elucidation of this theory is presented in John Livingston Lowe's book, *The Road to Xanadu*.[14] In it, Lowe tracks down in extraordinary detail the sources of the images used by Coleridge in his poetry. He traces the images of sea serpents in "The Rime of the Ancient Mariner" to travelogues of explorers, to scientific treatises on fish, and even to the works of Shakespeare which Coleridge had read.

Carl Jung approaches the origin of new images from a different point of view. Rather than trace a particular image to a past perception, Jung speculates on why man is interested in a particular image at all. Jung divides artistic creation into two categories: *psychological art*, which "deals with materials drawn from the realm of human consciousness—for instance, with the lessons of life,"[15] that is with the experiences of life in the outer world; and *visionary art*, which "derives its existence from the hinterland of man's mind—that suggests the abyss of time separating us from pre-human ages, or evokes a super-human world of contrasting light and darkness."[16]

Jung is interested in the second category of artistic endeavor. He concerns himself with "images of the vision," which remind him of dreams and fantasies. As to the origin of these images, Jung speculates, "Is it a vision of other worlds, or of the obscuration of the spirit, or of the beginning of things before the age of man, or of the unborn generations of the future?"[17]

Jung feels that these primordial images are "true symbolic expression—that is the expression of something existent in its own right, but imperfectly known."[18] Believing in psychic reality (see page 8), Jung thinks these images are no less real than physical reality. Rather than theorize that visionary images are the result of a creative goal, he speculates that they often come unbidden, and certainly are not under the command of the ego: "Do we delude ourselves in thinking that we possess and command our own souls? And is that which science calls the 'psyche' not merely a question mark arbitrarily confined within the skull, but rather a door that opens upon the human world from a world beyond, now and again allowing strange and unseizable potencies to act upon man . . .?"[19] Jung feels that the artist

Carl Jung divided artistic creation into two modes: psychological and visionary. Psychological art deals with love, family, environment—the realm of conscious experience, the understandable. The photograph *Arizona Stovepipes*, by Michael Samuels, can be looked at as an example of this mode. Visionary art deals with images of happenings beyond the grasp of human understanding. Jung suggests that such images, which are not from everyday life, may be cold or foreign. *The Hunted Sky (Le Ciel Traqué)* (1951), by Yves Tanguy, is an excellent example of visionary art. Oil on canvas, 39⅛ × 32⅜ inches. Collection, The Museum of Modern Art, New York. Kay Sage Tanguy Bequest.

occasionally catches sight of spirits, demons, gods of the night world. And when an artist draws a mandala-like shape it is as objective a portrayal of inner experience as a bird picture is of a bird. Jung goes on to say that such basic shapes and designs, like myths, are truly the clearest expression of inner experience. ''The primordial experience is that source of his [the artist's] creativeness; it cannot be fathomed, and therefore requires mythological imagery to give it form.''[20] Furthermore, Jung believes that the primordial experience needs bizarre images in order to express itself. He believes that these visions are the expressions of the collective unconscious; that they are built into the body, inherited by each person, and therefore have primitive character. When an artist is able to see and express these visions, he transcends personal, single man and speaks as mankind to mankind. Jung believes that the artist is seized by a drive that works through him. The work of an artist has a life of its own, as if it were a unique person. When an artist creates a work of art, it becomes his ''fate and determines his psychic development. . . . [The artist] has drawn upon the healing and redeeming forces of the collective psyche . . . in a return to the state of *participation mystique*—to that level of experience at which it is man who lives, and not the individual . . .''[21] Thus, when mankind needs a particular image for its growth or health, Jung believes it comes through an artist and is expressed for mankind as the artist's creation.

In the rest of this chapter we will deal with some of the ways in which visualization can be used to increase a person's ability to receive creative ideas. All of the theories of creativity that we have discussed share the common assumption that creative ideas are formed in the unconscious, following an appropriate and necessary period of incubation. Likewise most psychologists working in the field of creativity agree that the incubation stage is the critical one—although, of course, the stages of preparation, illumination, and verification are essential. These theorists also concur that the creative idea comes to consciousness in a moment of illumination. This moment is thought to take place in a state of non-ordinary consciousness, known variously as transliminal mind (Rugg), primordial mind (Jung), an altered state of consciousness, or the reverie state. Visualization is a means of willfully putting oneself in this particular state of mind —specifically to become aware of images from unconscious. In terms of creativity, the images that are experienced are unique new images that the unconscious mind forms in its natural tendency to solve problems (Rugg), create order (Sinnott), and harmonize the universe (Jung). The moment of illumination is itself a visualization experience—a dense, wordless, sensory experience symbolic of a highly complicated concept.

Many famous people have written about their creative experiences. Indeed such writings are the basis for the theories of creativity that we have discussed. The accounts that we are most interested in deal specifically with the periods of incubation and illumination. Many accounts have been written—a number of which have become famous examples frequently quoted in the literature. Several fascinating books have been published from these chronicles. Perhaps the best, most readily-available book, Brewster Ghiselin's *The Creative Process*, contains forty such accounts.[22] These reports come from people in widely diverse fields—science, the visual arts, writing and music—throughout history. We will quote from a number of them in order to give a more personal feeling for the nature of the creative experience.

Bertrand Russell, the 20th century philosopher and mathematician, has said, ''In all the creative work that I have done, what has come first is a problem, a puzzle involving discomfort. Then comes a concentrated voluntary application involving great effort. After this, a period without conscious thought, and finally a solution bringing with it the complete plan of a book.''[23]

Henri Poincaré, a 19th century French mathematician who discovered fuchsian functions, has written, ''Every day I seated myself at my work table, stayed an hour or two, tried a great number of combinations and reached no results. One evening, contrary to my custom, I drank black coffee and could not sleep. Ideas rose in clouds; I felt them collide until pairs in-

When people deal with the invisible and unknowable, they must resort to metaphor. This occurs at the frontiers of even the most quantitative sciences. It is said that Albert Einstein first realized the distortion of time and space by imagining himself riding on a ray, traveling the speed of light. Illustration by Susan Ida Smith.

terlocked, so to speak, making a stable combination. By the next morning . . . I had only to write out the results, which took but a few hours."[24] Another time, after a great deal of deliberate work, Poincare reports, "Disgusted with my failure, I went to spend a few days at the seaside, and thought of something else. One morning, walking on the bluff, the idea came to me, with just the same characteristics of brevity, suddenness, and immediate certainty." Poincare also discusses receiving ideas "in the morning or evening in bed while in a semi-hypnagogic state."[25]

Albert Einstein has said he discovered the theory of relativity by picturing himself riding on a ray of light. He has written (1925) that words did not play a role in his thought. "The psychical entities which seem to serve as elements in thought are certain signs and more or less clear images which can be 'voluntarily' reproduced and combined."[26]

The composer Wolfgang Mozart wrote in a letter in 1789, "When I am, as it were, completely myself, entirely alone, and of good cheer —say, traveling in a carriage, or walking after a good meal, or during the night when I cannot sleep; it is on such occasions that my ideas flow best and most abundantly. . . . My subject [music] enlarges itself, becomes methodized and defined, and the whole, though it be long, stands almost complete and finished in my mind, so that I can survey it, like a fine picture or a beautiful statue, at a glance. Nor do I hear in my imagination the parts successively, but I hear them, as it were, all at once."[27]

The composer Peter Tchaikovsky, in a letter of 1878, write, "The germ of a future composition comes suddenly and unexpectedly. . . . It takes root with extraordinary force and rapidity . . ." frequently in a somnambulistic state. "I thought out the scherzo of our symphony—the moment of its composition —exactly as you heard it."[28]

The Impressionist painter Vincent Van Gogh once wrote to his brother Theo, "I have a lover's clear sight or a lover's blindness . . . I shall do another picture this very night, and I shall bring it off. I have a terrible lucidity at moments when nature is so beautiful; I am not conscious of myself any more, and the pictures come to me as in a dream . . ."[29]

Max Ernst, a 20th century abstract painter, has written, "The sight of an imitation mahogany panel opposite my bed had induced one of those dreams between sleeping and waking. . . . I was struck by the way the floor . . . obsessed my nervously excited gaze. So I decided to explore the symbolism of the obsession, and to encourage my powers of meditation and hallucination I took a series of drawings from the floorboards by dropping pieces of paper on them at random and then rubbing the paper with black lead. As I looked carefully at the drawings that I got in this way—some dark, others smudgily dim—I was surprised by the sudden heightening of my visionary powers, and by the dreamlike succession of contradictory images that came one on top of another with the persistence and rapidity peculiar to memories of love. . . ."[30] Ernst said that he worked by "excluding all conscious directing of the mind (towards reason, task, or morals) and reducing to a minimum the part played by him formerly known as the author of the work . . . the artist's role is to gather together and then give out that which makes itself visible within him."[31]

D. H. Lawrence, the English writer, in describing his paintings, said, "Art is a form of supremely delicate awareness . . . meaning at-oneness, the state of being at one with the object. . . . The picture must all come out of the artist's inside . . . it is the image as it lives in the consciousness, alive like a vision, but unknown."[32]

Henry Moore, the English sculptor, wrote that the sculptor "gets the solid shape, as it were, inside his head. . . . He mentally visualizes a complex form *from all round itself*: he knows while he looks at one side what the other side is like; he identifies himself with its center of gravity, its mass, its weight; he realizes its volume, as the space that the shape displaces in the air."[33]

Samuel Taylor Coleridge, describing himself and how he wrote his poem "Kubla Khan," said, "In consequence of a slight indisposition, an anodyne [opium] had been prescribed, from the effects of which he fell asleep in his chair at the moment that he was reading the following sentence, or words, of the same substance, in 'Purchase's Pilgrimage': 'Here the Khan Kubla

Vincent van Gogh has said that he painted *The Starry Night* (1889) as in a dream. Indeed, the radiant energy of his mystical view of the heavens is an unearthly vision. And we, like he, are mesmerized by it. Oil on canvas, 29 × 36¼ inches. Collection, The Museum of Modern Art, New York. Acquired through the Lillie P. Bliss Bequest.

commanded a palace to be built . . .' The author continued for about three hours in a profound sleep, at least of the external senses, during which time he has the most vivid confidence, that he could not have composed less than from two to three hundred lines; if that indeed can be called composition in which all the images rose up before him as things. . . . On awakening he appeared to himself to have a distinct recollection of the whole, and taking his pen, ink, and paper, instantly and eagerly wrote down the lines that are here preserved.''[34]

Amy Lowell, an American poet and critic, wrote of her creative experiences, ''The first thing I do when I am conscious of the coming of a poem is to seek paper and pencil. It seems as though the simple gazing at a piece of blank paper hypnotizes me into an awareness of the subconscious. . . . I find that the concentration needed for this is in the nature of a trance. . . .''[35]

Another 20th century American poet, Stephen Spender, has said, ''A poem is like a face which one seems to be able to visualize clearly in the eye of memory . . . [The poet's] job is to

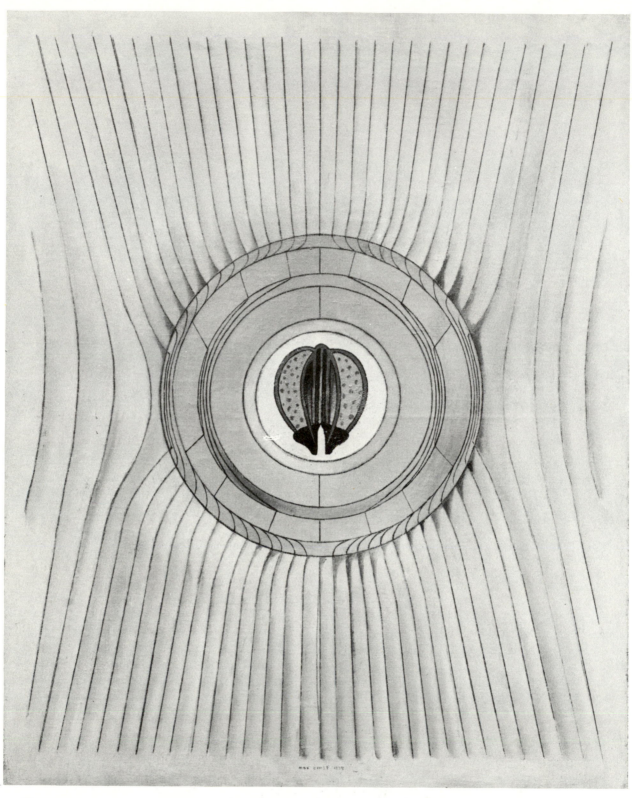

The artist Max Ernst used *frottage,* a process which involves recording the texture of
materials by dropping paper on them and rubbing the paper with charcoal or lead pencil.
The outlines and textures thus recorded stimulated Ernst to see hypnotic visions which
Ernst would highlight on the rubbing. Ernst has described himself as a "blind swimmer,"
who has made himself clairvoyant and has seen. *The Blind Swimmer,* 1934; oil on canvas,
36⅜ × 29 inches. Collection, The Museum of Modern Art, New York. Gift of Mrs. Pierre
Matisse and Helena Rubenstein Fund.

recreate his vision."[36]

Dr. John Yellot, a research engineer studying glass and steam, has written that he worked very hard, without any success, on a problem and was becoming obsessed with a fear of failure. Then, "I was riding on a crowded bus, much absorbed in these [personal] matters so irrelvant to my scientific work, when suddenly the solution of the problem came to me. In a flash I visualized the drawing of the proper design of the apparatus, immediately drew out a notebook, and, without consciousness of my surroundings, wrote down the answer. I knew it was right . . ."[37]

One element common to all these accounts is that the creative people were looking back on their creative experiences. As a result of this retrospective contemplation, the artists occasionally realized that the creative moment is not purely a matter of chance or utterly beyond their control. Many of the artists became aware of certain recurrent characteristics of the illuminative situation. None of them were actively seeking the solution to the particular problem at the moment of their illumination. Rather, they all were thinking of other matters, relaxing, taking walks in the country, gazing at something, or were half-asleep, under the influence of drugs, or dreaming. In short, they were engaged in situations and activities that we described earlier (page 136) as being productive of receptive visualizations. Some of the creative people even noted that they could manipulate the images that came to them in their illuminative flash. We will have more to say about this later in this chapter.

In the last twenty-five years research psychologists have begun to study the possibility of increasing people's creative abilities. Dr. Alex Osborn developed a technique that he called *applied imagination*, which became the basis of thousands of problem-solving courses. Sidney Parnes, a psychologist at the University of Buffalo, conducted a series of experiments using Osborn's technique of *deferred judgment*. This technique separates idea formation from evaluation or judgment of the worth of the idea. In the first part of the technique, called the "green light stage," students are instructed to free themselves of any inhibition, to open their minds, and to let their imaginations soar. In the

second stage, students are told to evaluate the ideas they have come up with, retaining those that seem even remotely possible.

This applied imagination technique was purposely designed to allow time for ideas to incubate. Results of Parnes' experiments showed that, in relation to a given problem, students who used the technique of deferred judgment got over twice as many unique and useful ideas as students who did not.[38] The green light stage works by uncensoring the subjects' thought, thereby freeing them from habit, labeled thought, and the fear of failure or ridiculousness that is associated with ego-bound thought. In this respect the green light stage is similar to such altered states of consciousness as the reverie state.

Another technique developed to increase personal creativity is discussed in the book by W. J. J. Gordon called *Synectics*. The Synectics technique involves free association around the subject of a problem, concentrating on metaphors and analogies. Gordon gives the example of a group that is trying to invent a new kind of roof that will be white in summer (reflecting heat) and black in winter (absorbing heat). The free associations of the group included discussion about things in nature that change color such as weasels, chameleons, flounders. One group member said that the flounder changes color by releasing pigment from lower layers of skin to higher ones. Another group member, hearing this, had a flash of insight: build the roof out of black material with tiny white balls in it which will expand when the roof gets hot, rise, and turn the roof white. The Synectics experience seems to allow people to become aware of metaphors, similarities, and images from their unconscious without ego censorship.

Results from courses using deferred judgment and Synectics provide experimental evidence that people can increase their ability to receive creative ideas. Researchers in the field have found in the accounts of creative people conditions that seem to foster the emergence of creative ideas. These conditions can be divided into two categories: mental attitudes and actions. Mental attitudes provide the background for receptive visualizations. Jerome Bruner, a Harvard University psychologist

253

Henry Moore, the British sculptor, says that a sculptor must be an expert in visualizing three-dimensional form. Moore suggests that the sculptor must visualize his work as if he were holding it completely enclosed in the hollow of his hand and respond to form in three dimensions. As a person walks around a Moore sculpture he feels a rhythm to the rise and fall of every angle and curve which makes him feel that the piece has been visualized from every viewpoint by the artist. The *Family Group* (1948-49)—bronze (cast 1950), 59¼ × 46½ inches. Collection, The Museum of Modern Art, New York, A. Conger Goodyear Fund—is remarkable in the complexity and harmony of its three-dimensional vision. The Moore etching, *Rocks, Arch and Tunnel* (Plate XVI, from *Elephant Skull*, 1970) shows the extent to which Moore visualizes his pieces in advance as three-dimensional forms. Etching, printed in black, 13⁹/₁₆ × 9¾ inches. Collection, the Museum of Modern Art, New York. Gift of the artist and Galerie Gerald Cramer, Geneva.

and educator, suggests a number of conditions for fostering new ideas, of which the first are *detachment* and *commitment*. By detachment Bruner means disengaging oneself from conventional or known ideas; by commitment he means having a deep need to understand the problem or express new ideas. The second set of conditions Bruner suggests is *passion* and *decorum*. By passion Bruner means the "willingness and ability to let one's impulses express themselves in one's life through one's work;"[39] by decorum he means respect for the forms and materials that limit one's work. Next Bruner stresses the importance of *freedom to be*

dominated by the object, by which he means permitting the creative work to develop its own life, and being willing to serve it. Bruner also talks about *deferral* and *immediacy*. He says that one must have an urge to find the problem's solution immediately, but at the same time must have the ability to wait for the "right" solution. The last condition Bruner describes is *internal drama*. By that he means the ability to become aware of mental figures that personify different aspects within oneself and that approach the problem in different ways. Bruner suggests that an interchange between these figures often produces novel solutions to problems.

In his book, *How To Think Creatively*,[40] Eliot Hutchinson, a Cambridge University researcher, has included a number of "hints" about the attitudes that underly the birth of a creative idea:

- increase your motivation by anticipating the satisfactions of achievement.
- increase your preparation by believing the problem is not insoluble for you.
- believe the answer will come, although you may have to wait or grow.
- realize that rest is essential when you feel defeated by a problem.

During the resting period—the stage of incubation—there are certain things people can do to increase the natural flow of inner images. That is, in terms of this book, there are things people can do to make it most likely that they will receive spontaneous visualizations. Hutchinson makes the following suggestions:

- organize your time so as to give yourself as complete freedom as possible.
- be alone and silent.
- determine the conditions under which you are most likely to spontaneously visualize, and watch for images.

In many of the accounts we quoted earlier creative people were aware of specific physical conditions or actions during which they got their ideas. Mozart commented that his ideas often came while riding in a carriage or walking after a good meal. Some of the conditions most frequently cited by creative people include the following:

- riding in a car, train, or airplane
- walking at leisure
- bathing
- reading (not with an eye to solving the problem), watching television or a movie
- listening to music
- napping, waking in the middle of the night (hypnagogic state)
- dreaming
- under the influence of drugs
- meditating
- gazing or staring at an object

The basic state of relaxed attention fostered by such activities corresponds with the non-ordinary states of mind that we said earlier accompany the visualization state and creative illumination.

Beyond these more general conditions, many creative people have written of personal, idiosyncratic conditions that they believed fostered their creative visualizations. Many of these conditions are sensory in nature—the psychologist McKellar has referred to them as sensory cues.[41] In an earlier chapter we mentioned that the poet Schiller was stimulated by the odor of decomposing apples, which he always kept in his desk. Knowlson, in 1917, wrote a book in which he collected examples of such idiosyncracies.[42]

- Samuel Johnson spoke of needing a purring cat, an orange peel, and a cup of tea in order to write.
- Proust wrote in a soundproof room.
- Kipling needed jet black ink to write.
- Kant wrote at precise times of day, in bed, staring at a tower (and was so disturbed when trees began to obscure the tower that he had them cut down).

Hutchinson lists further examples:

- Rousseau thought bare-headed in full sunshine.
- Beethoven poured cold water over his head, believing that it stimulated his brain.
- Rossini covered himself with blankets while composing.
- Dickens turned his bed to the north, believing that the magnetic forces helped him to create.

The poet Stephen Spender has written that he depended on coffee and tobacco while writing. These eccentricities, he believed, provided "a kind of anchor of sensation with the physical world . . . [because during concentrated creative effort] one completely forget[s], for the time being, that one has a body."[43]

Whatever the reason for such eccentricities, they seem to be characteristic of creative effort. Many creative people have speculated that such conditions increase concentration, which, as we have discussed, increases the ability to visualize (see page 136). Another theory explaining the universal usefulness of these phenomena is simply that creative people themselves have faith in them—faith being an important condition underlying visualization. One can even speculate that, through conditioning, these idiosyncratic actions come to act as stimuli which trigger or induce a visualization state. The whole process is then reinforced by the occurrence of visualizations and by the usefulness of them.

We have included many details concerning the conditions associated with creative effort in order that readers can develop their own conditions for receiving spontaneous visualizations and thereby increase their creativity.

We believe that the conditions surrounding creative effort, the conditions under which people receive spontaneous visualizations, can be consciously created, reproduced, and controlled. The door to the creative state is receptive visualization. Receptive visualization occurs at a level of non-ordinary consciousness which produces inner imagery. The receptive visualization state has all the characteristics associated with the stages of incubation and creative illumination:

- access to images from the unconscious
- lack of ego censorship
- freedom from labeled ideas
- identification with the object-image
- autonomy of imagery
- symbolization

Here then is a receptive visualization for creativity. Find a quiet space where you will be undisturbed, which has been favorable for past creative work. Make yourself comfortable. Let your eyes close. Breathe in and out deeply, allowing your abdomen to rise and fall. As your

The tantric artist uses visualization to realize his images. The artist first ceremonially purifies himself, then proceeds to a solitary place. There he invokes the gods, meditates on friendliness, compassion, sympathy, impartiality, and emptiness. Then he calls upon the deity he wishes to portray. Only when a brilliant mental image of the deity appears before him does he begin to paint. Tibetan tanka, *Green Tara,* 18th century. Asian Art Museum of San Francisco, The Avery Brundage Collection.

breathing becomes slow and even you will feel relaxed. Now deeply relax your whole body in stages by whatever technique works best for you. Deepen this heavy, warm feeling of relaxation by slowly counting backwards from 10 to 1. As you mentally say each number you will become more and more relaxed.

You are now at a level where you can easily receive images. The images will be vivid; they are images which will provide you with inspirations for artistic endeavor, scientific work, or creative problem-solving of any kind. As the images appear before you, you will feel even more relaxed; the images will become clearer and clearer; and they will flow more and more easily. At this creatively receptive level of mind let the images flow, watching them appear and disappear, combine, coalesce, merge and separate. Let the images play before your inner senses. As you continue to see the images, allow your receptive state of mind to open the doors of your psyche. At this deeper level of mind, let the images have access to all

the perceptions of your mind and body, of mankind, and of the universe. Stay at this level as long as you wish. When you return to your ordinary level of consciousness you will remember clearly the images you have visualized. Allow your receptive unconscious to choose the images you will remember most clearly. Each time you receptively visualize in this way, the images will be clearer, flow more easily, and be more useful to you in your creative work.

To return to your ordinary level of consciousness, count from 1 to 3, and gently move some part of your body. Allow yourself to return slowly and open your eyes when you feel ready to do so. You will feel rested, full of energy, and ready to do whatever work is necessary to put your creative ideas into form.

A variation on this receptive visualization run might include creating a mental studio or laboratory, visualizing sensory cues that will stimulate the flow of ideas, using time distortion or *accelerated mental processes* (AMP) to

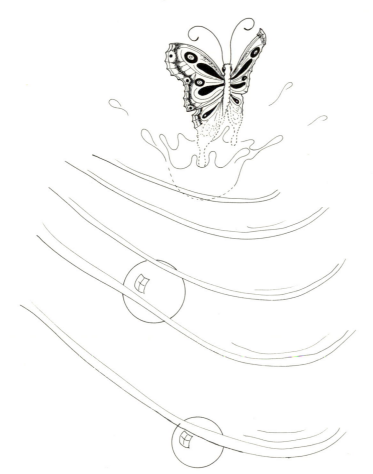

Releasing images from the unconscious and bringing them to awareness is basic to the creative process. Illustration by Susan Ida Smith.

do a large amount of creative work in a short time, or meeting an inner guide to help a person with his or her work.

Mind Games, a book by the psychologists Robert Masters and Jean Houston, provides several visualization runs dealing with creativity, and with AMP in detail. Part of one of Masters and Houston's exercises deals with meeting a teacher under accelerated time conditions: "And now you will be given one minute of clock-time, and this will be sufficient to give you the experience of meeting in the world of images a most exceptional artist who is also a very good art teacher, and this teacher will ask you to draw. You, the artist, will draw. And then you will receive from this teacher instruction about how to make your artwork more effective. You will practice, doing more drawings, receiving more criticism and instruction, and benefiting from it, and you will have all these experiences beginning now!"[44]

The characteristics of the images that people receive during receptive visualization are the same as those of images received by creative people in a moment of illumination. These characteristics include the following:

- a feeling of correctness
- a feeling of surprise
- a sense of the answer appearing whole
- a sense of the answer appearing in short-hand form—one image or word expressing a complicated concept
- a sense of the answer appearing in symbolic form
- a feeling of release and joy if the image relates to an important problem

Programmed visualization gives creative people a chance to work with and perfect their creative ideas. It can be the counterpart to and/or a continuation of the receptive visualization state. During programmed visualization creative people can work with their images, manipulate them, and evaluate changes without having to resort to material form. In programmed visualization, people can be guided by their feelings in selecting which changes are

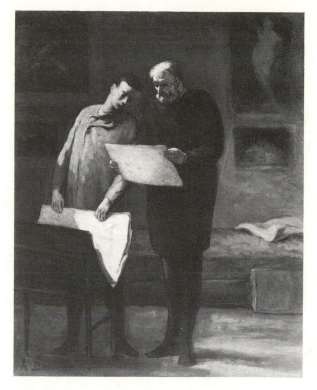

The image of *Advice to a Young Artist* is a useful visualization which can help a person with his art work. A visualized art teacher can act as a Muse and critic in a person's own mental studio. Honore Daumier, 1808-1879, The National Gallery of Art, Washington. Gift of Duncan Phillips, 1941.

"right" and which should not be used. Using feelings as a guide corresponds to the artists' intuition and to the organizing center we discussed earlier in this chapter. Using programmed visualization to play with images and evaluate them can make it possible for artists and creative people to achieve a final image even though they did not initially visualize the image as a whole. People can even develop an image entirely, based on no initial visualization, by building it up piece by piece, keeping "lines" that feel good and erasing those that do not. In this way, people can bring to awareness images that exist in their unconscious that they have previously been unable to visualize.

"Once I saw a spotted lady whose belly was round like a ball."

"I dreamed I saw a man with bats in his hands and three birds stuck in his head."

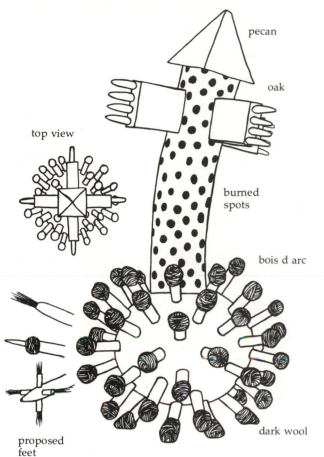

pecan

oak

burned spots

bois d arc

top view

dark wool

proposed feet

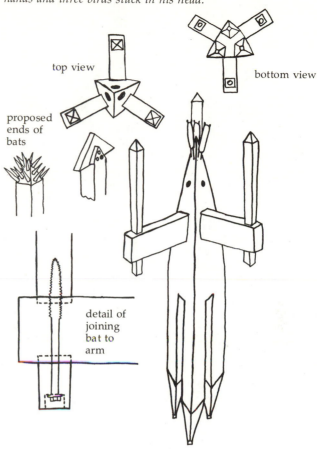

top view

bottom view

proposed ends of bats

detail of joining bat to arm

James Surls, an American sculptor, says that his images come from two sources. The outward source is physical reality, things people see. When a person sees things outside he can rearrange the images in his mind, catalogue the images, file them, pull them out periodically to think about them, and some day use them for a sculpture. *Once I Saw a Spotted Lady Whose Belly Was Round Like A Ball* is from an outward source. Surls saw a lady in a Safeway store who had three spots on her neck and was pregnant. She looked like she had a basketball under her dress, her belly was firm and round. Surls felt that this was a strong image, a phenomenon that had significance. A week later he made the sculpture. Photograph courtesy of Dallas Museum of Fine Arts.

I Dreamed I Saw A Man With Bats in His Hands and Three Birds Stuck in His Head came from the inward source, from a waking dream. Surls was lying on a couch, listening to music, floating in space, letting images come by. The image for this piece was a sentry guard. When Surls first saw the birds he didn't understand what they were about and doesn't have any explanation now. He saw them on his image and didn't see any reason to take them off. Before Surls fixed this image in his mind concretely enough to say that he was going to build it he manipulated the image around in his mind. He saw it tumbling and rolling, took an arm off, put an arm on, changed the bats from pointed to dull. When Surls visualizes his sculpture he keeps in mind the limitations of logs, chainsaws, and drills, and doesn't visualize anything he can't do with these tools and these materials. Photograph courtesy of Delahunty Gallery, Dallas, Texas (page 262).

Here is a programmed visualization for creativity: Close your eyes. Breathe in and out slowly and deeply. Allow yourself to relax. Go to a level where you can visualize, where images flow freely and easily. Allow an image to come to mind that you are working on or that you saw in a receptive visualization. Move your eyes over the image and allow it to become more and more vivid and clear. As you scan the image, you may see it change before you or you may get an idea for changing it. Now look at the changed image. If the image feels "right,"

retain the new form. If the image does not feel "right," allow it to return to its previous form. In changing the image you may find yourself mentally using the tools inherently required by the materials, or you may find the image changes without the need of such tools. Continue working in this manner, making changes, until you feel the image is complete. When you have finalized an image or images, return to your ordinary conscious state by counting slowly from 1 to 3 and gently moving a part of your body.

FOOTNOTES

1. Green, E. From a speech at De Anza College, Cuperinto, Cal.: Oct. 30, 1971.
2. Patrick, C. *What Is Creative Thinking*, New York: Philosophical Library, 1955.
3. Vernon, P. E. *Creativity, Selected Readings*. New York: Penguin Books, 1970, p. 109.
4. Vernon, P. E. p. 111.
5. Ghiselin, B. *The Creative Process*. New York, New American Library, 1952, p. 237, from R. W. Gerard, "The Biological Basis of Imagination."
6. Ghiselin, B. p. 242.
7. Ghiselin, B. p. 243.
8. Ghiselin, B. p. 244.
9. Ghiselin, B. p. 230.
10. Ghiselin, B. p. 246.
11. Rugg, H. *Imagination*. New York: Harper & Row, 1963, p. 309.
12. Rugg, H. p. 309.
13. Rugg, H. p. 297.
14. Lowes, J. *The Road To Xanadu*. Boston, Mass.: Houghton, Mifflin, 1927.
15. Jung, C. G. *Modern Man In Search of A Soul*. New York: Harcourt, Brace & World, Inc., 1933, p. 155.
16. Jung, C. G. p. 156.
17. Jung, C. G. p. 157.
18. Jung, C. G. p. 162.
19. Jung, C. G. p. 162.
20. Jung, C. G. p. 164.
21. Jung, C. G. p. 172.
22. Ghiselin, B. *The Creative Process*.
23. Hutchinson, E. *How To Think Creatively*. New York: Abingdon-Cokesbury, 1949, p. 26.
24. Ghiselin, B. *The Creative Process*. p. 26 from H. Poincaré, "Mathematical Creation."
25. Ghiselin, B. p. 38.
26. Ghiselin, B. *The Creative Process*. p. 43, from A. Einstein, "Letter to Jacques Hadamard."
27. Ghiselin, B. *The Creative Process*. p. 45, from W. Mozart, "A Letter."
28. Vernon, P. E. p. 59.
29. Stone, I. *Dear Theo.: The Autobiography of Vincent Van Gogh*, New York, New American Library.
30. Ghiselin, B. *The Creative Process*. p. 64, from M. Ernst, "Inspiration to Order."
31. Ghiselin, B. p. 65.
32. Ghiselin, B. *The Creative Process*. p. 72, from D. H. Lawrence, "Making Pictures."
33. Ghiselin, B. *The Creative Process*. p. 74, from H. Moore, "Notes on Sculpture."
34. Ghiselin, B. *The Creative Process*. p. 85, from S. Coleridge, "Prefatory Note to Kubla Khan."
35. Ghiselin, B. *The Creative Process*. p. 111, from A. Lowell, "The Process of Making Poetry."
36. Ghiselin, B. *The Creative Process*. p. 116, from S. Splender, "The Making of A Poem."
37. Hutchinson, E. p. 22.
38. Parnes, S. *Creative Thinking*. New York: Scribner's, 1962.
39. Gruber, H. *Contemporary Approaches to Creative Thinking*. New York: Atherton Press, 1962, p. 12.
40. Hutchinson, E. p. 229.
41. McKellar, P. *Imagination and Thinking*. London: Cohen & West, 1957, p. 125.
42. Knowlson, T. S. *Originality: A Popular Study of the Creative Mind*, Wroner Laurie, 1917.
43. Ghiselin, B. p. 114.
44. Masters, R. and Houston, J. *Mind Games*. New York: Dell Publishing Co., 1972, p. 139.

OTHER READING

1. Gordon, W. *Synectics*. New York: Harper & Row, Publishers, 1961.
2. Sartre, J. *Imagination*. Ann Arbor, Mich.: University of Michigan Press, 1972.

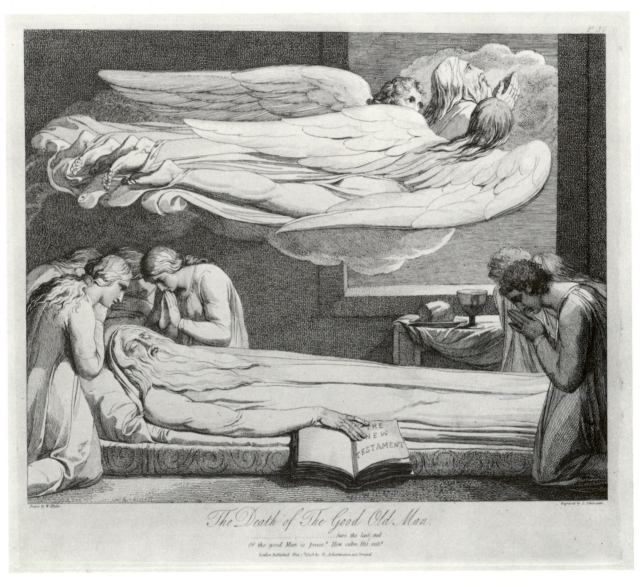

The Death of The Good Old Man.

Sure the last end
Of the good Man is peace! How calm His exit!

London Published Mar. 1st 1813 by R. Ackermann, 101 Strand

Parapsychology has always invoved itself with the question of survival after death. This print by the British artist, William Blake (1757-1827), is called *The Death of the Good Old Man*. It shows two angels escorting the man's soul to heaven. This particular vision is Christian in orientation: the presence of the Bible and the bread and wine symbolize the old man's faith. Each person has a visualization of what will happen to him after death; this visualization affects all that he does in life. The Metropolitan Museum of Art, New York. Harris Brisbane Dick Fund, 1917.

Chapter 16

PARAPSYCHOLOGY

Parapsychology is a term adapted from the German by the famous Duke University scientist, J. B. Rhine, to describe extraordinary phenomena including extrasensory perception, mental telepathy, clairvoyance, psychokinesis, and survival of the personality after bodily death. The description is a scientific one but, paradoxically, the field of parapsychology deals with an area that has long been avoided by scientists: the relationship between mind and matter. Paranormal phenomena are ones that, up till now, have eluded explanation by commonly held scientific laws and theories.

Extrasensory perception (ESP) refers to a response to or awareness of an event not based on known sensory perception or logical, rational thought. *Mental telepathy* refers to the transmission and/or reception of thoughts and mental states from one person to another, without inference or known sensory means (ESP of mental states). *Clairvoyance* refers to knowledge of an object or events without inference or known sensory means (ESP of objects and events). *Psychokinesis* (PK) deals with direct mental influence on material objects. Parapsychology also embraces other phenomena which science has heretofore left unexplained: faith or psychic healing, precognition or prediction of the future, the existence of auras, levitation, water-witching and dowsing, Kirlian photography, and the existence of spirits and ghosts.

All of these phenomena have been discussed, debated, and/or believed in since the time of primitive man. Priests and shamans were believed to have special powers—including power over objects. Egyptian priests had a well-developed magic whose tradition has continued to the present day in the form of secret occult societies and mysticism. The Indian Yoga Sutras of Patangali devote a major section to "supernatural" powers, discussing knowledge of past and future, knowledge of the

The *Korwar Figure* from West Irian, New Guinea is believed to contain the spirit of a deceased person. The figure serves as a means of communication between the living and the dead, by which the living can seek advice from the spirit and secure protection. M. H. de Young Memorial Museum, San Francisco. Gift of Henry J. Crocker Estate.

mind of any living being, and knowledge of previous lifetimes. The Yoga Sutras assume that such powers are experienced by everyone who practices yoga and attains spiritual realization. In fact, the Yoga Sutras caution against becoming involved with powers as a primary focus, because they can turn the mind from one's spiritual progress.[1] The spontaneous experience of psychic phenomena by lay people throughout the ages has likewise led to widespread legends and superstitions about, and belief in, paranormal phenomena.

Science as we know it today is based on prediction, experimental verification, and duplication. When scientific methodology first began developing around the time of Galileo the Catholic Church was the most powerful social and political institution in the Western world. Scientific historians, such as J. Bronowski, have speculated that the Church felt that science posed a threat to its doctrines and allowed science to continue its work unheeded only after the scientific establishment declared it would leave matters of God and the soul to the Church, and confine itself to the realm of matter.[2] As a result of this de facto agreement, science, whose authority grew tremendously over succeeding centuries, became an establishment based solely on the exploration of material reality. Today, science has the social and political force the Church had in the 1600's; like the Church then, the bulk of the scientific establishment in recent times has been slow to consider new ideas and phenomena that do not fit within the relatively narrow confines of known scientific laws. This same hesitancy confronted the great discoveries of evolution, the divisibility of the atom, the discovery of the unconscious, and the theory of relativity as well. It confronts parapsychology today.

In spite of this kind of resistance, a small group of scientists and a number of well-known laymen began scientific studies into parapsychological phenomena in the late 1800's. The center for this early parapsychological research was the Society for Psychical Research in London. The board of this society included at times several Nobel prize-winning scientists

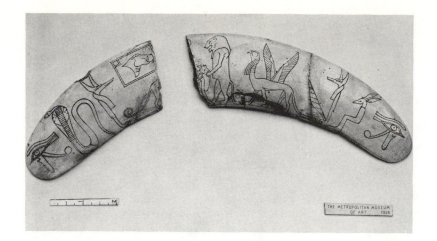

An Egyptian magic wand decorated with fantastic animals and amuletic signs, including the Eye of Horus, a visualization symbol. 12th dynasty. (2000–1788 B.C.). The Metropolitan Museum of Art, Carnarvon Collection, Gift of Edward S. Harkness, 1926.

such as J. J. Thompson, the discoverer of the electron, and Lord Rayleigh, the discoverer of argon. The society's psychic studies included the collection and examination of spontaneous occurrences of parapsychological phenomena, description of and experimentation with specially-gifted psychics and mediums, and ESP experiments with cards and word-guessing.

In 1930, J. B. Rhine set up a parapsychology laboratory at Duke University and began a tradition of mathematical quantification that has typified American parapsychology until recently. Researchers have conducted a large number of experiments concerning ESP, clairvoyance, telepathy, and psychokinesis—including most recently studies using computers. These studies have proven to

researchers and many scientists in other fields the existence of psychic phenomena. The experiments have also demonstrated some characteristics of the phenomena: ESP is not limited by space, time, or material barriers such as electromagnetic wave shields; people who believe in ESP have been shown to score a higher percentage of correct answers on any experiment than those who do not. Despite the quality and quantity of these experiments there are many scientists who are skeptical of such results and who even deny the existence of the phenomena. The most common contemporary arguments against affirmative data are fraud and poor experimental construction and control.

This picture shows a "soul ship" from the Asmat tribe in New Guinea. The soul ship is believed to provide transportation to the supernatural world for dead people's souls. The ship is used in a ceremony in which souls of people who have recently died are sent out of the village. The figures in the ship are visualizations of animal spirits. Courtesy of The Museum of Primitive Art, New York.

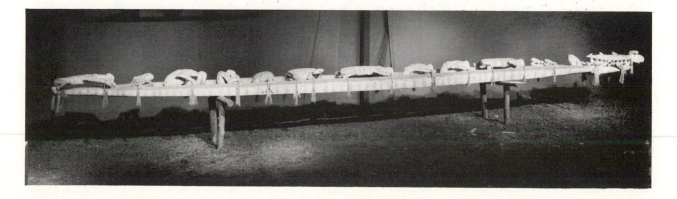

One of the most basic visualizations in all history is the resurrection of Christ. This miracle was confirmed by the disappearance of his body from the sealed tomb. The lefthand panel from this early 15th century altar piece by a Master active in Aragon shows *The Resurrection of Christ.* Scientists are just beginning to study the survival of life after death. M. H. de Young Memorial Museum, San Francisco. The Samuel H. Kress Collection.

Parapsychology has always investigated reports of people appearing after their death. This is an area that the scientific establishment had avoided since the early 1600s. The righthand panel, *Christ Appearing to the Magdalen,* is based on New Testament accounts of Christ appearing to his followers following his crucifixion. M. H. de Young Memorial Museum, San Francisco. The Samuel H. Kress Collection.

While this experimentation and controversy was going on in the West, a number of researchers in Russia, Bulgaria and Czechoslovakia carried out a large volume of work on all manner of psychical phenomena. These experiments were chronicled in Ostrander and Schroeder's book, *Psychic Discoveries Behind the Iron Curtain.* Many of these studies concentrated on the physics and the physiology of psychic phenomena, in addition to attempting to obtain statistical proof of their existence. Knowledge of and enthusiasm about this research has created a new field in the West, paraphysics, which attempts to deal with the explanation of psychic phenomena in terms of energy. EEG's (brain waves) and Kirlian photography have been extensively studied. Kirlian photography, which studies high frequency electrical fields, has visually demonstrated that energy fields seem to surround objects and living things. The energy fields around people's fingers have been shown to vary with mood, and to be stronger around psychic healers while they are healing. Brain wave recordings (EEG's) have shown changes in telepathic receivers similar to those in their senders.

Researchers have not yet developed theories that fully explain parapsychological phenomena, but a number of theories have been put forth. In fact, since the beginning of parapsychological research, each researcher has had his own theory about the phenomena. Most of these have been more in the nature of philosophies or beliefs than actual scientific hypotheses. Like philosophies, these theories have dealt with cause and effect, the mind-body problem, predestination and free will, and the relationship between spirit/energy/matter. One theory holds that the brain puts out electro-magnetic waves similar to radio waves. This theory does not account for the fact that telepathy is unaffected by distance and can operate through a variety of shields.[3] Another postulates the existence of a new type of energy —psychic energy. The Czechs have called it psychotronic energy; the Russians, bioplasmic energy. This is the energy believed to be visually represented by Kirlian photography. As yet, no one has been able to measure this energy, and its method of action is not under-stood. But there is a possibility that it corresponds to that phenomena yogis refer to as prana or kundalini.

A number of researchers have recently postulated the existence of *psi-fields*. These are thought to be fields that emit or receive extremely small quantas of energy, and that, like gravitational fields, surround every object.

Gardner Murphy, a Harvard psychologist and prolific author on parapsychology, hypothesizes that paranormal phenomena may depend on relationships between people; that sender, receiver, and situation form a matrix in space, and that a real form or trace is left when an event takes place in that matrix. The Oxford University professor of logic, H. H. Price, has speculated that a part of each person's mind— the collective unconscious—connects with all other minds in the world and is continuous. Price says that the human mind in ordinary consciousness represses information from this area and that such censorship is released in non-ordinary states of consciousness, when paranormal phenomena seem to occur.

G. Tyrrell, an English electrical engineer and parapsychologist postulates that each person has an unconscious part of his personality, called the *subliminal self*, which exists beyond space, time, and language. Tyrrell believes that during paranormal phenomena subliminal selves enter into relationships with one another by means of vehicles—dreams, hallucinations, mental images, or emotions. J. B. Rhine speculates that the mind "goes out" and makes contact with objects. He also believes that there is a mind energy which is different from physical energy.

A British neo-Freudian psychoanalyst, Jan Ehrenwald, theorizes that there is a level of personality in the unconscious called the *psi level*. He believes that this level is a part of every person and is beyond the confines of space and time. He suggests that highly emotional information, such as the death of a close friend, is more likely to come to awareness at the psi level. This could explain the instances of spontaneous telepathy or clairvoyance that often occur surrounding a death.

Another theory, put forth by Thouless and Weisner, British psychologists, holds that both ordinary sensory perception and paranormal knowledge are the result of the same brain processes. The brain interprets both kinds of information as an image. In sense perception, the sensory system sends data to the brain to interpret; in parapsychological cognition, there is direct contact between the subject and the object. Thouless and Weisner believe that a part of the mind they call *shin* goes out and makes contact with the object.

Lawrence LeShan, a New York psychologist and psychic healer, theorizes that paranormal events occur in "clairvoyant reality," as opposed to "sensory reality."[4] He believes that clairvoyant reality is a different metaphysical state, in which paranormal phenomena are viewed as normal. Like a number of other researchers, he believes clairvoyant reality to be a non-ordinary state of consciousness.

C. G. Jung felt that because paranormal phenomena don't depend on time or space, they can't be thought of as causal. So he postulated that synchronicity, which operates as a non-causal relationship, provides a better explanation. "Synchronicity takes the coincidence of events in space and time as measuring something more than chance, namely, a peculiar interdependence of objective events among themselves as well as

In this print by the Dutch artist Rembrandt (1606–1669) Christ is shown with a large aura around his head, radiating tremendous energy. This picture is a detail from *Christ With the Sick Around Him, Receiving Little Children.* Recently scientists have shown auras around healers through kirlian photography. The Metropolitan Museum of Art, Bequest of Mrs. H. O. Havemeyer, 1929. The H. O. Havemeyer Collection.

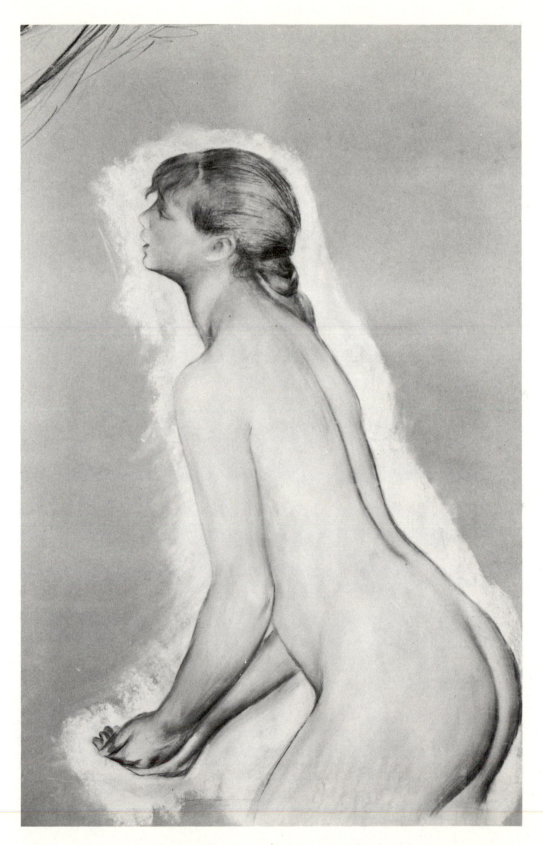

This pastel study, *Nude,* by the French artist Auguste Renoir conveys the feeling of an
energy field surrounding the young woman. Many parapsychologists have theorized that
a form of energy—*psi* fields or *bio-plasmic* energy—accounts for parapsychological
phenomena. Courtesy of The Art Institute of Chicago.

with the subjective (psychic) states of the observer or observers."[5] Jung's concept of synchronicity looks at simultaneous events of matter and mind, for example "the coincidence of inner and outer events," as meaningful. Dr. Marie-Louise von Franz, a professional colleague and close friend of Jung, says these "meaningful coincidences" occur when an archetype is activated in the unconscious of the individual concerned, and synchronistic events almost always accompany crucial phases of personal growth. Thus events involving mind and matter that seem coincidental have been found to be strongly associated with images from the inner center. The implications of this type of event are that when a person clearly holds an image in mind, the energy of his visualization can influence the external world. In terms of the Jungian concept of synchronicity, the release of

energy surrounding the freeing of an archetype —bringing the image from the inner center to awareness—is accompanied by spontaneous changes in the material, external world. These changes can appear to a person to be coincidences—they seem to occur naturally.

Precognition, the ability to predict future events, provides another stimulus for theories of paranormal phenomena. These theories all deal with time, and to account for precognition, they postulate new theories about it: for instance, that the present is not a point, as is generally thought, but an area; that time is a fourth dimension of space; that time is a form of energy; that there are particles which travel faster than light, which move from the future to the past.

Despite the variety of these theories, certain characteristics of the paranormal experience are

One explanation given for telepathy and clairvoyance is that thoughts actually have form. Theosophists believe that each thought gives rise to vibrations which gather matter from the surrounding atmosphere into various forms and colors which can be seen by clairvoyants. Spiral shapes, for example, are believed to indicate a desire to understand, to know more. Illustration by Susan Ida Smith.

A number of modern artists and musicians have allowed their works to create themselves through the laws of chance. They believe that chance is not random but relates in a pure way to their inner center or to a cosmic reality. Working in this manner bypasses the narrow view of the ego and allows universal images to be created. *Collage with Squares Arranged According To The Law of Chance*, Jean Arp, 1916-17. Collection of the Museum of Modern Art, New York, Purchase.

generally agreed upon. First, that it is associated with the unconscious part of the mind. Second, that paranormal experiences tend to occur during non-ordinary states of consciousness, such as trances, dreams, or hypnagogic states. Third, that the information received in a paranormal experience comes in the form of images—generally visual, but also auditory and sensory. Researchers have found other evidence linking paranormal experiences with characteristics of both non-ordinary consciousness and visualization. Paranormal experiences seem to be increased and strengthened by a relaxed state of body and mind, by

faith in the phenomena, and by an expansive, imaginative frame of mind.

At the Maimonides Hospital Dream Laboratory in New York LeShan trained subjects to be able to achieve a state he calls "clairvoyant reality." This training involved relaxing the subjects' beliefs in conventional time and space, increasing their faith in paranormal psychology and teaching them to achieve an altered state of consciousness through meditation and concentration exercises. LeShan found that after such training the subjects increased their clairvoyant ability.

Milan Rzyl, a pioneer Czechoslovakian parapsychologist now working in the United States, has used hypnosis to train people to experience such paranormal states as clairvoyance and telepathy. He took subjects who showed no previous paranormal ability and trained them through self-hypnosis. After their training, the subjects scored very high on ESP card-guessing tests.

Both Rzyl's and LeShan's work back up the assumption that paranormal experiences take place in an altered state of consciousness. Moreover, it demonstrates that paranormal abilities can be learned. Rzyl, in his hypnotic training, used visualization extensively. "Like many Communist researchers, Rzyl believes that the ability to visualize sharply is central to good psychic performance." In his training, Rzyl first hypnotized his subjects, then trained them to visualize objects—such as flowers, naked women, or racing cars—chosen according to each subject's interest. After the subjects had learned how to visualize imaginary objects, Rzyl asked them to visualize real objects or situations, such as a clock in the room hidden behind a screen or whatever was going on in an adjacent room. As the subject experienced these visualizations, Rzyl encouraged them with positive suggestion.

In the *Persistence of Memory* the Spanish Surrealist Salvador Dali shows a world where space and time have lost their linear qualities and shadows of events past and future exist alongside the happenings of the transient present. Through visualization Dali has journeyed to his inner world and seen a view of time and space that 20th century physicists have begun to explore. Oil on canvas, 1931; Collection of the Museum of Modern Art, New York.

Then he guided them on imaginary trips to real places, asking them to "see scenes as they would really look in everyday actuality."[6] In so doing, his subjects were able to accurately describe real scenes occurring across town, find lost objects, and correctly guess ESP cards.

Rzyl found that his subjects showed only chance abilities when they were not hypnotized. Therefore, the next step in his training was to teach his students to achieve a state of consciousness, by themselves, in which they could experience paranormal phenomena: a state of "active mental inactivity." One subject was taught to "balance on a gray thread between sleep and wakefulness. All thought inhibited, she must wait patiently, passively for the psychic impression to appear. After the images formed, she must switch on the active, critical side of her mind to evaluate and report on what filled her psychic screen."[7]

We believe that the state of consciousness achieved by subjects of LeShan and Rzyl's

Clairvoyance is based on the ability to visualize distant scenes and places as if they were perceptions of everyday life. This photograph shows a Guatemalan market at dawn. The early morning haze on the mountains and the black shadow of the door frame heighten the visionary quality of this image. The first sun rays of morning striking the figures in the center of the image evoke the feeling of suddenly realizing a clairvoyant image. Photograph by Michael Samuels.

training is the one we call receptive visualization. The receptive visualization state is a state in which a person can receive extrasensory perceptions of another person's mind states (telepathy), of objects or events (clairvoyance), of future events (precognition), and of psychic diagnosis. The programmed visualization state we have talked about corresponds to a state of telepathic sending, to aspects of psychic healing, and to mentally influencing physical objects (psychokinesis).

A number of psychics have described the role visualization plays in their mental telepathy. About receiving, Wolf Messing, a Russian psychic, says "people's thoughts come to me as pictures . . . I usually see visual images of a specific action or place . . . I first put myself into a certain state of relaxation in which I experience a gathering of feeling and strength . . . After an effort of will, I suddenly see the final result of some event flash before me."[8]

About telepathic sending, Uri Kamensky, a Russian biophysicist and sender, says, "I let both the feeling and sight of it [the object] sink into me. At the same time, I envision the face of Nikolaiev [the receiver]. I imagined he was sitting in front of me. Then I shifted perspective and tried to see the spring [the object] as if I were looking over Karl's [Nikolaiev's] shoulder. Finally I tried to see it through his eyes."[9]

"The ability to visualize easily, vividly, is key, according to the Soviets, in the successful transmission of telepathy."[10] Uri Kamensky advises senders to relax, become comfortable, put aside worries and emotions, become confident, and visualize vividly the receiver looking at and touching the object.

Lobsang Rampa, an English author of numerous books on parapsychology and the occult, advises people who wish to receive images to make themselves comfortable in a dimly-lit room, breathe deeply, clear their minds, and visualize the sender in front of them (a photograph may be used to aid in the visualization). Then he says to wait with faith for a message. "First you will be inclined to put it down to imagination but it is not imagination but reality. If you dismiss it as idle imagination you will dismiss telepathy."[11]

A psychic named Bob Hoffman and a psychiatrist named Ernest Pecci working together in Oakland, California have developed a system of psychic therapy called the Fischer-Hoffman technique. This system involves imagining an inner sanctuary and a spirit guide in order to aid in receptive visualization. Jean Porter, a Fischer-Hoffman teacher, in writing about telepathy says, "As the sender . . . make contact with the receiver by visualizing him or her and then send love and positive feeling energy . . . When ready, look carefully at the picture or object, repeat the details of it in your mind . . . [As the receiver] engage the attention of your conscious, intellectual mind by focusing on a symbol, a blank screen . . . Wait with receptive attention for the information to come."[12]

Joseph Weed, writing about Rosicrucian techniques, says that telepathy deals with love, mind, and primal energy. In his book, *Wisdom of the Mystic Masters*, he gives instructions for experiencing telepathy. The sender is instructed to send love to the receiver while visualizing that person's name or face. The sender is told to totally focus his attention, quiet his emotions, and visualize the idea to be transmitted. The sender should send the idea out on a stream of love to the receiver and dismiss any thought of how the process works, feeling that the idea has been transmitted. The receiver is told to send out a stream of love to the sender, which can be visualized as reaching out his hand to touch the sender. Then using his will, the receiver should lift his consciousness to the mental level and keep it there, free from emotional stress. The receiver should relax and assume an attitude of indifference rather than expectation.[13] Weed advises at first that the sender and recipient be near each other, and that they start with simple geometric shapes.

Telepathy has taken place across great distances—from the United States to England, for example. Not only shapes, but complex images and ideas have been transmitted under experimental conditions. Telepathy has also been demonstrated between humans and animals, and humans and plants. A number of instances of these phenomena were described at length in the book, *The Secret Life of Plants* by Peter Tompkins and Christopher Bird.

Visualization of geometric forms builds up intuition. Illustration by Susan Ida Smith.
Intuition is associated with heightened insight, clairvoyance, and telepathy.

Clairvoyance, that is extrasensory perception of objects, apparently involves receptive visualization in a manner similar to that employed by the receiver in mental telepathy. Clairvoyant experiences include correctly identifying ESP cards; psychic reading (getting information about a person); being able to describe the contents of a closed container such as an envelope or box; getting information about an object, such as mentally locating a lost object or describing characteristics of an object's owner; and describing the locale and occurrences of distant scenes. Special categories of clairvoyant ability involve describing events and objects of the future (precognition), or events and objects of the past.

The most widely-researched paranormal phenomenon to date is the reading of ESP cards. In 1933, the Duke University researcher J. B. Rhine invented the first ESP deck, consisting of twenty-five cards, each having one of five symbols on it, such as a star or a series of wavy lines. The procedure used by Rhine in the Pearce-Pratt Experiment (1934) became a model for future work in parapsychology. Briefly, a subject attempted to identify the symbols on cards which were manipulated by an assistant in a building over 100 yards away. The cards were shuffled by the assistant and laid face down, one by one. (In this way, the assistant himself did not see the symbol on the card.) In 1,850 trials the subject Pierce (who believed he had clairvoyant power and was congratulated when he correctly identified a card) scored 558 correct identifications or "hits." Chance expectations would have yielded 370 identifications. The probability that Pierce would have identified by guesswork so many cards above the chance expectation was 10^{-22} or *over* 1 in a million times a million times a million times a million.[14]

An experiment with even more striking

Max Ernst, in his collotype (printed in black, 19⅝ × 12½ inches, 1926) *The Fugitive*, shows a fantastic eye travelling over the earth. Ernst has written that clairvoyance enables the artist to travel far from everyday reality. Collection, The Museum of Modern Art, New York. Gift of James Thrall Soby.

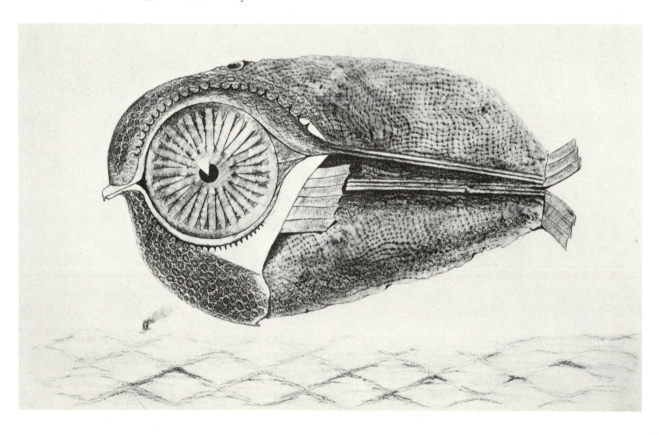

results was conducted by S. Soal, a pioneering British parapsychologist, in 1934. Soal had read about Rhine's experiments and was attempting to duplicate them, but found that the results he was getting did not deviate significantly from chance. A fellow researcher suggested that Soal re-evaluate the data for hits on the card immediately before or after the target card. Soal did this and found that one of his subjects had been very successful in guessing the next card. The experiment was repeated with this subject, and the subject correctly identified the next card (that is, the next one to be laid down) 1,101 times in 3,789 trials. Chance would be expected to produce 776 hits. The odds against the subject attaining his success were one in several billion billion.[15] Even more extraordinary, Soal found that the subject was identifying cards 26 seconds ahead of their being laid down. If the experimenter turned over the cards exactly twice as fast, the subject would then guess the cards two ahead. As the Pierce-Pratt experiment is the classic example of clairvoyance, Soal's is the classic of precognition.

Beyond and perhaps ultimately more significant than these experiments are the hundreds of spontaneous clairvoyant experiences reported in parapsychological literature, as well as the everyday experiences many people have had. Among the more common experiences are premonitions (sometimes in dreams) of unexpected events, deaths, or accidents which later happened; knowing the identity of a caller at the door or on the phone moments ahead of time; and hunches to keep a particular card in a game for no rational reason.[16] Many scientists and lay people believe that paranormal abilities are present in everyone, but are largely undeveloped. In fact, LeShan, Rzyl, Fischer-Hoffman instructors, and Silva Mind Control trainers (a course given for developing mind skills) have demonstrated that people with no apparent paranormal abilities can be trained to experience extraordinary paranormal phenomena.

Here is a receptive visualization run for opening yourself to extrasensory perceptions. Find a quiet space where you will be undisturbed, a place which you feel will be conducive to extrasensory perceptions. Make yourself comfortable. Let your eyes close.

Visualization allows a person to travel into the mind to a space where the possibilities of matter, time, and space are unlimited. Illustration by Susan Ida Smith.

Breathe in and out deeply, allowing your abdomen to rise and fall. As your breathing becomes slow and even you will feel relaxed. Now deeply relax your whole body in stages by whatever technique works best for you. Deepen this heavy, warm feeling of relaxation still further by slowly counting backwards from 10 to 1. As you mentally say each number you will become more and more relaxed.

You are now at a level where you can easily receive images. The images will be vivid; they are images which will provide you with information about people, objects, or events in the present, past, or future; they are images which will be beneficial to you and the world around you. Realize that you are connected with every object and every living thing in the universe and that they, in turn, are connected to you.

Matter, time, and space are different at this level; their possibilities are unlimited. People have received images about events, objects, and other people since the beginning of time; you are one of them. . . .

Allow your mind and emotions to become quiet. Now fix in your mind the image of a person, object, place, or event about which you wish to have information. Look attentively at this image. Now wait passively for other images to appear. Allow the images to appear, remain in your view, and disappear. Simply note the images that appear before you and accept them as having relevant information.

Stay at this level as long as you wish. When you return to your ordinary level of consciousness, you will remember the images you have seen. Each time you visualize in this way, the images will be clearer, flow more easily, and contain more information. To return to your ordinary level of consciousness, count slowly from 1 to 3, and gently move some part of your body. Allow yourself to return slowly, and open your eyes when you feel ready to do so. You now feel rested, calm, and ready to evaluate and interpret the images you have seen during the visualization.

This exercise can be used to find out information about a person—present or not. The technique is known as psychic reading. Psychic readers commonly describe events from a person's past; present situations involving the person; and less commonly, events from a person's future. Some readers give information about past lifetimes, karma, and the key problems or purposes of a person's life. If the subject of the reading is not present, the reader sometimes uses a photograph of the subject to aid their visualization (photometry).

A visualization or reading can also be used to determine information about the subject's health. The information may be general, involving weak and strong areas of the body, or it may be specific, involving actual medical diagnoses. One of the most commonly used techniques in body readings is to visualize the subject's body clearly. While asking for images relevant to the subject's health, the reader scans the subject's body from head to toe, concentrating on areas that attract attention. Some readers see healthy areas as light and problem areas as dark or murky. Others see actual bacteria or broken bones, auras, or energy blocks.

The basic exercise that we have given can also be used to find out information about objects. Through visualization psychic readers have located broken parts in complex machinery, found lost jewels and leaks in pipes buried within walls.

Another form of clairvoyance, one that involves the translation of images into ideomotor action, is dowsing, or the location of underground water or minerals. Dowsers commonly use a forked stick held in both hands; however, the ability lies in the dowser, who generally can use any forked twig. Well drilling companies commonly employ dowsers as their primary means for determining the most likely site for water wells. One of the most famous stories about dowsing concerns a Maine dowser who was brought to Bermuda. He correctly located the first underground water found on that island. Until then, Bermuda had depended solely on the collection of rainfall for its water supply.

Clairvoyance includes the ability to see distant scenes and places. One of the techniques used to accomplish clairvoyance involves a person mentally traveling to the place he wishes to see, and then looking around as if he were there. For example, if a person wanted to describe the contents of an unseen, unknown room across the street, he could visualize himself walking out of his house, across the street, into the house and into that room. Once in the room, he could look around as if he were actually there.

Rzyl calls this phenomenon "traveling clairvoyance;" the Rosicrucians refer to it as "mental projection." The Rosicrucians suggest that a person begin by using places with which he is already familiar, no matter how far away. In *Wisdom of the Mystic Masters*, Weed writes of the example of a man in New York who wishes to project himself to his sister's home in California. The man has been there and can visualize the house and grounds. When he does so he observes whether the sun is out or it is cloudy, whether there is a wind blowing, and so on.[17] Weed warns that the person should remain attentive and avoid the inclination to go into a dream state.

Odilon Redon, in his *Winged Head Over Water* Number 8 conveys the feeling of a person mentally travelling and clairvoyantly viewing distant scenes. Courtesy of the Art Institute of Chicago.

Clairvoyants throughout history have frequently used the aid of a crystal ball or a diamond ring in visualizing scenes. The ball or ring is stared into like a screen. The New Zealand psychologist McKellar, one of the foremost imagery researchers, says that visualizations seen in the ball are a kind of eidetic image and that they are three-dimensional and tend to appear in color. In his experiments McKellar found that subjects who were given verbal suggestions that they would experience "crystal imagery"[18] saw vivid scenes, although they had been otherwise unable to visualize.

Lobsang Rampa, the British occult author, gives the following instructions for seeing clairvoyantly: Seat yourself in a dark room and stare into the crystal—without trying to see anything—as if you were looking into the distance. He says the crystal will begin to appear cloudy, then spontaneously clear and reveal a scene, at which you are gazing down. You will move closer to the scene—possibly "landing" and feeling as if you are a person in the scene. He reassures that you should not be frightened —that you can't be hurt by the scene. He also advises that if you jerk your body at any point, the scene will disappear. Some people, Lobsang Rampa says, experience all the sensations of a scene without actually seeing it.

A different type of mental travel is known as *out-of-body experience* or *astral travel*. It is characterized by a person having "ordinary sense perceptions of actual things and persons (including very often his own physical body), from a point of view located in the ordinary space of nature outside the position occupied by his physical body at the time."[19] A person experiencing astral travel often feels as if he has another body during the experience. During astral travel, he becomes totally unaware of the sensations of his physical body. Another person, looking at him, would find his body in a comatose state. People working with astral travel believe that there is actually a second body, called the astral body, made of a fine, light material, which separates from the physical body but remains connected with it by a cord or thread. People who have experienced astral travel say they do so by visualizing themselves separating from their physical body, then floating away from it.

Once separated from the physical body, the astral or etheric body can travel at will, without regard for the ordinary laws of time and space. At its destination, the astral body can experience events with senses similar to physical reality. People writing about astral travel say that the astral body can sometimes be seen by people at its destination. Occasionally the astral body can be seen to materialize completely. Materializations of this type may explain famous accounts of people appearing in two places at once or appearing after death (since the astral body is believed to survive physical death).

Psychokinesis, the direct influence of physical objects by the mind, is another kind of paranormal phenomena that involves visualization. The first experiments in this area of parapsychology were conducted by Rhine at Duke University in 1934. They involved subjects attempting to throw high scores (8 or above) with ordinary dice. In 901 runs, subjects scored 446 more hits than would be expected by chance. The chances for this are computed to be a million billion to one.[20] Since then the Rhine experiment has been refined and duplicated many times. One variation done by McConnell, a biophysicist at the University of Pittsburgh, in 1955 involved the complete mechanization of the dice throwing and recording process. An even more elaborate experiment by Shmidt, a physicist who succeeded Rhine at Duke University, involved a subject attempting to influence a random-number generator, whose sequences of numbers were produced by decay of radioactive strontium 90 nuclei. The likelihood of the influence the subjects had on the numbers being due to chance was a thousand to one.

The Russians have extensively tested subjects with PK (psychokinesis) who have moved objects without touching them. One subject, Nelya Mikhailova, learned PK by using autogenic training relaxation methods. She was able to move compass needles, cigarettes, gold rings, cups, and match boxes. An American physician, William McGary, measured physiological changes of increased pulse and weight loss in Nelya while she was moving objects. A Russian physician, Dr. Zverev, also found changes in her EEG waves, blood sugar, and endocrine secretions.[22]

One technique for experiencing psychokinesis (PK) is to visualize an object in the mind's eye and picture it moving (process) or see it at the end of a process (final state) after it has moved. Here is a programmed visualization for experiencing PK. Sit down and make yourself comfortable. Close your eyes. Breathe in and out slowly and deeply. Allow yourself to relax. Deepen this relaxation by whatever technique works best for you. Go to a level where you can visualize, where images are clear, vivid, and stable.

Allow an image to form in your mind of the object you wish to concentrate on. If the object is in front of you, and you wish to, open your eyes and gaze steadily at it, while remaining in a relaxed and focused state of consciousness. Now picture the object moving to a new state or place. Visualize energy coming from you, ac-

complishing this change. Allow energy to flow through you. Imagine this energy focusing like a beam, pushing or affecting the object. If you visualize the energy flowing from your fingertips, you may even move your hands above the object. See the object move or change its state. Now visualize it in its changed state, see it clearly. Then rest. Visualize energy flowing into you, making you feel strong and calm. Hold this visualization as long as you feel necessary. To return to your ordinary state of consciousness, lift your eyes slowly and gently move your arms.

For some people, psychokinesis is the most physically demanding of paranormal experiences. Nelya Mikhailova loses as much as eight pounds in a 30-minute session.[23]

Psychic healing can be thought of as a special form of psychokinesis, in which the mind directly influences the tissues of a person's body.

Astral travel is said to involve separating from the physical body and travelling in a second, fine, light body which remains connected to the physical body by a slender cord. *Nude and Spectral Still Life*, 1939, by Victor Brauner. Oil on canvas, $36\frac{1}{8} \times 28\frac{5}{8}$ inches. The Sidney and Harriet Janis Collection, Gift to The Museum of Modern Art, New York.

This fresco by an unknown 12th century Spanish painter depicts Christ healing the blind man and raising Lazarus from the dead. The lefthand panel exemplifies spiritual healing by laying on of hands; the righthand panel exemplifies a miracle, bringing someone back to life, a feat not believed possible by modern science. There have been many theories attempting to explain these miracles, but none has been scientifically explained. The Metropolitan Museum of Art, The Cloisters Collection, 1959.

Robert Miller, an American chemical engineer, studied the well-known American psychic healers, Ambrose and Olga Worrall, in 1971. At a scheduled time the Worralls, in Baltimore, Maryland, visualized rye grass growing vigorously in white light. Miller, in Atlanta, Georgia measured an 840% increase in growth in his rye grass.[24] Other healers have been found to increase the speed of wound-healing in laboratory animals. We have mentioned previously that the aura recorded by Kirlian photography is much greater around the fingertips of healers while they are healing.

Here are some suggestions for how to use the programmed exercise that we gave for psychic healing:

- visualize the person you wish to heal surrounded by white light
- visualize yourself at one with the person you wish to heal, in an atmosphere of love
- visualize energy flowing from or through your body to the body of the person you wish to heal

A fascinating picture of the doctor as full of healing energy—*Dr. Dumouchel* (1910) by the French Surrealist Marcel Duchamp. The radiant aura around the doctor's hand looks remarkably similar to kirlian photographs of healers' hands taken in the 1970s. A person visualizing similar energies increases his own healing powers. Louise and Walter Arensberg Collection, Philadelphia Museum of Art.

Welcome to a world where inner and outer are one. Illustration by Susan Ida Smith.

visualize yourself, helpers, or tools going into the body of the person you wish to heal and changing a sick area to a healthy one (in coordination with psychic diagnosis—if you see a murky area, make it bright; if you see an infection, mentally drain it and visualize new tissue growing).

A Rosicrucian healer's visualization involves "visualizing psychic energy pouring into you . . . [and] opening a valve into an unlimited supply of energy which will continue to flow through you into the patient as long as your visualization is clear. The original accumulation by you is more in the nature of a pump priming. The continuing flow is far greater than your personal containment. . . . Make sure that love, a great, open-hearted, generous, dynamic love, takes over. . . ."[25]

This exercise illustrates several concepts about the nature of visualization healing. First, a person can direct healing energy within the body. Second, many visualizations make use of energy from outside a person—from God, from the universe, from another person. Third, a positive emotion—namely love—influences a person's ability to visualize and move healing energy.

In previous chapters of this book we viewed visualizations as memory images or imagination images. We could think of these images as being derived from sensory perceptions, from stored impressions from the past. This chapter forces us to look upon images in a new way—as literally seen with the mind's eye, that is, as an image directly perceived, not based on stored or immediate sensory perceptions but on an existent (past-present-future) real scene. Furthermore, we have seen that images held in the mind, such as those of a telepathic sender, have the power to *act* directly in the outer world. This phenomenon complements the Perky experiment that we discussed in the first chapter, in which a person could not tell internal visual images from "real" external images that were projected on the back of a screen. Here the inner image is as "real" as the outside object. Inner and outer have become one.

FOOTNOTES

1. Mishra, R. *Yoga Sutras*. Garden City, N.Y.: Doubleday and Co., Inc., 1973, p. 132.

2. Bronowski, J. *Ascent of Man* television show.

3. Rao, K. *Experimental Parapsychology*. Springfield, Ill.: Thomas, 1966. This theory and the following ones in our text are discussed in this book.

4. LeShan, L. *The Medium, The Mystic, and The Physicist*. New York, Ballantine Books, 1974, p. 86.

5. Wilhelm, R. *The I Ching*. Princeton, N.J.: Princeton Univ. Press, 1917, p. xxiv.

6. Ostrander, S. and Schroeder, L. *Psychic Discoveries Behind the Iron Curtain*. New York: Bantam Books, 1971, pp. 336, 337.

7. Ostrander, S. and Schroeder, L. p. 340.

8. Ostrander, S. and Schroeder, L. p. 47, 58.

9. Ostrander, S. and Schroeder, L. p. 15.

10. Ostrander, S. and Schroeder, L. p. 122.

11. Rampa, L. *You – Forever*. London, Gorgi Books, 1971, p. 159.

12. Porter, J. *Psychic Development*. New York: Random House-Bookworks, 1974, p. 12.

13. Weed, J. *Wisdom of the Mystic Masters*. West Nyack, N.Y.: Parker Publishing Co., Inc., 1968, p. 134.

14. Rhine, J. B. *ESP*. Boston, Mass.: Bruce Humphries, 1964.

15. Rhine, J. B.

16. ____ "Phantasms of the Living," Proceedings of the Society for Psychical Research, London, 1904. Chronicles of hundreds of spontaneous psychic experiences.

17. Weed, J. p. 191.

18. McKellar, P. *Imagination and Thinking*. London: Cohen & West, 1957, p. 28.

19. Broad, C. D. *Lectures of Psychical Research*. London: Routledge & Kegan Paul, 1962, p. 167.

20. Rhine, J. B.

21. Koestler, A. *The Roots of Coincidence*. London: Hutchinson, 1972.

22. Ostrander, S. and Schroeder, L. p. 407.

23. Ostrander, S. and Schroeder, L. p. 407.

24. Ferguson, M. *The Brain Revolution*. New York: Bantam Books, 1975, p. 350.

25. Weed, J. p. 85.

OTHER READING

1. Murphy, G. *The Challenge of Psychical Research*. New York: Harper & Brothers, 1961.

2. Schmeidler, G. *Extrasensory Perception*. New York: Atherton Press, 1974.

3. Muldoon, S. *The Projection of the Astral Body*. New York, Samuel Weiser, 1973.

Spiritual life is visualization. Spiritual life involves a quest toward a wholly different reality. This panel tells the story of St. Anthony's visit to St. Paul. Three scenes from the story are shown at once, thus conveying a feeling of time and space transcended. In the upper left St. Anthony sets out on his journey after having a vision of a fellow hermit, St. Paul, who was known as a man of great holiness. In the center of the picture St. Anthony meets a centaur whom he blesses and converts to Christianity. At the bottom right St. Anthony finds St. Paul. The overlapping of their halos graphically conveys the intensity of their meeting. This picture portrays a sacred visualization of the world. Sassetta and Assistant, *The Meeting of Saint Anthony and Saint Paul*. National Gallery of Art, Washington. Samuel H. Kress Collection.

Chapter 17

SPIRITUAL LIFE

In the chapter on daily life we said that visualization seemed almost an intruder. In daily life we were concerned with external realities, with objects in time and space, with the clearly known world of our senses. In this chapter we will deal with spiritual life, which *is* visualization. Spiritual life, which the University of Chicago religious historian and scholar, Mircea Eliade, calls the "sacred," deals with "the manifestation of something of a wholly different order, a reality that does not belong to our world . . ."[1] a reality that goes beyond space and time, that deals with paradoxes where things are themselves, but not themselves; that deals with the absolute unknowable One, with eternity, with powers. The sacred viewpoint requires looking at the world with a totally different eye than the secular. In the spiritual realm many of the philosophical premises by which man judges his reality become altered. It is as if man has evolved two different

models for describing his interaction with the world.

It is said that in the beginning of history, man's universe was totally sacred. Gershom Scholem, a religious scholar who has written extensively about Judaism, has called man's beginnings "the childhood of man, its mythical epoch . . . [In this epoch the world was seen] as being full of gods whom man encounters at every step . . . [where the] abyss between man and God has not become a fact of the inner consciousness . . . [and where] the interrelation and interdependence of things, their essential unity . . ."[2] was the way man experienced reality.

In time, man became separated from this unity—isolated from his gods and his origin. Suddenly there was "a vast abyss, conceived as absolute, between God, the infinite and transcendental Being, and Man, the finite creature. [This vast abyss or separation was only crossed

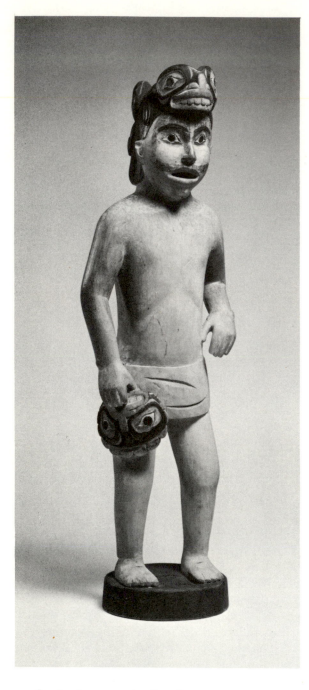

In ritual ceremonies the shaman experienced ecstasy, journeying from the everyday world to the sacred world of the spirits. Masks help the shaman contact particular spirits and invoke their aid. *Figure of Dancing Shaman*, North American Indian, 19th century, M. H. de Young Memorial Museum, San Francisco.

by] the Voice of God, directing and law-giving in His revelation, and the voice of man in prayer."[3]

At this point in man's history, says Scholem, mysticism appeared. Mysticism can be defined as knowledge gained through personal experience—experience that often involves seeing God. The mystic searches for a way to regain the old unity between man and God. In the beginning, all that there was, was unity; now unity must come from duality. This historical view is not unlike the myth of the fall from grace.

The basic means the mystical traditions found for bridging this duality were ascetic practices which produced a state of ecstasy. It was in this state that the practitioner experienced his God or gods. Ecstasy is a non-ordinary state of mind that includes trance states, sleeping dreams, visions, hallucinations, reveries, and deep meditation. Such ecstasy is understood by many people to be an inner experience, but it is felt by the practitioner to be more real than 'the world.'

The ecstatic state is important to this book because it can be reached through visualization. In the first section we said that visualization requires a non-ordinary state of consciousness in which the ego-mind no longer asserts itself, in which subject merges with object, participating in the experience rather than observing it. A person, that is the subject, feels that his experience is beyond space and time and that the object of his visualization comes from outside himself. These characteristics of the visualization state make it the ideal vehicle for the ecstatic experience. This is the reason why we said, at the beginning of this chapter, that spiritual life *is* visualization.

Probably one of the earliest examples in which visualization was used to bridge man's divided world lies with the shaman, the priest-healer-magician of primitive tribal life. Eliade has called the shaman "the great master of ecstasy" and has defined shamanism as the "technique of ecstasy." Shamans were called to their vocation because they demonstrated ecstatic powers; often they experienced visions or dreams of conversing with the gods, which foretold their future role. In these dreams they might die and be reborn, and be initiated as

290

shamans. Eliade says that " 'seeing spirits' in a dream or awake is the determining sign of the shamanic vocation . . ."[4] a sign to the tribe that the person has crossed the bridge to the sacred world. The shaman becomes familiar with the gods, can talk to them and invoke their aid, and often has spirit helpers or assistants. In a trance, the shaman causes his soul to travel to other worlds where he meets with spirits and gods. He does this in order to bring an offering from the tribe, to help the souls of sick or dead people, or to learn from higher beings. The shaman has supernatural powers: the ability to produce inner warmth or see things at a great distance; the ability to fly magically, to foretell the future, to heal; and the ability to perform feats of magic, such as physically disappearing, for the tribe.

Many of the powers described by shamans are similar to, and possibly forerunners of, powers described by Greek mystics, Sufis, and Indian yogis. Tantric yogans have described in detail how they achieve such powers through visualization. Indeed, descriptions by shamans reveal remarkably vivid visualizations. An Australian shaman of the Yaralde tribe has described a vision of spirits as follows: " 'When you lie down to see the prescribed visions, and you do see them, do not be frightened, because they will be horrible. They are hard to describe, though they are in my mind and my miwi (that is, psychic force) . . . some are like snakes, some are like horses with men's heads, and some are spirits of evil men which resemble burning fires . . . If you get up, you will not see these scenes, but when you lie down again, you will see them, unless you get too frightened. If you do, you will break the web (or thread) on which the scenes are hung.' "[5]

Much of the shamanistic tradition of ecstasy states and of the powers that accompany them was incorporated into the evolving religions of India, the Middle East, and Europe. As the modern religions of Judaism, and later, Christianity, grew in the West they formulated a doctrine which was rationally based. Western institutional religion has emphasized authoritative theology based on Biblical interpretation and elaboration of doctrine and policy. The priests have become mediators between man and God, and direct experience of

Man Inside of Fish, Northwest Coast American Indian. This sculpture represents the Indians' belief that inside the animal's shape can be found a man-like spirit who can speak to shamans and bestow powers on them. M. H. de Young Memorial Museum, San Francisco. Gift of Mrs. Eleanor Martin.

The Annunciation by the Master of the Retable of the Reyes Catolicos (Spanish, last quarter of the 15th century) portrays God the Father sending the image of the infant Christ child, cross in arms, on beams to the Virgin Mary. A dove, symbol of the Holy Spirit, hovers over her head. The angel Gabriel announces the Incarnation. M. H. de Young Memorial Museum, San Francisco. The Samuel H. Kress Collection.

God has been de-emphasized. However, visualization still plays a part in institutional religion. It can not help but do so because any religion, even an institutionalized religion, involves a concept of a spiritual universe not verifiable in the physical world. The Old Testament is rich with visions, dreams, and revelations; the New Testament is filled with accounts of ecstatic conversions and illuminations. In addition to these textual accounts of visualizations, the ritual practices involved in both Judaism and Christianity can be understood as visualizations. In Chapter 3 we discussed how the Christian Communion Service takes concrete objects—wine and bread—and (symbolically) transmutes them, in a visualization of the Last Supper that Christ shared with his disciples.

Alongside institutionalized religion, in both Judaism and Christianity, there has existed throughout history many rich mystical traditions. These traditions all developed techniques for achieving ecstatic states and a personal experience of God, techniques which involved detailed, deliberate visualizations. Christian and Jewish mysticism were undoubtedly interconnected and both drew on knowledge from Egyptian Hermetism, Greek Platonic philosophy, the traditions of the classic occult mysteries, and their forerunners, the primitive shamanistic traditions.

Jewish mystical tradition formed a movement called the Kabbalah that began in Biblical times and continues to the present day. Kabbalistic mysticism involves the use of symbolic doctrines, ascetic rites, magic and visualization. In early times Kabbalistic doctrines were considered to be heretical by institutional Judaism so Kabbalistic teachings were spread secretly. The following paragraphs describe two ascetic techniques that show the use of visualization in Kabbalistic mysticism.

From the first century B.C. to the tenth century A.D., Kabbalistic mysticism involved the "ascent of the soul from the earth, through the spheres of the hostile planet-angels and rulers of the cosmos, and its return to its divine home in the 'fullness' of God's light . . ."[6] To experience this ascent the practitioner fasts, whispers hymns, and sits with his head between his knees. " 'Then he perceives the interior and the chambers, as if he saw the seven palaces with his own eyes, and it is as though he entered one palace after the other and saw what is there.' "[7] The practitioner also sees the rulers of the palaces, and makes use of protective armor, weapons, and secret names in order to pass from palace to palace. He experiences his body being burned and finally reaches the original home of the soul where he sees and hears God. Scholem links this visualization to ones used by second and third century Gnostics and Hermetics, and traces it back to Greek texts and to earlier papyri written in Egypt.

From 1200 A.D. on a Kabbalistic movement in Spain centered around the teacher Avulafia. He developed a technique for achieving ecstasy which is similar to Yoga. With the aid of a master, a practitioner is taught ecstatic techniques of concentration that involve staring at, and recombining, Hebrew letters. After one-mindedness is attained, ". . . the visionary perceives the image of his spiritual mentor, usually visualized either as a young or as an old man, whom he not only sees but also hears."[8] The visionary may also "see the shape of his self standing before him and he forgets his self and it is disengaged from him and he sees the shape of his self before him talking to him and predicting the future."[9] The visionary may then experience himself as surrounded by light and/or experience God.

Christian Gnostic tradition paralleled Kabalistic mysticism in time and development.

This elaborate and beautiful Christian visualization, *The Nativity*, is from the workshop of the Early Netherlandish painter Rogier van der Weyden. In the right side of the central panel the wisemen see a vision of the Christ child's birth, while in the right wing the wisemen are shown paying homage to Him. The Metropolitan Museum of Art, Purchase, 1949. The Cloisters Collection.

Seven steps leading to enlightenment and knowledge were a symbol common to Kabbalistic, Gnostic and alchemical thought. The aspirant visualized himself ascending from step to step until he reached the goal. From Andrae's *Alchymia,* 1633.

Hebrew letters combine and recombine in this 16th century occult symbol from *Cor Agrippae De Occulta* by Henrici.

It also had roots in Hermetic and Platonic practices. Gnostic writings are filled with symbolism, magical rituals, visualizations of ascent and descent to other worlds, and direct experiences of God.[10] Christian mystics, writing about their experiences, often describe their detachment from external sensations, intense concentration, and visualization. Around the first century A.D., St. Ignatius, the Bishop of Antioch and a Church father, wrote a manual of spiritual exercises which recommended that the practitioner imagine a graded series of holy scenes, the highest of which was a visualization of Christ fully occupying the mind. St. Ignatius also wrote that "he saw in a distinct manner the plan of divine wisdom in the creation of the world. On another occasion, during a procession, his spirit was ravished in God, and it was given him to contemplate in a form and images fitted to the weak understanding of a dweller on the earth, the deep mystery of the holy Trinity."[11]

However the most highly developed visualization techniques in spiritual life come to us from the Tantric Yogic tradition. Tantra, which means *that which extends knowledge,* became a widespread philosophical and religious movement in India and Tibet around 600 A.D. Tantric thought fit in well with the prevailing Indian belief that man ordinarily no longer had direct access to truth. Tantra developed and perfected a series of techniques by which man could again experience the truth.

Tantrism, like all Indian religions, has as its goal liberation from the ephemeral unreality of the physical world as perceived by the mind and senses, and knowledge of the absolute spirit.[12] To realize liberation, the ego or the "I" must be left behind. The "I" that must be transcended is the "I" of both the conscious reality of the senses and the "I" of subconscious tendencies and memories. Like other religious thought, Tantrism differentiates between the secular world and the spiritual. To achieve liberation a person must see the difference between the illusory world of matter and the real world of the spirit; the person must cease to think of himself as matter and identify himself with the absolute.

Tantra sees the secular world, the entire cosmos, as *maya,* or cosmic illusion. The world

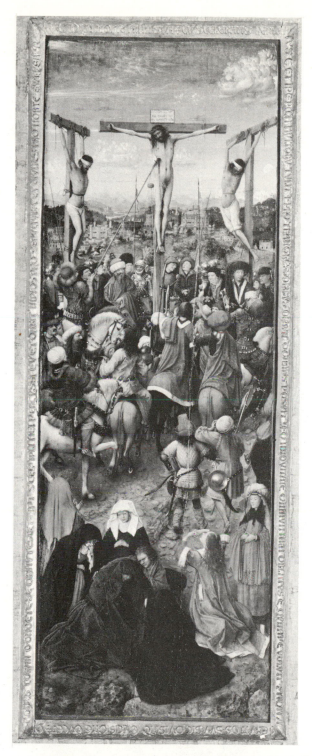 

The Crucifixion (left) and *The Last Judgement* (right) by the 15th Century Flemish artist Jan van Eyck is a richly orchestrated visualization. *The Crucifixion* shows the crucified Christ surrounded by callous soldiers and dignitaries at the top of the painting and the Virgin Mary comforted by Saint John in the lower part of the painting. *The Last Judgement* shows Christ the Savior, surrounded by angels, presiding over the court of heaven. The Twelve Apostles are seated in the center, surrounded by the saints and martyrs. The center portion of the painting depicts a barren earth and sea giving up their dead. St. Michael straddles a skeleton who represents the spectre of death. Beneath the skeleton the damned fall into a ghastly pit filled with terrifying demons. Viewers will experience very different feelings when they meditate on the upper or lower part of either painting. The Metropolitan Museum of Art, Fletcher Fund, 1933.

of our senses is maya, but so is the world of dream and hallucination. "The mind alone is the cognizer of sensuous impressions, and the mind makes no real distinction between these, whether they be internally [dream state] or externally [waking state] cognized. In the mind, as in a mirror, both the internal and the external sense objects are reflected, and apart from mind have no existence, being, as the Doctrine of Maya teaches, merely appearances."[13] Maya is in contrast with the absolute reality, which lies beyond matter and mind and is eternal and unchanging. The Tantric-Hindu theory of the creation of the world holds that "Nature as a whole is the Dream of the One Mind"[14] and that the dream itself is thought substance, which as it becomes coarser, and its vibrational level slows, becomes sound, then light, then matter. In this way the universe was created.

Tantra teaches that a person realizes liberation not through doctrine, but through personal experience. The basic techniques are meditation and visualization which lead to the ability to concentrate, control one's mind, and free oneself from the distractions of the senses. In Tantric visualization the practitioner is given

Andrae Del Castagno portrays Christ rising from the grave, surrounded by a radiant aura in *The Resurrection*. A Christian holding the image of this scene in his mind is uplifted. Copyright The Frick Collection, New York.

instruction by a master on visualizing an image of a god or an object. The yogin practices his visualizations until they are extremely vivid, which may take years. W. Y. Evans-Wentz, a religious scholar from Oxford who spent years studying in India and Tibet, says that for a yogin's visualization to be successful, it must appear to the person to be lifelike. Tibetan masters teach two methods for visualizing. In the first method, called the gradual process, the yogin forms his visualization around a central idea. This idea acts as a nucleus upon which the visualization is built step by step. The second method is called the instantaneous process. In this method the visualization seems to suddenly pop into existence.[15]

The mandala, of which we spoke earlier, is involved in many visualization exercises used by Tantric yogins. A mandala is a complex design made up of concentric circles, enclosing squares and triangles. It may also contain images of divinities or objects such as flowers. Mandalas act as concentration devices to help the yogin visualize. " 'There exists no form of concentration more absolute than that by which images are created. Direct seeing of a tangible object never allows of such an intensity.' "[16]

The *yantra* is a simple mandala composed of triangles and other geometric shapes. It "is a piece of psychological apparatus to call up one or another aspects of divinity."[17] The Yantra has specific colors and mathematically

Sitatapatra (Invincible Goddess of the White Parasol). 18th century Tibetan tanka. Asian Art Museum of San Francisco, the Avery Brundage Collection.

299

Yamantaka Mandala (18th century) is an example of a Tibetan mandala. Mandala means circle and designates a consecrated area which is protected from hostile influences. A central deity is portrayed surrounded by his emanations and entourage. Every deity has his mandala or sphere of power. During a ritual the devotee identifies with the deity and assumes his powers. In geometric mandalas circles represent spiritual planes and squares symbolize the world pervaded by spirit of the One. The mandala brings order out of chaos and helps the devotee re-establish his true relationship with the original creative order. Asian Art Museum of San Francisco, the Avery Brundage Collection.

geometric proportions. The Yantra form is constructed to induce, bear, and convey a particular pattern of thoughts and forces. To visualize that form is to understand that thought. To understand that form is to realize the impact of the forces which that form creates. "The principle behind this is that, just as each form is the visible product of an energy pattern rooted in sound so, reciprocally, each visible form carries with it its own implicit power-pattern."[18] Becoming one with the mandala allows the yogin to experience the force behind the forms. "When we close our eyes we can really look at things. We see without seeing, to be exact. In the ultimate act of vision the body meditates as well as the mind."[19] "By such inward contemplation, man acquires the power to remake his vision both of himself and of the world."[20]

The mandala's contents symbolize aspects of Tantric doctrine, such as illumination, rebirth, and the burning of ignorance. Each mandala represents basic principles of the universe, such as receptivity, action, tension, or wholeness. Visualizing a mandala involves becoming one with these principles. The yogin uses the mandala as a base for visualization. He also constructs mandalas as part of his religious rites, and visualizes the mandala projected into parts of his body.

When the yogin is initiated into his sect, a mirror, called the Mirror of Karma, is held before him. On this mirror is painted the likeness of a goddess. The yogin is instructed to let his visualizations become as vivid as this likeness. He is told that his visualizations will appear like an image reflected in a mirror, but that they will appear to be between the mirror and himself. With practice the visualization not only looks like a vivid projected reflection, but may even become animated and substantial enough to touch. Yogins believe that extremely vivid visualizations can materialize, becoming palpable. These visualizations can then exist on their own, even acting like spirit figures. "Thoughts being things, the yogin, by use of visualization yogically directed, causes his mentally-created images of protecting deities to assume concrete form on the fourth dimensional, or psychic, plane."[21]

A yogin is instructed to regard his visualizations " 'with exalted regard, veneration, and devotion, looking upon the Devatas (that is, the visualized deities) as real, holy, and divine. They are none the less so because mind-produced for the mind ultimately is That [absolute reality] and its ideas forms of That.' "[22] At the same time, the yogin is told these Devatas, though palpable, are also part of the world of Maya. After visualizing the deity, the practitioner is told to identify himself with the deity, or to identify the deity with the Dharma, the laws of his teachings which are the path to liberation. This process of visualization and identification is not simply mental exercise; rather, it awakens the divine nature within the yogin. This awakening enables the yogin to see beyond Maya to the Absolute Reality. Visualization functions as a vehicle for taking man from the physical world to the mental world. And in realizing that neither the physical world nor the mental world of his visualizations is real, the yogin attains liberation.

Shri Yantra. The four triangles with apex pointing up symbolize the male principle Śiva; the five triangles pointing down symbolize the female principle Śakti, the central point symbolizes the undifferentiated Absolute. The Yantra then symbolizes cosmic manifestation from unity to form.

Tibetan Tanka. Courtesy of the American Museum of Natural History, New York.

It is the specific content of his visualizations which give the yogin the power to find liberation. The masters give each yogin detailed descriptions of just what he is to visualize. The yogin may also be shown detailed drawings of deities to visualize. Each object, shape, and color in the visualization is purposeful. Each symbolizes concepts that the yogin must understand. This understanding must occur beyond a rational level, within the yogin's being.

The shape and colors of the visualization are believed to affect the yogin directly, including altering his physiological state. These visualizations, being an evolved form of thought, draw the yogin to the root thought. For example, the visualization of a particular goddess in a certain shape and color will lead the yogin to understand the emptiness and illusory nature of his own body. The visualization acts as a power figure, transforming the yogin into a changed being. At the same time, the yogin receives the powers associated with that particular visualization. For example, in visualizing fire, the yogin receives the power to generate internal heat or withstand external heat. Thus supernatural powers come to the yogin as a natural result of his visualizations. These powers, if properly used, aid the yogin on his path to liberation. If improperly used or sought as ends in themselves, the powers will stop all his spiritual progress and they will often disappear.

In the book *Tibetan Yoga and Secret Doctrines*, W. Y. Evans-Wentz includes translations of several ancient Tantric texts which describe in detail visualizations to be used by yogins. The purpose of one of these visualizations is to understand that the human body is illusory. "Imagine thyself to be the Divine Devotee Vajra-Yogini [a goddess of intellect and energy], red of color; as effulgent as the radiance of a ruby; having one face, two hands, and three eyes [the yogic third eye being included]; the right hand holding aloft a brilliantly gleaming curved knife and flourishing it overhead, cutting off completely all mentally disturbing thought-processes; the left hand holding against her breast a human skull filled with blood [symbolizing renunciation of the world]; giving satisfaction with her inexhaustible bliss; with a tiara of five dried human skulls [symbolizing highest spiritual discernment] on her head; wearing a necklace of fifty blood-dripping human heads [symbolizing severance from the round of death and re-birth]; her adornments, five of the Six Symbolic Adornments [the tiara of human skulls, the necklace of human heads, armlets and wristlets, anklets, the breastplate Mirror of Karma], the cemetery-dust ointment [symbolizing renunciation of the world and conquest of fear over death] being lacking; holding, in the bend of her arm, the long staff, symbolizing the Divine Father, the Heruka [the male power]; nude, and in the full bloom of virginity, at the sixteenth year of her age [unsullied by the world]; dancing, with the right leg bent and foot uplifted, and the left foot treading upon the breast of a prostrate human form [treading upon ignorance and illusion]; and flames of wisdom forming a halo about her.

"[Visualize her as being thyself], eternally in the shape of a deity, and internally altogether vacuous like the inside of an empty sheath, transparent and uncloudedly radiant; vacuous even to the fingertips, like an empty tent of red silk, or like a filmy tube distended with breath.

"At the outset, let the visualization be about the size of thine own body; then, big as a house; then, as big as a hill; and, finally, vast enough to contain the universe. Then concentrate thy mind upon it.

"Next, gradually reduce it, little by little, to the size of a sesamum seed, and then to the size of a very greatly reduced sesamum seed, still having all the limbs and parts sharply defined. Upon this too, concentrate thy mind."[23]

Another, similar exercise involves the yogin visualizing his body as being the body of the goddess, with a nerve canal going from between his legs to the top of his head. "Imagine the median nerve as possessing the following four characteristics: redness like that of a solution of lac, brightness like that of the flame of a sesamum oil lamp, straightness like that of an inner core of the plantain plant, and hollowness like that of a hollow tube of paper."[24]

This next exercise is one for achieving the Yoga of the Psychic Heat: psychic heat enables the yogin to be impervious to the elements of weather which would otherwise distract him during prolonged meditation. "To obtain the benefit of the warmth from the Art of Visualizing, proceed according to the directions which now follow . . . imagine at the centre of each of the two palms of the hands, and at the centre of each of the two soles of the feet, a sun; and then place these suns one against the other. Then visualize in the tri-junction of the three chief psychic-nerves [below the naval nerve-center, in the perineum, at the base of the organ of generation], a sun. By the rubbing together of the suns of the hands and feet, fire flareth up. This fire striketh the sun below the navel [in the tri-junction]. A fire flareth up from there and striketh the half-A. A fire flareth up from the half-A and permeateth the body. Then, as the expiration is going out, visualize the whole world as being permeated with fire in its true nature [as invisible psychic-heat, or psychic-fire] . . . By meditating thus, for seven days, one will undoubtedly become able to endure [the most extreme cold] with only a cotton cloth on the body."[25]

Evans-Wentz tells stories of yogins who, with the power of psychic heat, could sit naked in the snow and dry sheets soaked in icy water that were wrapped around them. Evans-Wentz says that as a result of the exercises leading to the ability to produce psychic heat, the yogin also gets the power to have knowledge of past, present, and future events; mind-reading; and the ability to understand one's own short-comings.

Tantric visualization exercises devote considerable attention to realizing the illusory nature of the world (Maya). The following exercise, like the visualization of Vajra-Yogini, deals with realizing that the physical body is not real: "In a mirror, attached either to a stake or some other support in front of thee, let thy body be mirrored.

"Inasmuch as applying to the mirrored body such pleasing things as honor, fame, and adulation affecteth it pleasurably, and depriving it of some of its belongings and applying to it deprecatory and displeasing epithets affecteth it adversely, therefore, visualizing it as being between thyself and the mirror, apply these pleasant and unpleasant things to it. Then regarding thyself as in no way unlike that mirrored form, apply to it the Sixteen Similes [such as, it is like a mirage, like clouds, like the moon reflected in water, etc.];

thereby habituating the mind to regard one's own body as being maya, and, therefore, unreal."[26]

Tantric doctrine has similar exercises for realizing the maya of the visualization. In other words, the yogin's visualizations—including those of gods and goddesses—although considered purer than the physical body, are produced by mind, and thus are maya. Tantric practice aims at systematically peeling back or seeing through one layer of illusion after another. To realize the nature of illusion, the yogin strengthens himself and appeals to the spirits of gurus (legendary teachers) to help him. In one such exercise, the yogin visualizes a circle around him which protects him from the wrathful deities and strange dangers encountered on the path to liberation. Another exercise involves picturing gift-waves—waves of psychic energy that stimulate spiritual development—coming telepathically from famous gurus to the yogin practitioner.

In order to understand illusion thoroughly, the yogin also examines the dream state. He does so by endeavoring to experience an unbroken continuity of consciousness throughout the waking state, the dream state, and the state between the two. Before going to sleep, the yogin suggests to himself that he will understand his dreams and that their content will be whatever he wishes it to be: "Then, at night, when about to sleep, pray to the guru that thou mayest be able to comprehend the dream state; and firmly resolve that thou wilt comprehend it. . . . Visualize a red dot as being within the throat psychic center [dreams are believed to result from motion in an area between the heart and the throat], and firmly believe that thereby thou shalt see whichever of these Realms [various paradises of the Buddha] thou desirest to see, with all its characteristics, most vividly."[27]

Next the yogin is advised to transform images in his dreams to other forms. By this experience the yogin learns that dreams, like matter, are subject to the mind's will. When he realizes the maya of both the awake and dream states, and reaches liberation, the yogin sees clear light, which is the goal of all his previous visualizations.

The Yoga of the Psychic Heat enables a yogin to generate incredible body heat and withstand freezing temperatures. To achieve psychic heat the yogin visualizes a sun in the tri-junction of the three chief psychic nerves. Illustration by Susan Ida Smith.

The Wheel of Existence, 17th century (?) tanka. This tanka symbolizes the endless cycle of birth and rebirth. Yama, the god of impermanence and death, holds the wheel in his clutches. The animals in the hub of the wheel symbolize the causes of rebirth. Around the hub the conditions of rebirth are depicted; from the top, clockwise, they are the realms of the gods, the titans, the tortured spirits, the hell dwellers, the animals and finally, humans. The outer wheel shows scenes which symbolize the twelve causes of rebirth. Outside the wheel, in the upper corners are the deities who help man become free. The wheel of becoming was visualized by Buddha as he meditated under the tree of wisdom and is a basic image of Buddhism. Details in this tanka show the influence of Christian and Tibetan art. A painting of the wheel of existence appears in the vestibule of Tibetan temples and is often carried about to illustrate the teachings. Collection of the Newark Museum.

The yogin is likewise instructed to experience an unbroken continuity of consciousness between life and death. Many visualizations for this practice are contained in the *Tibetan Book of the Dead*.[28] Tantric thought also contains visualizations for helping the conscious principle of another person reach clear light when they pass from life to death, and for transferring one's consciousness into the body of a dead person or animal.

Tantric yogins perform a ritual called the Chod Rite which, like other visualizations, demonstrates the illusory nature of mind and body. The yogin goes into the wilderness and, in visualization, evokes and conquers strange beings. This ritual involves the yogin's visualization of the sacrifice of his own body. In one form of this ritual the yogin first visualizes that his body contains all worldly pleasures and goals, and then visualizes that the flesh falls away from his body, revealing his own skeleton. This rite is not to be undertaken lightly, for the strange beings evoked are extremely powerful once they are manifest, and the yogin risks madness or death if he is not able to vanquish them.

This Tibetan tanka (scroll) depicts one of the fierce deities visualized by yogins. Asian Art Museum of San Francisco. The Avery Brundage Collection.

307

This picture, *The Graded Way of the Assembly Tree,* is a painting from a Tibetan Tanka, a hanging scroll made by Tibetan priests to meditate upon. This tanka shows the major lines of Tibetan gurus, Lamas, Bodhisattvas, and deities. This tanka was produced during yogic meditation in which the disciple visualized the vast assembly as living beings, blazing with light. When a disciple is able to visualize all of these holy beings in perfect detail, the beings merge into one another and the disciple merges with them and all is merged into the Absolute. Collection of the Newark Musuem.

This rite, which involves symbolic death of the physical body and rebirth of a spiritual one, is a basic spiritual visualization shared by many religions. In fact, it is almost identical to many shamanistic rites. The visualization of one's own skeleton, for example, is common to shamanistic rites in Australia, North America, and Siberia. In a similar way, Christians are exhorted to spiritually die and be reborn in Christ, as he physically died for them.

The final goal of all mystic spiritual practices is liberation, that is, union with God. The experience of union itself often takes place as a visualization. A turn-of-the-century Canadian psychiatrist, Bucke, in his book *Cosmic Consciousness*,[29] delineates the characteristics of this experience. Chief among them are a sense of being immersed in light, and the experience of a vision outlining the meaning of the universe. Yogananda Paramahansa, author of *Autobiography of a Yogi*, and founder of the Self-Realization Fellowship in Los Angeles relates the emotional effects of the visualization of union and cosmic consciousness. Once Yogananda was meditating with his mind concentrated on the Goddess Kali at a temple which contained her image in stone. For five hours he sat outside the temple, inwardly visualizing her, and despairing because he experienced no response to his visualization. "Then, to my amazement, the temple became greatly magnified. Its large doors slowly opened, revealing the stone figure of Goddess Kali. Gradually the statue changed into a living form, smilingly nodding in greeting, thrilling me with joy indescribable. As if by a mystic syringe, the breath was withdrawn from my lungs; my body became very still, though not inert.

"An ecstatic enlargement of consciousness followed. I could see clearly for several miles over the Ganges River to my left, and beyond the temple into the entire Dakshineswar precincts. The walls of all buildings glimmered transparently; through them I observed people walking to and fro over distant acres. I realized anew, standing there in the sunny courtyard, that when man ceases to be a prodigal child of God, engrossed in a physical world, indeed a dream, baseless as a bubble, he reinherits his eternal realms."[30]

FOOTNOTES

1. Eliade, M. *The Sacred and the Profane*. New York: Harper and Row, 1959, p. 11.
2. Scholem, G. *Jewish Mysticism*. New York: Schocken Books, 1961, p. 7.
3. Scholem, G. p. 8.
4. Eliade, M. *Shamanism*. London: Routledge & Kegan Paul, 1964, p. 4.
5. Eliade, M. *Shamanism*. p. 86.
6. Scholem, G. p. 49.
7. Scholem, G. p. 49.
8. Scholem, G. p. 139.
9. Scholem, G. p. 142.
10. Jonas, H. *The Gnostic Religion*. Boston, Mass.: Beacon Press, 1958.
11. James, W. *The Varieties of Religious Experience*. New York: University Books, 1963, p. 410.
12. Eliade, M. *Yoga, Immortality and Freedom*. New York: Pantheon Books, 1958, p. 4.
13. Evans-Wentz, W. Y. *Tibetan Yoga and Secret Doctrines*. London: Oxford University Press, 1967, p. 165.
14. Evans-Wentz, W. Y. p. 164.
15. Evans-Wentz, W. Y.
16. Mookerjee, A. *Tantra Art*. Paris, Ravi Kumar, 1971, p. 13.
17. Mookerjee, A. p. 13.
18. Mookerjee, A. p. 23.
19. Mookerjee, A. p. 36.
20. Mookerjee, A. p. 11.
21. Evans-Wentz, W. Y. p. 179.
22. Evans-Wentz, W. Y. p. 44.
23. Evans-Wentz, W. Y. pp. 173–175.
24. Evans-Wentz, W. Y. p. 176.
25. Evans-Wentz, W. Y. pp. 203–204.
26. Evans-Wentz, W. Y. pp. 209–210.
27. Evans-Wentz, W. Y. p.
28. Evans-Wentz, W. Y. *Tibetan Book of the Dead*. London: Oxford University Press, 1969.
29. Bucke, *Cosmic Consciousness*, New York: E. P. Dutton, 1969.
30. Paramahansa, Y. *Autobiography of a Yogi*. Los Angeles, Cal.: Self Realization Fellowship, 1946, p. 216.

APPENDIX

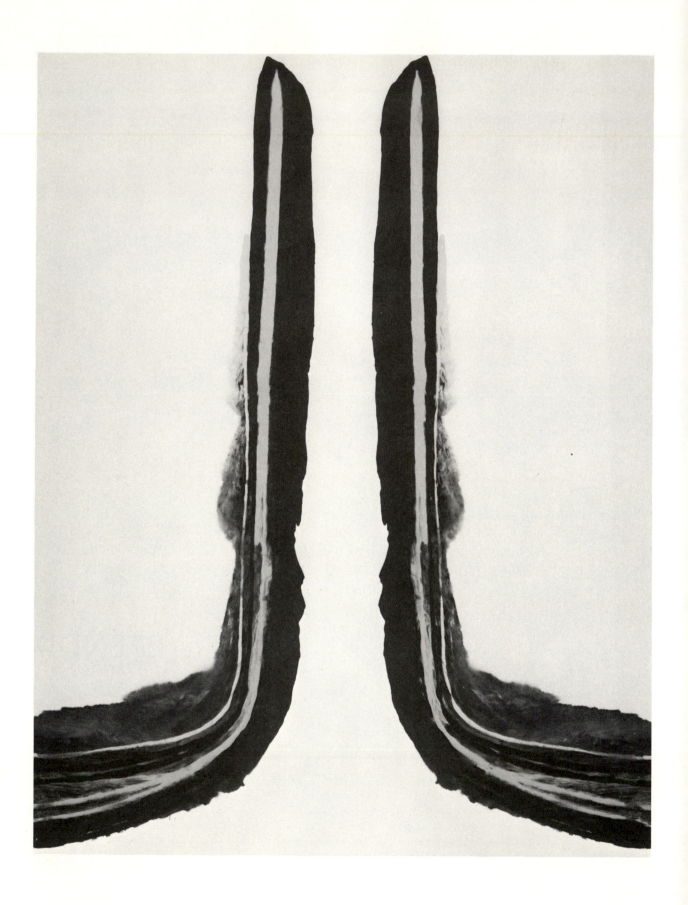

Receiving a visualization from one's inner center is an event of great importance. With each visualization a person comes into greater harmony with himself, furthering the process of personal growth. This process has associations with birth, ascendancy, and joy. Murray Reich. *Annunciation (for KM)*. 1969. Synthetic polymer on canvas. 104 × 80 inches. Collection of Whitney Museum of American Art. Gift of Mr. and Mrs. Sam Golden (and purchase).

GOING FURTHER

Throughout the book we've talked about how visualizations manifest themselves in the external world. In essence, what people visualize is what they get. Likewise, what they have is the result of what they have previously visualized. And that is why we think that a way of choosing which life areas and which visualizations to concentrate on is important.

The third section of this book deals with the six broad areas of a person's life. Each chapter in that section contains specific visualizations pertinent to a particular area. There are several ways for people to choose which area to use as a subject for their visualizations.

Personal interests or intuition. In looking through the third section a person may immediately see one area that interests him strongly, for example, *Medicine and Healing*. It may be because he has a problem in that area, such as an actual illness. Or it may simply be an area he's thought a lot about—for example, he may have read a number of books dealing with illness or with keeping healthy. In any event, he will have a clear motivation for picking that area as a subject for his visualizations. Or a person may find himself attracted to one area for no particular reason that he is aware of. That category may simply "feel right" to him or he may find himself coming back to it. When a person's intuition draws him to a particular category in this way, it is helpful to follow it.

Receptive visualization. If a person does not find himself immediately struck by a particular area, he can tune in his intuition by putting himself in a receptive visualization state (see p. 152). Once in the receptive state he can ask himself which area would be useful for him to visualize on. He may even picture the list of areas from Section III and their symbols in his mind's eye. One area or its symbol will probably seem to stand out. The person may get a strong feeling about this area, like an inner voice. Or he may visualize an image which by its subject matter—directly or symbolically—suggests an area.

Chance or synchronicity. A person can even choose an area to concentrate on at random. For example, he might pick a number from 1 to 6 and work on the material in the corresponding chapter. He might roll dice. Or he might even spin a pencil, like a dial, on the Life Areas Chart (see p. 160) and go to the area that the pencil tip points to. These methods are similar to the ones used to consult the Chinese *Book of Changes,* the *I Ching.* They employ the concept of synchronicity. For an explanation of synchronicity by Carl Jung, (see p. 270).

Using feelings as a guide. People's feelings, their reactions to their visualizations, tell them which visualizations to program, to hold. If people respond to a visualization with positive feelings, they know that this visualized state or condition is one to maintain (if it already exists) or a state to seek, to hold the image of (if it does not presently exist). If people respond to a visualization with negative feelings, they know that this visualized state or condition is not one to pursue or to continue (if it already exists). People's feelings in the visualization state enable them to test out an image. If they visualize a

situation that presently does not exist in the external world, their feelings will tell them whether or not to work (to visualize and/or to take action) to bring about that situation. If they visualize a situation that does exist in the external world, their feelings will tell them whether or not to leave or change that situation (and the visualizations behind it).

A metaphor for feelings guiding people toward becoming aware of a pure inner image, and that image manifesting itself in the world, is provided by the artist at work. An artist making a sketch will draw a line, stand back and look at it, and *know* whether or not it is right. If an artist is asked how he knows what makes a line *right,* so that he leaves it, or *wrong,* so that he redraws it, the artist will answer that the line feels right, or it feels wrong. It is as if the artist has an inner image of the finished picture below his level of awareness. When a line matches his inner image, it feels right; when there is "no match," it feels wrong. When it feels wrong, the artist tries out one line after another until a match occurs which feels right. In a similar way, people can look upon themselves as having images in their inner center applicable to all areas of their life—images that show them what directions to take for harmony and growth. The images they see when they visualize are like the artist's sketch. People can receive or create a detail in an image and change it if it is wrong, until they create an image that feels right. Just as an artist's images manifest in the world as a drawing, people's visualization images manifest in the world as the parts of their life.

Here is an exercise for completing an inner vision. Close your eyes. Breathe in and out slowly and deeply. Allow yourself to relax. Deepen this relaxation by whichever technique works best for you. Go to a level where you can visualize, where images flow freely and easily. Imagine yourself doing work that you enjoy, that makes you feel comfortable. It may be the work you are presently doing, or work that is similar—or it may be work that is quite different. Let a series of images flow through your mind—images of different aspects of the work. Notice whether you are working alone or with other people, whether the work is primarily physical or mental. Notice whether you are working outdoors or in a building or in your

A list of the areas in Section III. Receptive visualization can help a person choose which area to concentrate on in visualization.

DAILY LIFE

PSYCHOLOGY

MEDICINE AND HEALING

CREATIVITY

PARAPSYCHOLOGY

SPIRITUAL LIFE

home. Are you working for yourself or are you employed by someone? Visualize your work schedule—the hours and days you work, the speed at which you accomplish tasks. Visualize the amount of money you'd like to make, the kind of ego-gratification you'd like to get from your work. Be open and alert toward any images that come to your mind.

Visualization gives you a chance to try out work situations without actually doing them in the external world. You can imagine yourself in any job situation you can think of. And you can immediately change any aspect of the job, or visualize a whole other job. As you do this, you can see how each situation and each change makes you feel. When you experience strong positive feelings such as satisfaction, excitement, and heightened interest, you are touching your pure inner images. When you experience negative feelings such as anxiety, stress, or boredom, you are becoming aware of areas that are far from your vision. You can let these negative images pass, or you can change aspects of the image until it makes you feel good again.

A person can choose areas to visualize on through chance. He can use a method similar to that used in consulting *The I Ching*. The coin oracle is a short method of choosing a hexagram (and reading) in *The I Ching*. A person throws down three coins together. Each throw gives one of the six lines in the hexagram. The inscribed side has a value of two; the reverse side has a value of three. *I Ching Throw*. Photograph by Michael Samuels.

The artist uses his intuition in shaping a work of art. This process can occur externally, using chosen tools and materials, and it can occur internally, using visualization. In a similar way people can get in touch with the internal images that shape their life.

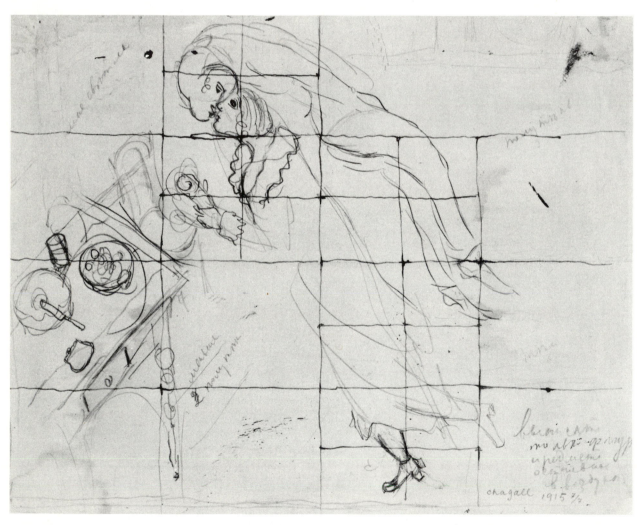

Marc Chagall. Study for *Birthday*. 1915. Pencil, 9 × 11½ inches. Collection, The Museum of Modern Art, New York. Gift of the artist.

Marc Chagall. *Birthday*. (1915). Oil on cardboard, 31¾ × 39¼ inches. Collection, The Museum of Modern Art, New York. Acquired through the Lillie P. Bliss Bequest.

If you did not visualize your present work situation in the beginning of this exercise, you can do so now. By paying attention to your feelings and by making changes in the images, you can locate the aspects of your work that bring you the greatest satisfaction. You can also locate the aspects that make you uncomfortable and, through manipulation of the images, discover ways to improve those aspects of your work. When you identify ones that make you feel good, hold the images in your mind. The images will tend to manifest themselves.

We have discussed three ways of choosing an area for visualizing. These same methods can be used to select a particular visualization exercise within a chapter. The method for choosing a visualization exercise might work like this. You've been feeling tension in your work (school courses, job, or everyday responsibilities) for several months and feel that this is an important area for you to work on. So you decide to look through the chapter on day-to-day life and you find the check list and exercise dealing with work. Then you might relax deeply by one of the exercises we've given (see page 108) and go to a level of mind where you can receive spontaneous visualizations from your inner center (see page 152). At this point you suggest to yourself that you will receive images related to work. You may see an image of yourself at your present work; you may see specific details of that work. Or you may see yourself doing a different kind of work. As you watch the visualizations, you become aware of the way you feel. For example, when you visualize one part of your job, you may notice yourself becoming tense, anxious or uncomfortable. When you visualize another part of your job (or another job), you may notice feelings of relaxation, calmness, and well-being. These feelings surrounding the visualization give you insight as to how your working situation might be improved; negative feelings indicate areas where changes in the visualization and in the external world would be beneficial, while positive feelings indicate areas that should be pursued or expanded by holding the visualization in mind and by action in the external world. Often it is difficult in a situation in the external world to pinpoint the cause of a particular feeling; visualization gives you the ability to focus in on a situation in a clear mental space, free of distractions and the need to interact. Visualization also gives you the ability to see yourself in, and experience the feelings of, situations that do not exist in the external world. This property allows you to see one visualization after another and respond to them and/or to create and respond to changes in your visualizations. Using your feelings as a guide, you can evaluate and modify your visualizations until you become aware of a visualization of your work that feels intensely right to you, one that is accompanied by strong positive feelings. It is this visualization that you would hold in mind, that is, program, to help you manifest it in the external world.

For example, say you are a student and you saw a visualization of yourself in a language course and noticed that you felt anxious and tense. You then saw another visualization of yourself in a physics course and felt more relaxed. By trying out other visualizations you might then home in on exactly what aspects of physics you enjoy and/or what aspects of language you don't enjoy. You might picture yourself memorizing a vocabulary list and feel tense, picture yourself solving a physics problem and feel good, picture yourself in a physics laboratory building a device to measure sound waves and feel very relaxed. You might picture yourself working as a laboratory physicist and feel relaxed and happy. This could indicate that you enjoy a combination of theoretical and practical work, and dislike memorization. You could then hold the visualization in your mind of yourself working in a physics lab solving specific problems. This would be the visualization, the mental act, the coming to awareness of your inner vision. The freeing of your inner vision would bring about a change in the external world that would improve your life and promote your personal growth. These changes would take place naturally and might involve spending more time in the laboratory and less time doing language work, spending the time in the language course reading physics papers in that language, dropping the language course, or leaving school to go to work in a physics lab.

The visualization exercises in this book are of several kinds. They involve receptive visualizations as well as programmed visualizations. They may be either general or specific. In addi-

318

People can relax deeply and go to a level of mind at which they can receive images from their inner center. When people become aware of such images they can make life changes which are beneficial. *Untitled*. Photograph by Michael Samuels.

The Andromedia Galaxy (Messier 31, NGC 224), taken with a Crossley reflector. Lick Observatory, University of California, Mount Hamilton and Santa Cruz, California.

tion, they may deal with processes involved with attaining a goal or they may deal with experiencing a final goal state. As we've said, receptive visualizations are images that come spontaneously. Programmed visualizations are images that are held consciously in the mind's eye. Generalized visualizations deal with symbolic images such as pure shapes, colors, or scenes in nature. Specific visualizations deal with actual situations, events, and feeling states. Process visualization deals with events occurring in time, such as bacteria in a cut being engulfed by white blood cells in the process of healing an infection. Visualization of final goal states involves images of a situation that has occurred, is fixed in time, is done. They characteristically do not involve motion or action through time. For example, a person might imagine healthy, new skin where there is an infected cut. In any specific situation, a person may find one kind of visualization easier and more vivid (and therefore more effective) than another.

For instance, a person might find it difficult to visualize a final goal state. In that case he could try visualizing the processes involved in attaining that state or he could try visualizing a more generalized state. For example, a woman has an infected cut and she's having difficulty visualizing it as fully healed (final goal state). She could try visualizing steps in the healing process, the white blood cells at work, a scab forming and then sloughing off. Or she might simply visualize her whole body feeling radiantly healthy. Again, her feelings are her best guide in choosing which form of visualization to use in this situation.

If she finds herself having difficulty with any form of visualization that deals with healing the cut, it may be because she has opposing visualizations that she is unaware of. In that case, a receptive visualization dealing with the cut might bring to light images that will help her understand what is going on. For instance, she may see an image of herself taking several days off from work because of the infection. This could indicate to her one of the reasons that she had difficulty picturing the healing. Having realized this and decided to take a day off from work, she might then find it easy to imagine the cut healing.

Likewise, at times it may be difficult to clearly visualize whole, intact images from the inner center—particularly images of final goal states. Like the artist in the metaphor a person may visualize fragments of a vision that feel right to him. These fragments correspond to steps in the process leading to a goal. Based on these fragments he will eventually reach the goal, filling in the image around the fragments. This filling-in may occur in the form of active visualization, or he may become aware of new parts of the puzzle when he is doing something unrelated.

In the child's game known as "hot and cold," a child is not at first aware of the ultimate goal, only of the directions "hot" or "cold" which tell him whether he is going toward the goal or away from it. When the child hears, "Hot, hot, hot" as he walks toward the goal he may suddenly realize the goal and go directly to it. Similarly, people may receive visualizations about which they feel good, and, following their feelings, may pursue a course which leads them to be able to see a whole visualization which fits together. And a whole visualization always leads people toward what Jung calls one's "personal myth," one's reason for being, one's "proper place" in the universe.

FOOTNOTES

1. Jung, C. G. *Memories, Dreams, Reflections*, New York, Vintage Books, 1963, p. 3.

ADDITIONAL SOURCES

1. Wilhelm, R., trans. *The I Ching*; Princeton, New Jersey; Princeton University Press; 1967; p. 723 discusses consulting the coin oracle.
2. Samuels, M. and Bennett, H. *Be Well*, New York, Random House/Bookworks, 1974, p. 79 discusses the "feeling pause," a technique for using feelings as a guide.